The Theater of Terror

Mass Media and International Terrorism

Gabriel Weimann
Haifa University

Conrad Winn
Carleton University

Longman
New York & London

**The Theater of Terror: Mass Media
and International Terrorism**

Longman, 10 Bank Street, White Plains, N.Y. 10606

Associated Companies:
Longman Group Ltd., London
Longman Cheshire Pty., Melbourne
Longman Paul Pty., Auckland
Copp Clark Pitman, Toronto

Acquisitions editor: Kathleen M. Schurawich
Production editor: Linda W. Witzling
Cover design: Joseph DePinho
Cover illustration: Joseph DePinho
Production Supervisor: Anne Armeny

Library of Congress Cataloging-in-Publication Data

Weimann, Gabriel, 1950-
    The theater of terror: mass media and international terrorism
    /Gabriel Weimann, Conrad Winn.
        p.   cm.
    Includes bibliographical references and index.
    ISBN 0-8013-1101-2
    1. Terrorism in the press—United States—History—20th century.
2. Terrorism in the mass media—United States—History—20th
century.   3. Terrorism—Political aspects.   4. Telecommunication—
Social aspects—20th century.   I. Winn, Conrad, 1945-
II. Title.
PN4784.T45W45   1993
303.6'25—dc20   92-46571
                                                           CIP

1 2 3 4 5 6 7 8 9 10-AL-9796959493

Contents

Acknowledgments

The authors wish to acknowledge the assistance of the RAND Corporation, especially Brian M. Jenkins, Bonnie Cordes, and Bruce Hoffman, for making available the RAND database on international terrorism and for updating it with new entries. We would also like to convey our gratitude to dozens of students at Haifa and Carleton universities for their essential, fastidious contributions to content analysis. The Ontario Arts Council kindly provided a seed grant. Two Longman Publishing Group reviewers provided valuable counsel beyond the call of duty: Deborah Gerner, University of Kansas and Donald Sylvan, Ohio State University. We warmly acknowledge family forbearance over the course of the project.

Chapter 1

Introduction

"The terrorists won, right?" ABC News's anchor Sam Donaldson pressed a former Reagan administration official.[1] It was a day in July 1985 when 39 hostages from the TWA flight 847, hijacked to Beirut, were set free. In the context of American television coverage of the hijacking, later described as "terrorvision" and "prime-time terrorism," Donaldson's statement phrased as a question did not seem out of place.

Donaldson's question contained several levels of ironic meaning. In one sense, it could be construed as a chastisement of the U.S. administration for succumbing to terrorism in its encouragement of Israel to free its Shi'ite prisoners. At a second level of irony, Donaldson's query could be interpreted as an apparently unconscious self-criticism. If the terrorists won, their prize was the terrorvision supplied by the networks.

Television's treatment of TWA flight 847 was to become an archetype in the evolving history of "the theater of terror." The story had the elements of an effective dramatic script. The back-and-forth shuttle Athens/Beirut/Algiers/Beirut/Algiers/Beirut, the plight of 39 ordinary Americans in an extraordinary situation, the undercurrent of death, and the media's access to the terrorists themselves made the episode one of the most widely viewed of television miniseries.

It was a miniseries. During the 16 days of the hijacking, CBS devoted 68% of its nightly news broadcasts to the event while the corresponding figures at ABC and NBC were 62% and 63% respectively. On the first day, CBS assigned three major newscasts and 10 special reports to the subject. NBC trailed with 9 special reports. On the second and third days, the

---

1   The quotations and content data from coverage of the TWA hijacking that are presented in this chapter are drawn largely from four articles in the September 21, 1985 issue of *TV Guide*: Edwin Diamond, "The Coverage Itself—Why It Turned into *Terrorvision*"; Roderick Townley and John Weisman, "The Reporters' Rat Race—Danger, Chaos, and Rumors of Payoffs"; Neil Hickey, "The Impact on Negotiations—What the Experts Say"; and David Halberstam, "The Bottom Line: How To Do It Right Next Time."

number of special reports at CBS rose to 13 and then 17, in addition to frequent "newsbreaks" and expanded evening coverage. Between newscasts, dramatic intensity was sustained by station break promotions and "teasers" such as "Are positions hardening? Details later tonight."

Throughout the ordeal, the Western media provided ample evidence of their organizational skills. Hundreds of reporters supported by high technology equipment and camera crews converged on Beirut. ABC led with 40 people, followed by NBC with 25 and CBS with 20. Satellite channels were established for instantaneous communication with the field. Network head offices located the families of the hostages, interviewed experts on terrorism, and scoured their archives for material on the Shia branch of Islam and on the local political, religious, and communal movement from which the hijackers were drawn.

The terrorists provided evidence of their own logistical and technical capabilities too. The terrorists managed to stage interviews, meetings, and press conferences with hundreds of different reporters while remaining fastidious about what content they would permit to be uplifted to the satellite links for potential broadcasting in the various home countries. With a concern for detail, the Shia organization carefully edited the American tapes, deleting hostages' comments that they did not endorse.

The American networks' investment in coverage yielded dividends: all the networks' news programs secured major audience increases. During the first week of the crisis, CBS evening news augmented its viewership by a full rating point, i.e., 849,000 households. The Cable News Network subsequently revealed that it had established a ratings record on the weekend of the hostages' release.

Of the three American networks and hence among all the networks covering the crisis, ABC was the undoubted leader in the "scoop count." The network's previous Beirut correspondent, Charles Glass, flew in from London for the event. Thanks to his connections with various Shia militia leaders, Glass was able to secure exclusive televised interviews with the TWA crew, the hostages, and Nabih Berri. The articulate and U.S.-educated Berri headed Amal, a political, religious, welfarist, and military organization that vied with the more fundamentalist Hezbollah for the affections of Lebanon's Shia population. NBC celebrated on air "the going away dinner" and found itself in a position to fly relatives of four hostages to West Germany for tearful family reunions in an exclusive story for the "Today" show.

If the networks felt that they had gained from coverage of the hijacking, so too did the hijackers feel that they had gained. The hijackers believed that their skills at newsmaking and media management were pivotal. The intensity of media interest in the dramatic events and the enormous size of the press contingent were almost a press agent's dream. The terrorists could influence the content of broadcasts in part by a thoughtful selection of individual journalists in whom they had confidence. As a spokesman for a militia group allied to Amal explained: "We helped reporters who showed friendliness. They got our cooperation because they'd be more willing to show our point of view."

In addition to selecting friendly reporters, the terrorists could also select friendly hostages for the interviews. Hostages were allowed to be interviewed if they feared sufficiently for their lives to cooperate or underwent the Stockholm syndrome and identified with their captors. Speaking on behalf of his fellow hostages, Allyn Conwell addressed his countrymen on the air: "We as a group...want to beseech President Reagan and our fellow Americans to refrain from any form of military or violent means as an attempt...to secure our freedom. That would only cause...unneeded deaths among innocent people....We understand that Israel is holding as hostage a number of Lebanese people who undoubtedly have as equal a right and as strong a desire to go home as we do."

Mr. Conwell's comparison of ordinary airline passengers who are hijacked in innocent passage with armed Shia who are captured in a state of belligerency was soon repeated uncritically all over the Western media. With their own lives in jeopardy and with thoughts of their families undoubtedly crossing their minds, the TWA passengers and crew quite understandably accommodated their kidnappers' wishes in what they said. This had an effect. Former Secretary of State Alexander Haig observed that in such situations "the emotional climate created by television...leads to national pronouncements in which the lives of the hostages take precedence over the broader interests of the American people. The first principle in a terrorist situation... should be what is in the best interest of the American people as a whole, not a particular group of victims. TV tends to reverse those priorities. It certainly did in the recent crisis."

In this particular crisis, the hijackers exercised influence. They secured and retained the media's prolonged attention. They acquired preferential access to airtime for journalists whom they judged to be sympathetic. They were able to select the hostages for interviewing and then edit their remarks. Finally, conscious or unconscious limits were placed on the themes that objective journalists would pursue.

The ability to set limits on permissible discourse is illustrated by David Hartman's interview with Amal leader Nabih Berri on ABC's "Good Morning,

America." Hartman concluded with the question, "Any final words to President Reagan this morning?" Hartman thus implied that his guest and the president were interlocutors, moral equivalents, or analogues of each other in some fashion. Berri was not confronted with the fact, and the audience was not told, that he commanded militia who had slaughtered women and children in the Palestinians' Sabra and Shatila camps, who had been responsible for at least eight previous hijackings, who had murdered two Palestinian nurses during the course of the current TWA hijacking, and who were responsible for countless other reprehensible acts.

As a result of the conscious or unconscious limits placed on the TV host's discussion with Amal leader Nabih Berri, the "Good Morning, America" audience could learn little from the program about the moral or political consistency of the man being presented to them as the U.S. head of state's interlocutor.

Ultimately the "hard" aspect of the hijacking subsided and the hostages were reunited with their families. The media then experienced what has become an established routine of theatrical self-flagellation. Typical of the dramatic headlines of the denouement were "The Network Circus" (*Newsweek*, July 15, 1985), "TV in the Hostage Crisis: Reporter or Participant?" (*New York Times*, July 2, 1985), and "The Bottom Line: How to Do It Right the Next Time" (*TV Guide*, September 1985). On July 30, ABC's special "Viewpoint" aired an analysis whose title could have constituted the network's line of defense for its own role in the miniseries: "Reporting Under the Gun."

A Philosophical Consideration

The essence of terrorism is the actual or threatened use of violence against victims of symbolic importance in such a way as to gain psychological impact for the purpose of achieving political objectives.[2] Symbolism and psychological impact are both key.

The practitioners of terror can be the defenders of a regime or the regime's antagonists. For both sides, the appeal of terrorism is its economy. Efficient, inexpensive psychological intimidation substitutes for much more costly organizational, military, and other methods of capturing attention or

---

2   See Donna M. Schlagheck, *International Terrorism* (Lexington, Mass.: Lexington Books, 1988), 1-5.

controlling minds. Through terror, the antagonists of a regime can achieve psychological impacts far out of proportion to the antagonists' own strength. A small antiregime or nonstate group could oblige an entire country or potentially a global audience to pay heed to the group's political agenda even if the group were in fact too weak, say, to seize and occupy a small village or, if fair elections were held, to achieve electoral success. For its part, a repressive regime can sow fear among a timorous populace and hence exact compliance at a fraction of the cost necessary to place a guard on every street corner and a listening device in every dwelling.

The psychological aspect is a source not only of terrorism's strength but also of its complexity. To both proregime and antiregime terrorists, it is not always clear who should be victimized in order to achieve maximum advantage. In some situations the most psychologically resonant victim is a powerful representative of an opposing group. Destroying a powerful antagonist enhances one's claim to power in a primitive quasi-cannibilistic way. Italy's Red Brigades had this in mind when they kidnapped and murdered Aldo Moro, former prime minister and mooted president to be. Irish republicans had this in mind when they assassinated Lord Louis Mountbatten, military hero and member of the royal family. Soviet leader Joseph Stalin had this in mind when he arranged the axe-murder of his principal competitor in the communist movement in Leon Trotsky's own haven in Mexico.

In other situations, terrorist acts achieve psychological resonance through the victimization of apparently innocent civilians. By choosing the innocent, the practitioner of terror demonstrates a unique capacity for rage and unforeseeable action against which no defense is possible. Stalin utilized such a stratagem in his fraudulent show trials, where transparently innocent civilians or loyal Communist officials were found guilty of treasonous conspiracy. Some loyalists actually pleaded guilty, thus heightening the psychological impact. On various occasions, Palestinian, South Moluccan, and other nonstate terrorists have selected children as targets to demonstrate their capacity for rage and hence implicitly the injustices that purportedly brought about their rage.

Apart from having to choose between high- and low-profile victims, the practitioners of terror must decide how much publicity to cultivate. For nonstate terrorist groups, maximizing the psychological impact is usually achieved by maximizing publicity. Terrorist governments, on the other hand, may desire just enough publicity to sow fear but not so much as to provoke domestic opposition and foreign opprobrium or reaction. For example, the white supremacist police state in South Africa drew just enough attention to its practices of torture and assassination to discourage potential black militants but not enough to arouse the consciences of white liberals within the country and abroad.

Sowing fear is often a complex process. For international terrorists, achieving a psychological impact may entail several stages. For example, the intended victims of violence may be different from the audience for violence, who may in turn be different from the intended objects of intimidation.

The intended objects of intimidation may vary considerably. Nonstate terrorists may do battle with their own governments, foreign governments, and/or foreign communities. Authoritarian states practicing terror may target their own populations, foreign populations, expatriate communities, and/or foreign governments.

The scholarly fallout from the extraordinary complexity of terrorism as a subject includes a cornucopia of definitions, analytic frameworks, and perspectives. A comprehensive treatment of terrorism would require a fulsome discussion of the hundreds of existing definitions of the subject. We will return to the subject of definitions in the next chapter.

This book is not a study of terrorism or international terrorism in particular. We do not do justice to the wide range of factors that motivate terrorists or shape their actions.[3] We do not explore the manifold psychological, sociological, economic, and political forces at the root of terrorism.[4] We do not focus on organizational matters, technology and

---

3   For thoughtful discussions of the range of political and psycho-organizational goals that drive terrorist groups, see David C. Rapoport, ed., *Inside Terrorist Organizations* (New York: Columbia University, 1988), especially the chapter by Martha Crenshaw on "Theories of Terrorism: Instrumental and Organizational Approaches" and Section II on "Motivations and Justifications." For an overview of psychological and personality explanations of terrorism and a discussion of their limitations, see Martha Crenshaw, "The Psychology of Political Terrorism" in Margaret G. Hermann, *Political Psychology* (San Francisco: Jossey-Bass, 1986), 379-413.

4   On the belief structures of terrorists, see David C. Rapoport and Yonah Alexander, eds., *The Rationalization of Terrorism* (Frederick, Md: University Publications of America, 1982), and David C. Rapoport, "The International World as Some Terrorists Have Seen It: A Look at a Century of Memoirs," in Rapoport, ed., *Inside Terrorist Organizations*, 32-58.

violence, the impact of interstate relations, or the impact of counterter-rorism strategies.[5] A comprehensive understanding of terrorism would require a comprehensive consideration of these and other factors.

This book concentrates on one category of terrorist conduct, international acts of violence by nonstate actors, and one aspect of terrorism, mass communications. The book assembles and analyzes statistical and anec-dotal information on the emergence of modern international terrorism. It examines how terrorists have sought to make use of the media, and how and why the media have made use of terrorism. In turn, the book assesses the impacts of this *ménage à deux* on public opinion, government decision makers, and the terrorists themselves.

A study of terrorism and the media overlaps several scholarly disciplines. A study of the media is of course at the core of the related disciplines of journalism and mass communications. Violence, terrorism, and counterterrorism are concerns of political science and to some extent public administration. Our examination of the terrorism-media nexus discusses such questions from political science as freedom of the press, the public's right to know, journalists' responsibilities in a liberal democratic society, press law, the relations between government and the press, setting the public agenda, access to the media, and advocacy through media manipula-tion. The influence of the media on governance is a vital issue for political science as well as its offshoots, public administration and public policy. The impact of mediated terrorism on public opinion is a significant matter for political science, sociology, and to a lesser extent the other social sciences as well.

Our analysis reflects the growing public and scholarly concern about the behavior of the mass media. Scholars and citizens may not all agree on the diagnosis of a malaise or even whether a malaise exists at all. But there is an increasing recognition that mass media reporting is too important a subject to be left to ordinary reporters. The journalism profession's recog-nition that the media do more than mirror society is reflected in the existence of long-standing codes of conduct as well as in the emergence of dedicated media columnists. Whether at the *Washington Post* or *Ottawa*

---

5   On the impact of internal organizational dynamics, see the essays in Section I on "Internal Structure and Conflict" in Rapoport, ed., *Inside Terrorist Organizations*. On the impact of counterterrorist tactics and strategies, see the crossnational study in Christopher Hewitt, *The Effectiveness of Anti-Terrorist Policies* (New York: University Press of America, 1984).

Citizen, such media columnists are mandated to comment independently on the impact of their profession on society.

The emergence of media self-criticism may be a necessary protective device because journalists have good reason to be wary when criticism comes from outsiders. Outside scrutiny is often a prelude to attempts to diminish rather than enhance journalistic standards. Even the casual student of the history of journalism is aware of the harm that has been done to the integrity of the profession by outside forces. Well-intended democratic governments have succumbed to the temptations of news manipulation and overt censorship when their patriotic impulses were kindled by war or its anticipation. Because of their frequently hidden economic agendas, private media owners and advertisers are a sometime threat to standards of performance. Still another potential threat to objectivity and fair play comes from citizens' groups whose highmindedness about what should properly appear on television or in print sometimes betrays a touch of the vigilante.

The various direct threats to the autonomy and objectivity of journalists constitute one problem for the profession. Another problem arises from the paradoxical nature of news itself. Though news is portrayed by journalists and understood by audiences as essentially spontaneous and naturally occurring, in fact most news is artificially *subsidized* by the newsmakers themselves.

Many news events are created by newsmakers with the motivation, resources, and personal connections to make the manufacture of news possible. Government stories based on press conferences, election stories based on staged campaign events, and business stories based on company documents fall under the category of subsidized news. The phenomenon of news subsidization is illustrated even by the most famous example of investigative journalism, the *Washington Post*'s exposé of the break-in at the Democratic party headquarters in the Watergate building complex during Richard Nixon's presidency. In this particular instance, the news was not subsidized by a government, company, election campaign, or other organization but by an idiosyncratic individual, the insider code-named *Deep Throat*.

The complement to the idea of subsidized news is the idea of profit-optimizing news. In national broadcasting systems that have a private broadcasting component, both private and public broadcasters seek for financial reasons the largest possible audiences for any given expenditure. For private broadcasters, large audiences are of course a path to advertising revenue. For government-owned systems, large audiences are a means of justifying annual budgets before elected officials. The audience-maximizing behavior of broadcasters leads them to emphasize content with theatrical character and "good production values" in order to retain the marginal viewer, poised to switch to more exciting fare on a competitor's channel.

Journalists have tended to respond to criticism of their performance by pointing to their rights under "freedom of the press." A deservedly powerful idea, the concept of freedom of the press needs an adequate response. One method of reconciling the valid principle of freedom of the press with the necessity of informed criticism of the media is to amend the concept of freedom of the press to take into consideration the insights of the late Oxford scholar Isaiah Berlin on the nature of liberty.

For centuries, Western civilization treated John Locke's concept of liberty as if it were an indivisible whole, as if it guaranteed only freedom *from* oppression or tyranny. Isaiah Berlin bifurcated the concept of liberty into freedom *from* and freedom *to*.[6] Thus, for Berlin, freedom could mean the absence of tyrannical impediments to existential choice as well as the presence of the medical, economic, and social requisites for the ability to exercise choice. This modern concept of liberty recognizes that the absence of oppression is not a sufficient condition for liberty. Humans require nutrition, health, education, and safety before they can exercise freedoms of which they are not specifically deprived.

Berlin's elaboration of the concept of liberty provides a way of critically evaluating the mass media without doing injury to the concept of press freedom. Paralleling Berlin's concept of negative freedom or freedom *from*, freedom of the press can be defined in part as freedom from governmental, corporate, and other coercive interventions in news production whose motivations or consequences are incompatible with professional neutrality.

Akin to Berlin's concept of positive freedom or the freedom *to do*, freedom of the press can be defined as the freedom to exercise journalistic judgment and initiative. Thus, the media acquire a right to transmit meaningful information on the widest possible range of events irrespective of the event-maker's resources, personal connections to journalism, or ability to

---

6   See, for example, his *Four Essays on Liberty* (New York: Oxford University Press, 1969). For an overview of alternative conceptions of media responsibilities, see Fred S. Siebert, Theodore Peterson, and Wilbur Schramm, *Four Theories of the Press* (Urbana: University of Illinois Press, 1956), especially Chapter 3 on "Social Responsibility Theory."

fulfill a media organization's economic requirements for audience-maximizing news.

This positive press freedom surpasses the classical liberal's or libertarian's conception of press freedom. The libertarian idea has been presented by private broadcasters and publishers as a property right. In the words of one-time *Wall Street Journal* publisher William Peter Hamilton, "A newspaper is a private enterprise owing nothing whatever to the public....It is therefore affected with no public interest. It is emphatically the property of the owner, who is selling a manufactured product at his own risk...."[7]

Both the granting of property rights by the nation-state and the understanding of property rights by economic thinkers have evolved since the industrial revolution. The belief that property rights are strongest when undiluted has been superseded by an awareness that rights are often secured by appropriate obligations. To offer a simple example, the car owner's right to drive a vehicle in safety and comfort is enhanced by such reasonable limitations on car ownership and use as requirements for driving permits, automobile registration, and safety checks.

Capitalism as a whole flourishes in part because of the enhanced predictability and rationality of behavior resulting from heightened legal, self-regulatory, and ethical constraints. It is no accident, for example, that strong equity markets tend to exact robust standards governing the reliability and volume of accounting, insider-trading, and other business information to be made routinely available to the public.

Just as property rights have evolved to accommodate more complex capital markets, press rights are evolving to accommodate the new exigencies of contemporary democratic political systems. Contemporary democracies require a free flow of accurate disinterested information in order to contend with environmental and military perils that were unknown in the nineteenth century, not to mention during the age of Enlightenment, when modern ideas of freedom began to take hold.

In light of the dangers facing a more vulnerable and interdependent planet, the libertarian idea that the newspaper "ow[es] nothing whatever to the public" may be a risky indulgence. The concept of the press's freedom

---

7   Quoted in Theodore Peterson, "The Social Responsibility Theory of the Press," in Fred S. Siebert, Theodore Peterson, and Wilbur Schramm, *Four Theories of the Press* (Urbana: University of Illinois Press, 1956), 73.

from is no longer satisfactory. Even the concept of the press's freedom *to* may fall short of a proper description of the necessary role of the media in democratic society. Ultimately, the media bear special responsibilities to provide the very wide range of meaningful information that democratic societies need as a basis for their portentous policy choices. Because of the importance of the media, news ought no longer to be conceived as a commodity, but rather as a social good.[8]

The notion of special media responsibilities is not new to journalists. The idea of the social obligations of the media is at least implicit in the many canons of press conduct and in the raison d'être of journalism schools. As early as 1904, Joseph Pulitzer justified the establishment of a school of journalism in the United States in terms of "a sincere sense of moral responsibility...[to] save journalism from a subservience to business interests, seeking selfish ends, antagonistic to public welfare."[9]

Classical liberal thought on the freedom of the press emerged from a pluralist concern about absolutism. Apprehension about the potential abuse of governmental power has as much validity today as ever. For this reason, we would recommend avoiding legal, regulatory, or even paragovernmental pathways for delineating the societal responsibilities of the press.

A commitment to a societally responsible media emerges best from within journalism. The commitment to a sense of media responsibility needs to be driven by an acceptance by journalists that they ought to be guided by the likely impacts, sometimes dramatic, of news coverage on newsmakers and bystanders alike. In practice, the elite and nontabloid press often abide by this self-constraint, especially in their coverage of local and domestic affairs. They may be respectful of the desire for privacy of victims in high profile cases of personal abuse. They may avoid highlighting ghoulish aspects of gruesome crimes in order not to inspire imitators. They may downplay reports of violent threats against members of their own profession for similar reasons.

The media need to become as sensitive in their international reporting as they have sometimes been in their coverage of local and national affairs. The need for self-restraint in international coverage derives from the

8   On this point, see A. P. Schmid, "Terrorism and the Media: The Ethics of Publicity," *Journal of Terrorism and Political Violence* I (Winter 1990), 539-65.

9   Quoted in Peterson, "The Social Responsibility Theory of the Press," 83.

inchoate intimacy of the planet. International events no longer take place in "far off lands" because nothing is "far off" any longer.

Self-restraint in international reporting needs to be grounded in objective knowledge about how such reporting impacts upon newsmakers and bystanders. A commitment to an ethic of media responsibility needs to be informed by an objective factual understanding of how newsmakers acquire media attention and how media coverage in turn affects newsmakers' behavior. Both the ethic of commitment and the factual understanding of behavior are particularly important in the case of international events that involve life and death. Our book looks empirically at the mutual relationship between coverage and newsmaking in the particular case of international terrorism.

The Data

The essence of our book is a quantitative study of how, why, and with what consequences the media have covered international terrorism. Two different types of data are examined: *behavioral data* on the violent transnational actions of hundreds of nongovernmental terrorist groups and *content data* on how these actions were reported in 12 electronic and print media in four regions of the world.

We analyze the RAND Corporation dataset on terrorist behavior between 1968 and 1986. This extraordinary dataset is a compilation of information on the behavior of hundreds of terrorist groups and over 5,000 international terrorist events. The data are drawn primarily from the press, journal articles, and other open sources, and are supplemented by classified U.S. government information and information from officials attached to other governments. Terrorist group behavior is measured operationally using more than 200 coded responses (see Appendix for fuller description of the database).

From this compendium, we are able to compare different groups according to the kinds of violent acts that they undertake (e.g., hijacking vs. bombing), where the events take place, the victims' occupation (e.g., diplomats vs. tourists) and nationality, and the kinds of targets involved (e.g., airlines vs. government buildings).

The quality of RAND's data collection effort receives recognition even from those who disparage the RAND Corporation's general approach to the understanding of terrorism. For example, E. S. Herman characterizes the RAND data program as "a relatively large and scholarly operation for the

the terrorism field" while at the same time condemning it for effectively excluding terrorism by governments against their own populations.[10] If our purpose were to examine the vital topic of state terrorism, we would share Herman's view of the insufficiency of the RAND database. However, our purview is nonstate transnational terrorism. The RAND dataset is well suited to this purpose.

The RAND Corporation has made prodigious efforts to assemble an unbiased population of all international terrorist events. All possible international media and nonmedia sources were used. Terrorist events taking place on the frontiers of neighboring states at war were excluded.

No dataset can ever be fully above question. It is fair conjecture to wonder if the RAND data might overrepresent slightly incidents involving U.S. victims and/or interests as a result of the unintentional omission of incidents not involving U.S. nationals or interests. The dataset is exceptionally large. For this reason, any omissions are apt to be proportionately very small in number. However nonrandom or skewed they might be, any conjectured omissions are therefore likely to exercise a trifling impact, if any, on overall conclusions.

Most of our causal findings would be unaffected by any evidence of a slight bias in the dataset. For example, one of our more prosaic causal findings is that a terrorist incident is more likely to receive media coverage when carnage is involved. The validity of this and other causal findings would not be affected in obvious ways by whether or not one assumes the dataset to overrepresent slightly events involving U.S.-related interests.

To the RAND dataset on terrrorist events, we married two datasets on the content of the media coverage of these events. One dataset consists of the Vanderbilt archive data on news coverage on the three principal American television networks, CBS, NBC, and ABC. The only archive possessing television data for the period in question, Vanderbilt did not track CNN or non-U.S. services. CNN and other television network coverage are not included in our study for this practical reason.

Complementing Vanderbilt data on the three American networks are our own content data on terrorist coverage in nine newspapers around the world: *New York Times, Times of London, Globe and Mail* (Toronto), *Daily Telegraph* (London), *Le Figaro* (Paris), *Frankfurter Allgemeine Zeitung, Yediot* (Tel Aviv), *Al Aharam* (Cairo), and the *Pakistan Times*. The seven papers

---

10   *The "Terrorism Industry"* (New York: Pantheon Books, 1989), 86.

published in liberal democracies are each large circulation, well respected, and at least somewhat independent of party lines. The Pakistani and Egyptian papers are also well respected, but their independence from government has varied depending upon the political climate of the day. Indeed, some of the variation in the nature of the *Pakistan Times*'s coverage of terrorism, we shall contend, is related to variations in the nature of the regime under which it has had to publish.

The systematic content analysis of the newspapers was an intensely laborious task made possible by the generous efforts of students at Haifa and Carleton Universities. Our goal of geographic and cultural diversity among the newspapers in the sample was necessarily tempered by the distribution of language skills among our volunteers.

Chapter 2 is devoted to the emergence of modern international terrorism. The chapter begins with a brief analysis of controversies in the definition of terrorism. After a discussion of typologies of terrorists, it proceeds to a quantitative analysis of the RAND Corporation's computerized chronology of terrorist events. The chapter explores which groups conduct most of the violence and are the most lethal, which groups are most apt to be victimized, where violence is most apt to occur, and what kinds of terrorist actions tend to be conducted.

Chapter 3 focuses on media coverage. The individual media are compared according to the volume and kinds of coverage they provide. Patterns of intermedia and cross-national similarity and dissimilarity are identified.

Chapter 4 departs from the empirical orientation of the book by looking at conceptual aspects of terrorism as communication. We utilize the construct of *media event* to help understand the content of terrorist appeals, the functions of the media, and the impacts of events and event coverage on audiences. The terrorist media event is presented as a new category of such events, the "coercion," as distinct from three previously conceptualized media events, "contests," "conquests," and "coronations."

Chapter 5 explores the factors affecting media coverage of terrorism. Combining data on the attributes of the events themselves and data on the nature of their coverage in the media, our analysis gauges the influence of different attributes on the presence and extent of reporting. The chapter presents empirical evidence of the degree to which coverage in various media and various countries is influenced by the type and intensity of violence, the degree of victimization, the nature of the victims, and the identity of the perpetrators. Out of our analysis emerges evidence of a media-minded terrorism, whose discourse is scripted and actions choreographed in order to achieve media attention and exposure.

Chapter 6 is devoted to the impact of mass-mediated terrorism on public opinion. Utilizing both experimental and observational evidence, our analysis considers such media effects as agenda setting, priming, awareness, status conferral, and attitude formation. Our evidence corroborates the prevailing scholarly paradigm that media effects are strongest when the public depends heavily on the mass media for information and understanding, a common occurrence in the case of terrorism.

Chapter 7 looks at the intricacies of coverage. Our analysis examines the phenomenon of emotionally loaded or affective labeling (e.g., *terrorist* vs. *freedom fighter*) and the reporting of terrorists' motives. Emerging from our data analysis comes evidence on the circumstances during which the different media will resort to positive, neutral, or negative labeling as well as the conditions under which journalists will accommodate the terrorists' desire for their ostensible motives to be retransmitted.

Chapter 8 provides evidence of a contagion effect in international terrorism. A growing academic literature lends support to the notion of contagion in suicide and in varied forms of crime, violence, and social disturbances as a result of the media's role in the modeling and teaching of deviance. In this chapter, we report the results of the statistical analysis of the probability that different types of terrorism will recur in the wake of different forms of media coverage. Our data analysis confirms that mass-mediated international terrorism does indeed qualify as a contagion.

Chapter 9 discusses the *critical* perspective on the media-terrorist nexus, expounded principally by Western neo-Marxist analysts. They focus on the terrorism of the West's intelligence agencies and of third world dictatorships allied with the West. The mainstream perspective focuses instead on the terrorism of anti-Western dictatorships or international terrorist groups, which are often anti-Western. The chapter explores to what extent the critical and mainstream perspectives are empirically complementary and to what extent the concept of a theater of terror can be an analytic bridge between the two schools of thought. International (nonstate) terrorists, we argue, are publicity maximizers whereas terrorist governments, whether allied with or hostile to the West, are publicity optimizers or publicity minimizers, depending on their strategies.

Chapter 10 explores the institutional stress experienced by security forces and political executives responding to the exigencies of terrorist events while faced with both the watchful eye of electronic journalism and journalism's own autonomy of action. In extreme instances, some critics of journalism and some elements of security and the political executive have deemed journalists to be facilitators of terrorism.

Chapter eleven, entitled "Must the Show Go On?", summarizes the empirical findings of our study. This concluding chapter also returns to the central issue raised at the outset: If it is empirically true that media coverage begets the replication of certain kinds of international terrorism, then how should the liberal democracies and their media respond to this dilemma?

Chapter 2

The Emerging Character of International Terrorism

Origins

The Middle East gave birth to the precursors of modern terror. One of the earliest campaigns was that of the Jewish Zealots against the Romans in ancient Palestine (A.D. 6-135), described in detail by the historian Flavius Josephus.[1] The Zealots' first uprising was prompted by a Roman census implemented for purposes of taxation. This was the same census mentioned in the New Testament as coinciding with the birth of Jesus. Roman occupiers responded vigorously to local protest, crucifying 2,000 Zealots.

According to conventional scholarship, the Zealots qualified as terrorists because they shaped their use of violence to create the psychological impacts that would help achieve their political objective, emancipation from Roman rule. In the words of D. M. Schlagheck,

> The Zealots used violence (assassinations, hit-and-run attacks) against Romans as well as Greeks and Jews who sympathized or collaborated with Roman rule. The attacks were unpredictable and the targets held symbolic value. The attacks often took place publicly or on a holy day so that the word of the Zealots' attack would spread as quickly as possible and as widely as possible.[2]

The Romans' successful suppression led to a half century of peace, followed by the emergence of a second group of Zealots, the Sicarii. They used assassination and kidnapping to incite a Jewish uprising against Roman occupation in A.D. 68. Vastly outnumbered, the Sicarii fled

---

1   *The Great Roman-Jewish War* (New York: Harper, 1960).
2   *International Terrorism* (Lexington, Mass.: Lexington Books, 1988), 16.

Jerusalem for the mountain fortress at Masada, ultimately choosing collective suicide over surrender.

The group drew its name from a short sword, the sica, which had been utilized against the Jewish peace party.[3] In large gatherings, the Sicarii would attack their quarry at close range and then disappear into the crowd. As Schlaheck notes, "The public relations impact of such murder was quite powerful."[4] A number of historians argue that the Jewish rebellion failed because the Sicarii and other Zealots replaced terrorist and guerrilla tactics, which placed them at an advantage, with conventional warfare, which did not.[5]

Between the eleventh and twelfth centuries, the Assassins emerged as an offshoot of the Ismaili sect of Muslims. Walter Laqueur has remarked on the increasing fascination with them among contemporary Western authorities. It is because "some of the features of this movement remind one of contemporary terrorist movements."[6] Their first leader, Hassan ibn al-Sabbah, acknowledged that his group was too weak to confront an enemy in open battle. He substituted a campaign of terror carried out by a small, disciplined group. Targets included prefects, governors, caliphs, and Conrad of Montferrat, the Crusader king of Jerusalem. *Fidalin* was the name given to those prepared to undertake political murder as their religious duty.[7]

The terms *Sicarii* and *Fidalin* reemerged in use in the middle of this century. In Mandatory Palestine, the anti-British terrorists took on the name *Sikarikim*. The term *Fidalin* was reclaimed first by Egyptian guerrillas battling British forces along the Suez Canal during the 1950s and later by Palestinians.[8]

---

3   For an important study of early terrorist groups, see David C. Rapoport, "Fear and Trembling: Terrorism in Three Religious Traditions," in *American Political Science Review* 78 (3) (1984), 658-77. See also Rapoport, "Terror and the Messiah: An Ancient Experience and Some Modern Parallels," in David C. Rapoport and Yonah Alexander, eds., *The Morality of Terrorism: Religious and Secular Justifications* (New York: Pergamon Press, 1982).

4   Ibid., 16.

5   See M. Avi-Yonah, *The Jews under Roman and Byzantian Rule* (New York: Schocken, 1984).

6   *Terrorism* (London: Weidenfeld and Nicolson, 1977), 8.

7   B. Lewis, *The Assassins: A Radical Sect in Islam* (London: Weidenfeld and Nicholson, 1967).

8   W. Laqueur, *Terrorism* (Boston: Little, Brown and Co., 1978).

According to accepted scholarship, neither the ancient nor modern manifestations of the Sicarii and Fidaiin rank as the most significant example of organized, nongovernmental fear-inducing violence. That honor is normally reserved for the Narodnaya Volya (People's Will or People's Freedom), operating in Russia from 1878 to 1881.[9]

The Narodnaya Volya were influenced by the anarchist and nihilist zeitgeist of the time, particularly by the writings of Bakunin and Nechayev and the *Revolutionary Catechism*, published in 1869. The *Revolutionary Catechism* inspires terrorist groups to this day, particularly its transcendence of social mores on the uses of violence. Bakunin's concept of "the propaganda of the deed" saw bloodshed as the means of awakening the masses and overthrowing a regime.

After their assassination of Czar Alexander II, Narodnaya Volya leaders were captured and executed. The terrorist mantle passed to the Social Revolutionaries, who created a semiautonomous terrorist group within their movement—a harbinger of the future. In combination, the party's conventional propaganda and its terrorists' histrionic violence had a potent impact on public opinion.

Russian anarchist writers extended their influence into Western Europe. Bombing and assassination were undertaken in France. An explosive detonated in a Parisian cafe in 1894, killing one person and wounding 20. When told that his victims were innocent of any capitalist crimes, the terrorist bomber proclaimed that "there are no innocents," a justification to be proffered by terrorists in the generations to follow.

Violence by terrorist groups grew sporadically in Europe during the early years of the twentieth century. It emerged in Ireland (Dynamiters), Turkey (Armenians, Macedonian IMRO), Poland, Hungary (Red Arrow), and Rumania (Iron Guard). The Croatian Ustacha and the German Freicorps resorted to terrorism on a small scale, as did French fascist groups.

After World War II, liberation movements in Africa and Asia found that simple acts of violence against their colonial masters could demoralize the imperial order out of proportion to the strictly military significance of the

9   G. Wardlaw, *Political Terrorism* (Cambridge: Cambridge University Press, 1982), 19-21.

violence.[10] Revolutionaries learned the value of a careful scripting of both action and location. As Algerian FLN leader Abane Ramdane asked rhetorically, "Is it better for our cause to kill ten of the enemy in the countryside of Telergma, where no one will speak of it, or one in Algiers that will be mentioned the next day in the American press?"[11] In the international arena, meanwhile, acts of violence led to pressure on the European powers by the United States, the Soviet Union, Canada, and other nations without a tradition of overseas empire. [12]

Terror as a Term

The etymological root of the concept is the Latin word *terrere*, which means to frighten or to cause to tremble and from which are derived the terms *terrible, deter,* and *terrify* as well as *terror*. The concept of deterrence stems from the Latin verb *deterrere*, which means to frighten away from.[13]

Accepted historiography holds that the first large-scale application of terrorism took place during the "popular" phase (1792-1794) of the French revolution. The "Reign of Terror" was formalized under a decree of September 5, 1793, declaring that "terror is the order of the day."[14] Facing anarchy, the new government feared foreign invasion, civil strife, and economic disorder. "Terror," asserted one of its members, "was a dictatorship of distress."[15] The principal agencies of terror were Robespierre's Committee on Public Safety and the Revolutionary tribunals. Both claimed the right to liquidate "enemies of the revolution."[16] More than 300,000 real or imagined opponents of the regime were arrested and 17,000 executed.

Executions were conducted before large crowds and were accompanied by sensational publicity, thus spreading the intended fright. When even

---

10   F. Fanon, *The Wretched of the Earth* (Harmondsworth: Penguin, 1967), 48.
11   Cited in G. Fairbain, *Revolutionary Guerrilla Warfare* (Harmondsworth: Penguin, 1974), 287.
12   B. Jenkins, *High Technology Terrorism and Surrogate War*, RAND Paper Series no. P-5339(1975), 7.
13   P. Wurth asserts that the term *terrorism* was first used by the fourteenth century French monk Bersuite. See Wurth, *La Repression Internationale du Terrorisme* (Lausanne: La Concorde, 1941).
14   D. M. Schlagheck, *International Terrorism* (Lexington, Mass.: Lexington Books, 1988), 18.
15   Hyppolyte Carnot, quoted in ibid., 19.
16   See J. H. A. Stewart, *A Documentary Survey of the French Revolution* (New York: Macmillan, 1951), 479.

revolutionaries called for an end to the fear and violence, Robespierre turned against them. By July 1984, the Reign of Terror became so unpopular that Robespierre himself was arrested and put to death. The machinery of terror was largely dismantled within a year.

Though scholars might well agree as to the etymological roots of terrorism and as to its archetypal practice during the French revolution, they do not share a common working definition. Walter Laqueur has protested

> the vagueness—indeed the utter carelessness—with which the term is used, not only in the media but also in government announcements and by academic students of the subject. Terrorism is used as a synonym for rebellion, street battles, civil strife, insurrection, rural guerrilla war, coups d'état, and a dozen other things. The indiscriminate use of the term not only inflates the statistics, it makes understanding the specific character of terrorism and how to cope with it more difficult.[17]

Bonanate has written that to decide "whether an action is terrorist...is more the result of a verdict than the establishing of a fact; the formulation of a social judgement rather than the description of a set of phenomena."[18] Out of this ambiguity emerges the cliche that "one man's terrorist is another man's freedom fighter."

For some activist-minded experts, the persistence of definitional debate is a cause for concern. Adam Roberts takes the view that there "are especially strong reasons for avoiding an excessive preoccupation with definitions....Often...a concern with defining terrorism or with explaining its causes has been the outward and visible sign of a reluctance to recognize the seriousness of the problem or to do anything at all about it."[19]

Despite their disagreements, scholars share a certain understanding of the phenomenon. Schmid and Jongman undertook a quantitative content analysis of 109 published definitions and found many common themes. The most frequent references were to violence or force (83.5%), political content (65%), fear or terror (51%), threat (46%), and psychological effects (41.5%). The next most common reference was to the fact that the victims and ultimate targets of violence are often unrelated (37.5%), while the least common reference was to terrorist demands on third parties (4%). In 1985,

---

17   W. Laqueur, "Terrorism—A Balance Sheet," *Harper's* (November 1976).
18   L. Bonanate, "Some Unanticipated Consequences of Terrorism," *Journal of Peace Research* 16(3)(1979), 197. For an antidote to Bonanate's skepticism, see F. G. Wardlaw, *Political Terrorism* (Cambridge: Cambridge University Press, 1982), 3.
19   Roberts, "Terrorism and International Order" in L. Freedman et al., *Terrorism and the International Order* (London: Routledge and Kegan Paul, 1986), 9.

Schmid solicited from 200 researchers on terrorism their reaction to his own proposed 200-word definition.[20] His definition began with the following opening sentence:

> Terrorism is a method of combat in which random or symbolic victims serve as an instrumental *target of violence*.

Approximately one-third of his panel of researchers found the definition acceptable in whole and approximately one-half in part while 12% rejected it outright.

Like many other influential paradigms, Schmid's definition acquired considerable currency by means of repetition, often in paraphrased form. Maxwell Taylor's adaptation of Schmid's definition merits citation:

> A terrorist action involves **violence**, or **force**, or **threat** of force as a **method of combat** directed towards some **political** end. That end is normally but not necessarily expressed as the action of a **non-state group or organisation**, and may be achieved through **coercion, extortion, intimidation**, or **induction of compliance** in some area of policy, addressed to either a government, organizations or third parties. It is essentially **criminal** in character, using the **publicity** generated by its acts as a potent weapon. In the public perception of the event **fear, apprehension** or **terror** is emphasized, through actual or potential **threat**. The threat intended is the result of **purposive, planned, systematic** and **organised action**, where the threat is expressed in terms of **extranormality**, and is **in breach of accepted rules without humanitarian constraints**. The violent actions undertaken by terrorists are often **repetitive**, or **serial in character**, and a critical election of the choice of action is **victim-target differentiation**, where **civilians, noncombatants, nonresisting, neutrals, or outsiders** are the **principal victims**. Terrorists action shows an **arbitrary, impersonal** and **random character**, where **indiscriminateness** in the choice of **innocent victims** is emphasised. Through its **clandestine** or **covert nature, incalculability, unpredictability,** and **the unexpectedness** of occurrence of violence constitutes an important feature (after Schmid).[21]

Much of the resistance of researchers to Schmid's proposal or to any other single definition stems from the complexity of the phenomenon. Identifying the victim or target may not be a simple task. Contemporary nonstate terrorist groups often follow a practice of multiple victimization. Thus, those who are victimized directly may be different from those in whom the terrorists wish to instill fear, who in turn may be different from those on whom the terrorists seek to impose a change in government direction.

The communications strategies of terrorists may be varied and complex as well. On the one hand, the nonstate terrorists of the third world normally

20 Alex P. Schmid and Albert J. Jongman, *Political Terrorism* (Amsterdam: North-Holland Publishing Company, 1988), 1.
21 Maxwell Taylor, *The Terrorists* (London: Brassey Defence Publisher, 1988), 71.

seek a maximum of media attention. On the other hand, both the pre-*glasnost* KGB in Eastern Europe and the CIA's terrorist allies in Latin America have been more circumspect in the dissemination of fear-inducing news. Their goal has been terror-optimization rather than terror-maximization—spreading enough knowledge of their cruelty to sow fear and panic among their local opponents, real or potential, but not enough to reach the electorates of the liberal democracies, where it might provoke mass revulsion against the perpetrators.

Some of the definitional disagreement among scholars has ideological roots. According to some Western Marxist scholars, the primary sources of terrorism are neither the various international "terrorist" groups nor so-called terrorist states such as Libya nor the Soviet bloc prior to *glasnost* but Western capitalist countries, especially the United States. According to Chomsky and Herman, the "western propaganda machinery" seeks to draw attention away from the grievances of the downtrodden and to obscure "the real network of terror," the violence of the CIA, and the coercive forces of allied governments.[22]

Conservatives may agree that emphasis should be placed on state repression, but they have viewed the Soviet bloc as the principal source of such repression. Claire Sterling argued that ostensibly spontaneous nongovernmental terrorism in the world was largely orchestrated by Moscow.[23] The practice of terrorism provided Soviet totalitarianism with a means of destabilizing the democracies without war. For some conservatives, the gulag, show trials, public confessions, enforced psychiatric hospitalization, KGB executions, and other manifestations of Stalinist-style terror were so important that conventionally understood terrorism amounted to little more than an epiphenomenon.[24] Terror-inducing totalitarianism was the issue, not "terrorism" itself.

22 N. Chomsky and E. S. Herman, *The Political Economy of Human Rights* (Nottingham: Spokesman, 1979), 85-87. See also E. S. Herman, *The Real Terror Network* (Boston: South End Press, 1982) and *The "Terrorism Industry"* (New York: Pantheon Books, 1989).

23 C. Sterling, *The Terror Network: The Secret World of International Terrorism* (London: Weidenfeld and Nicholson, 1981).

24 R. Conquest, *The Great Terror: Stalin's Purges of the 1930's* (London: Macmillan, 1968), B. Barber et al., *Totalitarianism in Perspective* (New York: Praeger, 1969), and I. Howe, ed., *1984 Revisited* (New York: Harper and Row, 1983).

Scholars have sometimes sought to surmount the definitional dilemmas in the field by avoiding definitions and developing typologies instead. A resulting predicament was that almost as many typologies seemed to materialize as there were analysts.[25] Wilkinson has produced a two-layered typology. At a higher level of abstraction, he distinguished among (a) *criminal* terrorism conducted for profit, (b) *psychic* terrorism on behalf of a religious cult, (c) *war* terrorism as an adjunct to conventional military strategy, and (d) *political* terrorism in order to achieve political goals. In turn, Wilkinson subdivided political terrorism into (i) *epiphenomenal* terrorism as in the unplanned by-product of insurrections, (ii) *repressive* terrorism as practiced by despotic states against their people, (iii) the *sub-revolutionary* terrorism of groups with limited political goals, and (iv) the *revolutionary* terrorism of the politically ambitious.[26]

Like Wilkinson, Sederberg also proposed a two-step typology. He first distinguished between *establishment* or pro-regime terrorism and *dissident* or anti-regime terrorism. Dissident terrorism was in turn subdivided into *criminal, nihilist, nationalist,* and *revolutionary* forms. *Nationalist* terrorism includes such politically motivated communal groups as the Quebec secessionist *Front de Libération du Québec* in the early 1970s and various Armenian, Palestinian, Croatian, Puerto Rican, and Irish organizations. *Revolutionary* terrorism encompasses such anti-regime groups as Germany's Red Army Faction, Italy's Red Brigades, or Peru's Shining Path. In practice, many of the nationalist groups have had organizational links with purely revolutionary terrorist groups and have supplemented their nationalist programs with ideological goals in order to broaden their potential appeal beyond their own community.

Sederberg subdivided *establishment* terrorism into *vigilante, covert official, overt official,* and *genocidal* terrorism.[27] The *vigilante* category includes such pro-regime extremists as Protestant terrorists in Ulster and Afrikaner white supremacists in South Africa. The distinction between *overt* and *covert official* terrorism pays homage to the difference between, say, the publicity-seeking show trials of Stalinist Russia and the publicity-avoiding cruelties of the same regime during the artificial famines in the Ukraine during the early 1930s. *Genocidal* terrorism would encompass both the

---

25   Chalmers Johnson, "Perspectives on Terrorism" in W. Laqueur, ed., *The Terrorism Reader* (New York: American Library, 1978), 276.
26   See Paul Wilkinson, *Political Terrorism* (London: Macmillan, 1974), 32-44, and *Terrorism and the Liberal State* (New York: New York University Press, 1986), 50-65.
27   Peter C. Sederberg, *Terrorist Myths* (Englewood Cliffs, N.J.: Prentice-Hall, 1989), 44-67.

state genocide of Nazi Germany against Europe's Jewish population during World War II and the nonstate genocide of Cambodia's Khmer Rouge in more contemporary times.

Both Wilkinson and Sederberg drew distinctions based on terrorists' objectives. Merkel proposed nine diverse attributes as a basis for what we consider to be a classification or taxonomy but what he termed "tabulation." Ranging from modus operandi to ideological objectives, Merkel's nine variables are as follows:

- *who*, i.e., the perpetrators of terrorist action
- *what*, i.e., kidnapping, bombing, or other type action
- *to whom*, i.e., diplomat, police, civilian, or other type of victim
- *symbolic addressee*, i.e., hated government, class, community, or other antagonist
- *claimed social basis*, i.e., communal or other broad constituency
- *sympathizers*, i.e., covert support stratum
- *small group organization*, i.e., key commando group or underground cell
- *large group organization*, i.e., formal organization to which the small group belongs
- *why*, i.e., ideological objectives or motives.[28]

Writing candidly, Merkel observed that creating a tabulation or taxonomy "in such a controversial and underresearched field is always a painful process...."[29] Whether or not the process is painful, it is certainly full of predicaments. One such predicament is the sheer number of available typologies to emerge from academics' diverse conceptual preoccupations. Another predicament is that many typologies have become exceedingly intricate in an effort to encapsulate terrorism in all its varieties. Encapsulating terrorism in all its varieties could require upwards of 50 distinct attributes, potentially yielding an unworkable million different combinations.[30]

---

28   P. Merkel, ed., *Political Violence and Terror* (Berkeley: University of California Press, 1986), 31-33.
29   Ibid., 31.
30   On the use and abuse of typology, see R. Friedlander, *Terrorism* (New York: Oceana Publications, 1979), Chapter 1.

Table 2.1 Categorizing Terrorism

		More than one nation involved	
		yes	no
government controlled or directed	yes	interstate	state
	no	international	domestic

Ultimately, a typology needs to be sparse enough to be workable and fair-minded enough to encompass both leftwing and rightwing preoccupations with terror. Mickolus offers such a reasonable typology.[31] His fourfold classification is based on two axes: presence or absence of government control and whether one country or more than one country is involved in a terrorist act (see Table 2.1).

Interstate terrorism is carried out by individuals or groups under the direction of a national government either against the citizens of another state or against its own citizens abroad. Examples include the violence practiced by Qaddafi's "death squads" against Libyans in exile, the North Korean sabotage of a South Korean airliner in flight over southeast Asia, and attacks by groups under the control of Saddam's Iraq in neighboring Kuwait a year after Desert Storm.

Intrastate terrorism likewise comes under the direction of a national government, but the violence takes place within its own borders. Examples are legion: the Armenian tragedy, Pol Pot in Cambodia, Stalin's liquidation of various Crimean nationalities for imagined treason and his conjuring of a (Jewish) "doctors' plot."

Domestic and international terrorism are practiced by nonstate actors. Although they may be handsomely supported by a state, they qualify as nonstate actors if they cannot actually be dissolved by their patron. International terrorism involves more than one country as in attacks against international flights. Domestic terrorism entails violence by nonstate actors within their home country, for example the kidnapping of American heiress Patty Hearst or the executions of dovish West Bank leaders by hawkish Palestinian groups.

31   E. Mickolus, "International Terrorism," in M. Stohl, ed., The Politics of Terrorism (New York: Marcel Dekker, 1983).

Our study of media and terrorism focuses on international terrorism in part for theoretical reasons. International terrorism actively seeks media coverage in order to influence an audience wider than and other than the population from which the victims may be drawn—hence, the concept of *theater of terror*. By contrast, state terrorism or, more precisely, *intra*state terrorism normally tries to restrict awareness outside the victimized group and may even desire the victimized group to be only vaguely cognizant. Stalin's "show trials" deviate from the general desire of dictatorships to shield their internal use of terror from the glare of the spotlight. Interstate terrorism may constrain awareness in order to limit the prospects of retaliation.

Domestic terrorism provides the closest parallel to international terrorism except in the case of despotic regimes, where access to the media is monitored carefully, thereby limiting media opportunities. For most domestic terrorist groups, publicity is an important objective in itself.

Peru's Shining Path or *Sendero Luminoso* is an apparent exception. Influenced by Maoist precepts, the movement sought the destruction of what it deemed a cruel, despotic, exploitive, capitalist regime. The group took form in 1970 as an offshoot of the Communist party led by an academic, Abimael Guzman. Violence began a decade later. The lethal *Sendero Luminoso* was initially publicity-shy, preferring actions to words, "armed propaganda" to press interviews.[32] During the 1990s, the group began to utilize attention-getting tactics and develop media networks.

Our emphasis on international terrorism derives in part from a focus on the media. For theoretical reasons, it makes sense for a book on terrorism and the media to focus to some degree on international terrorism. But the theoretical advantages of studying international terrorism should not be exaggerated. Indeed, the distinctions among international and the other forms of terrorism are to some extent analytic and in some sense arbitrary. The media- seeking behaviour of international and domestic terrorist groups are often similar. Indeed, in the pages below we highlight an occasional example of domestic terrorist behavior if it elucidates especially well the patterns we observe among international terrorists.

The reasons for focusing on international terrorism are rooted in practical realities as well as theoretical considerations. Extant datasets on international terrorist incidents are more comprehensive and reliable than those

---

32   Gordon H. McCormick, "The Shining Path and Peruvian Terrorism," in David C. Rapoport, ed., *Inside Terrorist Organizations* (New York: Columbia University Press, 1988), 110.

on domestic terror. Thus, it is more feasible to undertake reliable quantitative studies of international terrorism than of the other kinds. The study of international terrorism has the added bonus of readily contributing to cross-national analysis by permitting a comparison of the ways in which the national media in different countries respond to the same international terrorist events. By contrast, it is much more difficult to conduct a comparative study of the media treatment of domestic terrorism. The data are less reliable.

The Growth of International Terrorism

Rapoport has delineated three major periods of modern terrorism: an early period extending from 1879 to World War I, a mid-period beginning in Ireland after World War I and concluding with colonial guerrilla and terrorist activity in the two decades after World War II, and the current period, which began in the 1960s.[33] Our own analysis focuses on the wave of terrorism that began in the 1960's.

Figure 2.1 portrays the frequency of terrorist incidents from 1968 to 1986, according to data assembled by the RAND Corporation. The data show that 418 events occurred in 1986 as compared to only 135 in 1968—a threefold increase for the period. Some years manifested a slight decline from the preceding year. But, in general, terrorism was a "growth industry."

The RAND Corporation data are considered to be the most reliable in existence; the RAND dataset accordingly forms an essential component of our analysis. Nonetheless, we did consult other sources, principally the CIA and U.S. Department of State datasets.[34] Other sources of data confirm the pattern that emerges clearly from the RAND data—a continual increase in the incidence of terror.

Figures 2.2, 2.3 and 2.4 portray the incidence of injuries, fatalities, and victimization resulting from terrorist attacks during the period, all based on the RAND chronology. The data show an unmistakable growth. The

---

33   David C. Rapoport, *Assassination and Terrorism* (Toronto: CBC, 1971), passim and Rapoport, "The International World as Some Terrorists Have Seen It: A Look at a Century of Memoirs" in Rapoport, ed., *Inside Terrorist Organizations* (New York: Columbia University Press, 1988), 34ff.

34   The U.S. Central Intelligence Agency database known as ITERATE appears to report more terrorist events but this greater reporting frequency is an artifact of a different operational definition of the event data. Thus, when explosive mail is sent by a single organization on a given day to several targets, RAND codes this as one event while the CIA file codes it as several.

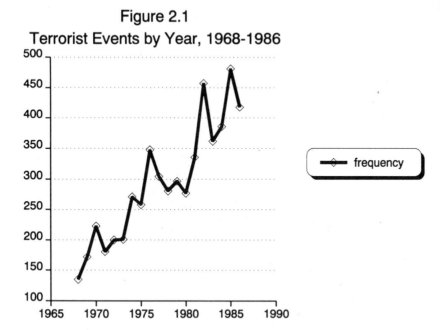

Figure 2.1
Terrorist Events by Year, 1968-1986

number of injuries grew by a factor of 17, from only 53 injured victims in 1968 to 868 injuries in 1986. Meanwhile the incidence of fatalities grew by a factor of 28, rising from 7 deaths in the first year of the statistical series to 196 in the last year. Figure 2.4 portrays the rate of victimization, the combined rate of deaths and injuries. The general rise in fatalities over the period under study results in part, as shown, from the general increase in the occurrence of terrorist events.

The general rise in fatalities also stems in part from the greater lethality of each individual event (see Table 2.2 and Figure 2.5). With the passage of years, each incident tends to have a higher likelihood of becoming fatal, as shown in Figure 2.5. For example, in the first four years, 1968-1971, the likelihood of one or more deaths was less than 50% for each event. By contrast, there was an average of more than one death per terrorist attack during the 1980s. Indeed, the years 1983 and 1985 witnessed for the first time a pattern of almost two deaths per terrorist incident.

Figure 2.2 Sum of Injuries

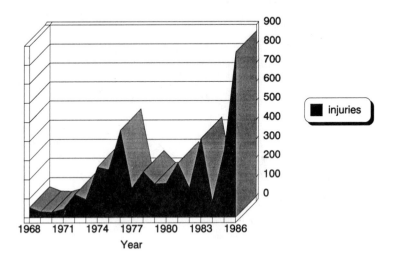

Table 2.2 Average Number of Fatalities per Act by Year

Year	Average
1968	.27
1969	.10
1970	.48
1971	.38
1972	1.13
1973	.53
1974	.92
1975	.51
1976	1.26
1977	.64
1978	1.02
1979	.57
1980	.71
1981	1.01
1982	.45
1983	1.86
1984	.58
1985	1.81
1986	.96

Figure 2.3 Sum of Fatalities

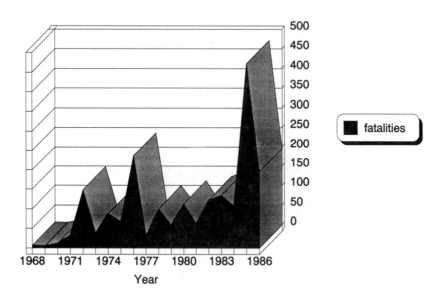

The continually increasing incidence of terrorism requires a satisfactory explanation. The social sciences normally offer two kinds of explanation for human behavior: either the behavior responds to a structural situation or it reflects a learning experience. Modern international terrorism emerged as a structural response by national liberation movements to the far greater conventional military power of the imperial rulers. But old-fashioned imperialism has been largely terminated, bringing to an end an important structural basis for international terrorism. Hence, it would seem as if the growth of postcolonial international terrorism is at least partly a case of *contagion*, whereby a pattern of warfare has diffused around the planet and has been adopted more and more widely even though its original raison d'être has largely subsided.

The Changing Occupational Targets of Terrorism

Conventional war is normally understood as violence between identifiable combatants in the service of belligerent nations. Guerrilla warfare is

Figure 2.4 Sum of Victims
Sum of Victims

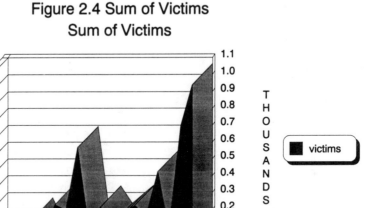

normally understood as the use of subterfuge and other unorthodox modes of operation by an inferior force against an occupying power. In both conventional and guerrilla warfare, combatants are the main targets of violence. The systematic application of violence against civilians is considered a sufficient transgression of military norms that conquerors wishing to do so usually resort to especially hardened troops for the purpose.

If terrorism were a special case of war being waged by inferior forces, one would expect combatants to remain the main targets of violence. The armies and police forces of the ostensibly subjugating states might be expected to provide a disproportionate share of the victims of terrorist violence. The military and especially the police embody the coercive and repressive power of every national government. *Police state* is the term normally reserved for the most repressive of polities. In many societies, mere mention of the office of minister of the interior may cause dread in polite conversation. During the nineteenth and early twentieth centuries, many revolutionaries made the assassination of the minister of the interior their chief aspiration. For

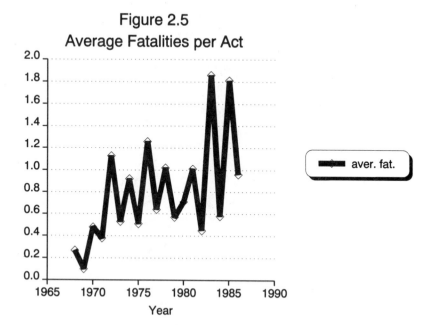

Figure 2.5
Average Fatalities per Act

the Social Revolutionaries of Czarist Russia, the execution of Sipyagin, the minister of the interior, was a pinnacle of accomplishment.

Our analysis of the RAND dataset shows that the police, far from being a principal target of terrorism today, are almost completely ignored. Of 5,589 terrorist attacks during the 1968-1986 period, police forces and individual policemen were targets of terrorist violence on only 27 occasions, i.e. less than 0.5% of the time (see Figure 2.6). The military were somewhat more frequent targets, but they were nonetheless the object of violence on fewer than 8% of occasions.

The range of real and potential targets for terrorist attacks is almost limitless. In view of these vast possibilities, it is interesting to compare the targets of traditional revolutionaries with the preferred targets of contemporary terrorists. Historically, railroads have been a favorite object of guerrilla forces seeking to disrupt an occupying power, but railroads and bus systems today are subject to only 3% of terrorist attacks. Local and national government leaders were historically a favorite victim of revolutionaries; for example, the Russian Narodnaya Volya reached their

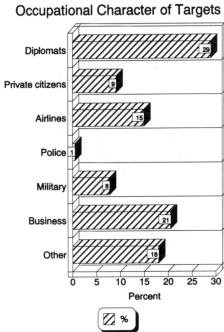

Figure 2.6
Occupational Character of Targets

apex, albeit temporarily, in assassinating Alexander II. Modern terrorists virtually ignore government leaders; all politicians together are the target of only 2.3% of attacks. In many countries, hydroelectric and other utilities are tempting military targets because of their economic importance and vulnerability, but they are largely ignored.

The single most important target of modern terrorists has been diplomats, who account for almost one-third of all attacks. As victims, diplomats embody a different symbolic meaning from that of policemen. In those autocratic countries that historically faced domestic terrorism, police forces represented violent repression, the flouting of law by authorities, and the abusive application of raw power. Contemporary diplomats do not conjure up the same imagery. They are by contrast the embodiment of conciliation, codes of conduct, and constraints on the use of power.

Violence against diplomats generates an intense theatrical impact in part because they embody the states that they represent and because diplomatic life is ritualistic. Embassies are sovereign territory, and their staffs are normally immune from local laws. New ambassadors cannot exercise their functions until their credentials are formally transmitted according to protocol. Ambassadorial conduct is strongly symbolic. Thus, the speed with which a country accepts a new representative's credentials is a measure of the amity between the two countries.

Over the centuries, the states of the international system have developed codes of conduct to insulate from violence their official representatives. Even the most brutal and murderous states normally stop short of attacks on embassy personnel. Given the symbolic importance of diplomacy and the historic protection provided to its practitioners, the targeting of diplomats by terrorists is a dramatic symbolic message crying out for media recognition. Both as a communications technology with specific strengths and weaknesses and as an economic system that sells audiences to advertisers, television is well suited to transmitting intensely dramatic symbolic messages.

Not all the targets of violence are as well suited as diplomats to the mass media requirements of terrorists. In terms of frequency of being chosen as a target, diplomats are followed by businessmen (20.5%), airlines (15%), and private citizens (9.2%). Of course, there may be an overlap among the three categories. Attacks on commercial airlines inevitably involve attacks on businessmen and private citizens as passengers even if these attacks are recorded in datasets only as actions against airlines. Hence, the data on the targeting of businessmen and ordinary citizens underestimate somewhat the degree to which the members of these two groups are actually victimized.

The common element among the four main target groups is that they are not military in nature. Private citizens, airlines, and businessmen have very little military significance. But, they do have a common symbolic meaning. As in the case of attacks on diplomats, attacks on civilians and on other militarily meaningless targets constitute a powerful repudiation of established conventions and therefore of customary patterns of thought. Like diplomats, national airline carriers are symbols of the state.

Over the period under study, diplomats and airlines have become proportionately less frequent targets of violence since the ministries responsible for foreign affairs and air transport have taken increased security precautions (see Figure 2.7 and Table 2.3). In 1968, attacks on diplomats and airlines accounted for two-thirds of all attacks, 40% and 27% respectively. In 1986, diplomats and airlines were involved in just over one-third of attacks, 27% and 9% respectively. Airlines in particular have become much

Figure 2.7
Occupational Targets by Year

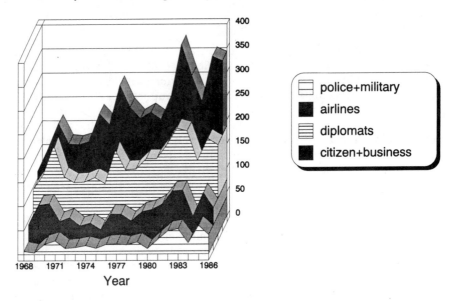

more secure. Meanwhile, the military have become more frequent targets of terrorism, partly because governments have instituted fewer measures to protect their armed forces than their diplomats. The proportion of attacks on military targets doubled from 5% in 1968 to 10% in 1986.

The greatest increase in victimization involves businessmen and ordinary civilians, on behalf of whom it is difficult for governments to undertake security precautions. Ordinary civilians and businessmen have replaced diplomats as the main targets of terrorism. In 1968, diplomats were targeted in 40% of cases while businessmen and citizens were targets in 13%. Eighteen years later, diplomats were still the single most frequent target, but their proportion declined to 27% while the combined share of attacks involving businessmen and citizens rose to 37%. International terrorism as a whole has increased by a factor of about 3 while attacks on businessmen have increased by a factor of approximately 5 and attacks on ordinary citizens by a factor of almost 10.

Table 2.3 Terrorist Acts—Occupation of Target by Year

Year	Police/military	Airlines	Diplomats	Citizens/business
1968	7	36	53	1
1969	3	80	44	34
1970	21	65	102	25
1971	28	21	73	49
1972	12	44	54	59
1973	14	25	72	64
1974	18	27	75	114
1975	12	19	77	103
1976	20	44	113	116
1977	21	42	73	111
1978	19	30	88	86
1979	25	43	91	77
1980	11	62	86	62
1981	30	54	104	83
1982	48	63	112	154
1983	52	61	104	95
1984	23	35	97	103
1985	59	49	93	151
1986	40	36	112	155

The emphasis on diplomats and the increased targeting of businessmen and ordinary civilians reflects the essence of international terrorism as a repudiation of conventional warfare with its elaborately developed and stylized code of conduct relating to the obligations of armies toward civilians. The avoidance of utilities as targets and the strictly limited nature of attacks on the military reflect the essentially nonmilitary purposes of international terrorists. The nature of the targets suggests that terrorists are little interested in achieving military conquest or causing serious material damage.

Achieving an extraordinary psychological impact is the real purpose of the terrorists' choice of unorthodox means and ends. As Jenkins observes, international terrorism "denigrates conventional military power by substituting dramatic violence played for the people watching. It violates the conventional rules of engagement: it reduces the category of innocent bystanders. It makes the world its battlefield: it recognizes no boundaries to the conflict, no neutral nations."[35]

35   Jenkins, *High Technology*, 8.

Table 2.4 *Victims' Occupations by Perpetrators*

Perpetrator	Dipl	Busin	Milit	Police	Air	Citizens	Other
Palest	19	9	5	0	16	21	30
Italian	29	42	13	0	5	3	8
German	12	16	54	0	4	3	12
French	6	51	1	12	8	5	18
Irish	11	17	25	1	1	14	31
Puerto R.	5	56	8	3	11	0	17
Spanish	19	44	1	1	3	13	21
Cuban	34	28	0	0	14	3	20
Latin Am.	38	37	3	0	6	6	10
Armen.	32	17	0	0	30	6	15
Middle E.	27	12	11	0	13	14	22
unknown	43	19	11	0	9	7	12

Overall, the period has witnessed an increased victimization of businessmen and ordinary civilians, but terrorists vary considerably in their target preferences (Table 2.4). Irish and especially German terrorists have focused their energies to a very considerable extent on military targets. More than half of German terrorists' targets were military. Apart from the Germans and the Irish, no single category of terrorist group selected the military for more than 15% of its targets.

Police targets are virtually ignored with one significant exception. The police did not once represent a target for Italian, German and Cuban terrorists but they represented more than 12% of the targets for French terrorists.

Businessmen and diplomats were targets for everyone. Businessmen figured more strongly than average for Puerto Rican and French terrorists and less strongly for Palestinian and other Middle Easterners. Diplomats figured more strongly for Cubans and Latin Americans and less strongly for French and Puerto Rican terrorists, who had their eye above all on businessmen. Airlines were targeted by everyone, especially by Armenians, Palestinians, and other Middle Eastern groups. Private citizens were earmarked especially by Palestinian, Irish, Middle Eastern, and Spanish terrorists.

The Location of Violence

Terrorist acts take place primarily in Europe and secondarily in Latin America and the Middle East. Highly populous Asia is far behind as is sub-Saharan Africa. Figure 2.8 shows that more than one-third of terrorist acts have occurred in Europe while between one-fifth and one-fourth have taken place in Latin America and the Middle East. Of course, to say that one-third of terrorist acts took place in Europe does not mean that one-third of the victims or one-third of the perpetrators were necessarily European. The identities of perpetrators and victims are discussed below in separate sections.

Within Europe, violent outbursts were concentrated among six countries in the west or south while they were virtually unknown among the communist states. Together, France (9%), West Germany (5%), the United Kingdom (4%), Italy (4%), Spain (3%), and Greece (3%) experienced 28% of the world's and four-fifths of Europe's acts of international terrorism in the period under study. France alone was host to almost one-tenth of interna-

Figure 2.8
Location of Terrorist Acts (%)

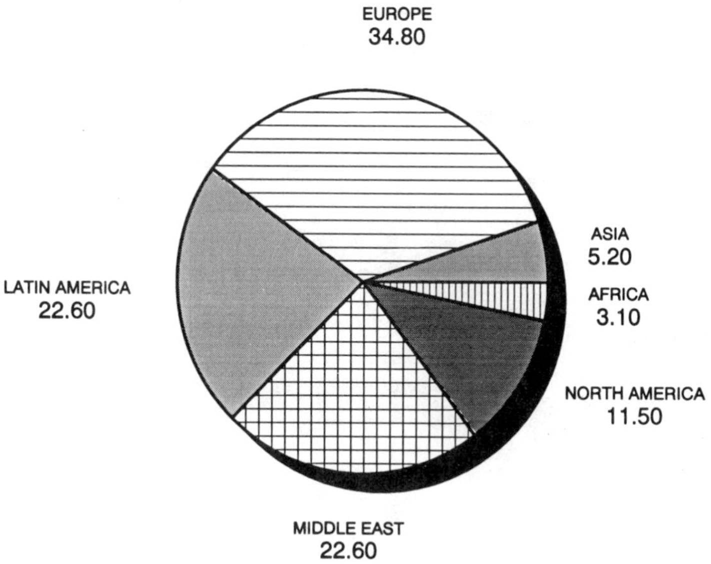

EUROPE
34.80

ASIA
5.20

AFRICA
3.10

NORTH AMERICA
11.50

MIDDLE EAST
22.60

LATIN AMERICA
22.60

tional terrorist acts, more than Lebanon and more than twice as much as Israel. Given the reasonably widespread image of Lebanon as a site of international terrorism, it merits mentioning that Lebanon suffered far more from domestic than from international terrorist acts.

Terrorism was somewhat dispersed in Latin America and the Middle East, albeit with some concentration. Argentina (6%) and Colombia (3%) accounted for about two-fifths of terrorism on their continent while Lebanese (8%) and Israeli (4%) territory were involved in about half the terrorism in the Middle East. Within North America, terrorist acts occur almost entirely in the United States. Canada was the site for less than 0.5% of international terrorist acts.

Over the period in question, terrorism on U.S. soil involved a hodgepodge of different groups, ranging from Croatians to anti-Castro Cubans. During the late 1960s, when the rate of international terrorism was lower than it would become, terrorism on U.S. soil accounted for a very high proportion of the world's total. But terrorism within the United States declined in a fluctuating fashion over the 18 years under study. By 1986, terrorism in the 50 states of the American union fell to 2% of the world total.

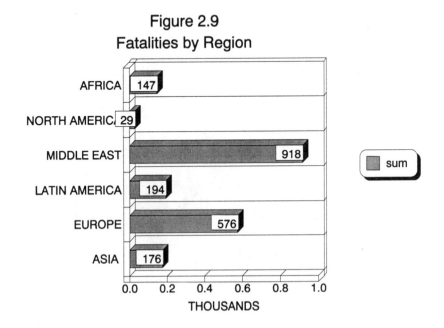

Figure 2.9
Fatalities by Region

Region	Value
AFRICA	147
NORTH AMERICA	29
MIDDLE EAST	918
LATIN AMERICA	194
EUROPE	576
ASIA	176

THOUSANDS

sum

Terrorism in Europe and the Middle East rose in the same period in a fluctuating fashion while it declined proportionately in Latin America. In the 1960s, Latin America was the site of 35 to 45% of the world's international terrorist acts as compared with less than 20% in the 1980s. In recent years, Middle East countries became the site for between 35% and 50% of terrorist acts. Meanwhile Europe began to host about one-third of the world's total.

The Middle East is not only significant because it is a region of growth in terrorist activity but also because violence in that region of the world is the most apt to be fatal (see Figures 2.9 and 2.10). For the entire period under study, only 22.6% of terrorist acts took place in the region. Yet, terrorism in the Middle East involved as much as 45% of the world's fatalities from this cause. By contrast, terrorism within North America was least apt to be deadly. North America accounts for 11.5% of the world's terrorist acts and 1.4% of deaths.

Figure 2.10
Sum of Victims by Location and Period

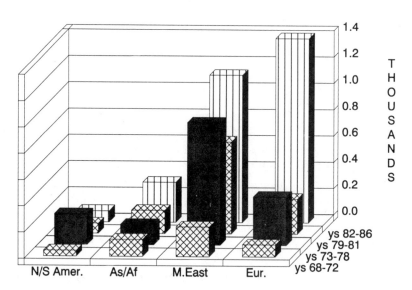

The Nationality of Targets

The nationalities of the victims of terrorism are far less diverse than the nations where terrorist acts unfold. A RAND Corporation report concludes: "One pattern of international terrorism established in the 1970's and continued in the 1980's: the United States remains the number one target."[36] Indeed, the RAND data show that American nationals were the objects of one-third of terrorist attacks throughout the period and that this ratio did not change much from year to year (*see* Figure 2.11).

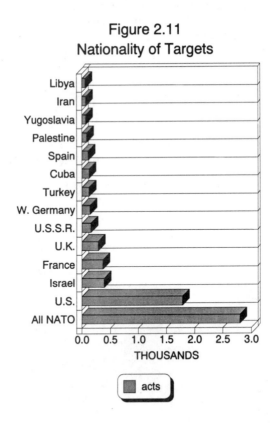

Figure 2.11
Nationality of Targets

THOUSANDS

acts

---

36   RAND Corporation Report: *Trends in International Terrorism* (August 1984), 2.

Americans and citizens of other Western alliance countries were the main victims, accounting for half of the world total. Of 5,589 attacks in the period under study, 1,790 were directed against Americans, 374 against Frenchmen, and 289 against Britons. Israelis were subject to 396 attacks, only fractionally more than the number involving citizens of France. Of the 13 countries whose citizens were most victimized, 6 were allies of the United States. For every major international terrorist grouping, American nationals were the most frequent victims (see Figure 2.12).

The citizens of three communist states were subject to terrorist attacks, albeit on a much smaller scale than the citizens of Western countries and with less lethality. The Soviet Union experienced 164 attacks, Cuba 129, and Yugoslavia 75. In most instances, these three countries were subject to violence perpetrated abroad by exiles.

Three third world groups were objects of repeated violence, primarily from terrorists in their own region. Thus, Palestinians experienced 93 attacks,

Figure 2.12 U.S. and Israeli Victims by Terrorist Grouping

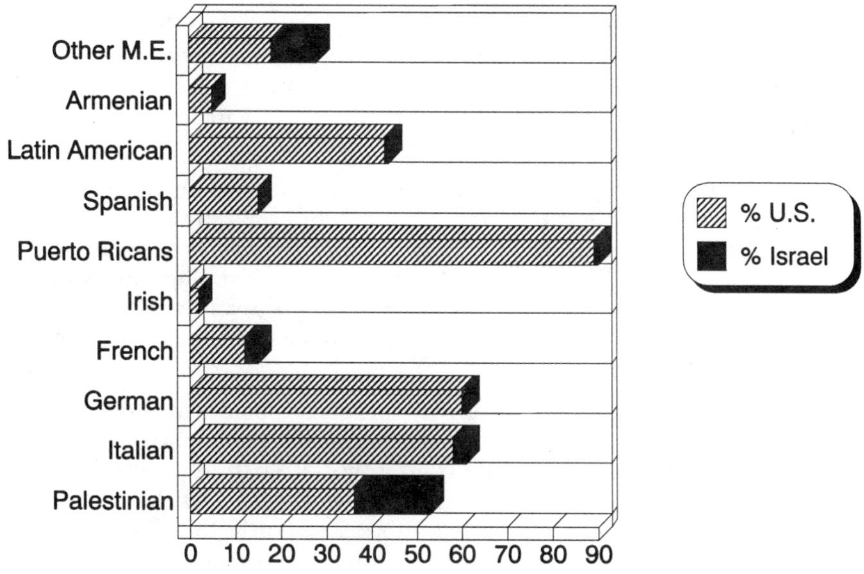

0 10 20 30 40 50 60 70 80 90

Other M.E.
Armenian
Latin American
Spanish
Puerto Ricans
Irish
French
German
Italian
Palestinian

% U.S.
% Israel

almost entirely from other Palestinian or Arab groups. Iranians and Libyans were involved as victims in 74 and 66 cases, respectively, of international terrorism.

We have not portrayed graphically the changes or trends in the targeting of victims because there are no changes or trends deserving of attention. American citizens were consistently the main target of attack throughout the study period (Figure 2.12). Other consistently important targets were Israelis, French, Britons, and West Germans. French citizens were almost as likely to be victimized as Israelis. However, as shown below in Chapter 3, the victimization of Israelis is far more apt to be reported.

Americans were the target of one-third of all attacks and yet fewer than 2% of these attacks have taken place on American soil. If the object of anti-American terrorism were to damage the American economy or military structure, attacks on American soil would be necessary. But if the object of anti-American terrorism were simply to attack American nationals, it is more cost-effective to do so abroad.

It is easier and safer to attack Americans in Europe and Lebanon than in the United States itself. It is true that Syrian, Iranian, and other diplomatic missions may be just as capable of transshipping concealed weapons to Washington and Ottawa as to Athens and Paris. But airport and general border security have been tighter in the United States than in much of Europe. Furthermore, the Red Army Faction, Baader-Meinhof, IRA, Red Brigade, Action Directe, and other groups have been able to provide weapons and safe houses in Europe. Comparable underground networks have not existed in North America. If captured in Europe, terrorists have greater hopes of escaping, being released, or being exchanged for hostages.

When victims are selected from nations other than those to which the perpetrators belong, they are chosen in part, but only in part, because they belong to ideologically strategic enemy nations. Britons are targeted by Irish terrorists because Great Britain is perceived to be an illegitimate occupier of Northern Ireland. Americans are targeted by Puerto Ricans, Israelis by Palestinians and other Arabs, Spaniards by Basques, and Frenchmen by Corsicans for analogous reasons.

Being a citizen of a strategic enemy nation or social class does not fully account for why individuals become victims. The Arab countries are ex-European colonies who, apart from Egypt after the Camp David Agreement, are in a quasi-permanent state of war with Israel. Yet American citizens fall victim to Arab terrorists more frequently than Israelis and far more frequently than Europeans. The United States played the lead role in the post-World War II denazification of Germany, and yet leftwing German terrorists channel much of their violence against Americans. Fascist Europe decimated the continent's Jewish population, and yet Europe's antifascist terrorists victimized the Israeli descendants of the survivors. Latin American terrorists set their sights on U.S. nationals even though their goals have been to achieve power in their own capitals rather than in the District of Columbia.

Victims are selected not just because they belong to ideologically reprobate nations but also because of their availability. For example, Soviet citizens were not particularly available because they travelled infrequently and were security conscious. American could be targeted in large numbers away from the sanctuary of their home country.

Victims are selected in part because of their propaganda usefulness. From a propaganda perspective, targeting Americans can display bravado by provoking the world's most powerful country with apparent impunity. Whether in Europe, Latin America, or the Middle East, targeting Americans can help mobilize indigenous nationalism on behalf of a broader alliance to bring about a change of regime.

Ultimately, any successful propaganda effort needs publicity. Attacking Americans helps assure attention from the increasingly U.S.-based international media systems. That some victims are more newsworthy and hence more useful than others is a vital theme to be addressed in the next chapter.

Although most of the major terrorist groupings target Americans to some degree, Irish terrorists are an exception. Irish Catholic terrorist groups have been in the unique situation of possessing constituencies of political and financial support within the United States. The IRA and its allies and competitors could not risk alienating U.S. supporters by being perceived to be doing harm to Americans.

The Perpetrators, Their Settings, Their Actions

The task of analyzing patterns of responsibility for terrorist activity is not insurmountable. Unlike criminals, terrorists are anxious for recognition. They normally make an overt claim of responsibility or at least make it easy for the press to infer it. For the period as a whole, the identity of the perpetrators was either unambiguous or eagerly volunteered in 62.7% of instances. In an additional 15.0% of cases, the identity of the perpetrators could be inferred with assurance. In only 22.2% of events have the terrorists neither made an overt claim nor left sufficient evidence to identify them with confidence. It is easy to make a preliminary identification of the perpetrators of terrorism because terrorists wish to be identified.

Although it may be easy to make a preliminary identification of the perpetrators of an act, making a complete identification can be very complicated. Major organizations such as the Amal in Lebanon or the Palestine Liberation Organization (PLO) sometimes produce splinter organizations that appear to act independently. It is not always clear to what extent a splinter organization is truly rebellious or actually a *front* group whose more bloodthirsty conduct is intended to make the original group appear more moderate or reasonable. Many splinter groups undertake one hijacking and are never heard of again.

The RAND Corporation dataset compiles information on four Irish groups and 14 Palestinian groups, ranging from the Popular Front for the Liberation of Palestine, General Command, to Black September and Eagles of the Palestinian Revolution.

Analyzing each individual group's conduct separately could become a nightmare of disentangling the true organizational relationships among the different groups. Analyzing each group could also become difficult statistically because no single group accounts for as many as 3% of the actions in the period. The most active groups, the Palestine Liberation Organization (PLO) and Irish Republican Army (IRA), were involved in only 2.2% and 2.4% of terrorist acts, respectively.

For ease of analysis, the various terrorist groups were clustered by nation of origin. Thus, all 14 Palestinian groups were clustered as Palestinian, Italian groups as Italian, and so forth. All Latin American groups were combined into a single category as were all Middle Eastern groups except for Palestinians and Armenians, who were each treated separately.

Responsibility for international terrorism is heavily concentrated. Palestinian groups are the source of more than one-third of all terrorist acts. Almost half of all terrorist acts originate with Middle Eastern groups, namely Palestinians (33.9%), Armenians (3.9%), and "other" Middle Eastern groups (9.1%). French, Spanish, Irish, Puerto Rican, German and Italian terrorists each account for fewer than 3% of incidents. All Latin American groups combined were involved in 16.8% of such acts.

Over the period under study, Palestinians retained their primacy as the most active and the most international group. The European groups remained parochial; virtually all their terrorist activity was conducted on the continent (e.g., 97.3% or higher in each case). By contrast, the Palestinians perpetrated their violent acts primarily away from home. Thus, only 35.5% of Palestinian terrorism was conducted in the Middle East as compared to 32.7% in Europe and 20.7% in Latin America. Armenian terrorists were less likely to undertake violence in the Middle East than the Palestinians (21.8% vs. 35.5%). But the Armenians were less diversified; two-thirds of their violence took place in Europe.

Other Middle Eastern and Latin American terrorism fell midway between the internationalism of the Palestinians and the parochialism of the Europeans. One-third of "other" Middle Eastern terrorist initiatives took place outside the home continent and one-fifth in the case of Latin American terror.

The RAND Corporation dataset compiles information on seven different types of terrorist actions: kidnapping, attacks on institutions, hijacking, bombings, barricades, assassinations, and threats. Bombings account for half (50.9%) the acts during the period under study. Other important shares are contributed by attacks on institutions (17.2%), assassinations (11.4%), kidnapping (9.0%), and hijacking (7.5%).

During the late 1960s, hijackings were frequent. Indeed, between 1968 and 1970, 36% of all terrorist acts involved the seizure of aircraft. By 1986, the rate of hijacking declined to a low of 1.2%. During the same period, kidnapping, attacks on institutions, bombings, and assassinations gradually increased while the frequency of barricades and threats remained static.

The United States was by far the most frequent target for each kind of violent act. In spite of their focused opposition to Israel, the Palestinian and other Middle Eastern groups seized only 3 Israeli aircraft throughout the period. By contrast, 134 U.S. airliners were hijacked.

Perpetrators' Styles: Traditional vs. Media-oriented

International terrorists can be subdivided into two broad categories: media-motivated terrorists, who script their violence to earn publicity, and traditional terrorists, whose main priorities are not publicity. Traditional terrorists, like traditional revolutionaries, might be expected to follow traditional rules of warfare in selecting their targets and to direct their violence against forces of repression, notably the police and military. Traditional terrorists might also be expected to target certain governmental authorities but not diplomats, who are more external symbols than internal governors of the state. Traditional terrorists concerned about class inequality or domination might focus on the business class. Above all, traditional terrorists might direct their violence against the nationals of the state with which they are in combat.

French, Irish, and some other European terrorists fit the traditional mold relatively well. The Irish focus on military targets (25% vs. 8% for all terrorist acts) and governmental ones (21% vs. 2%) while downplaying diplomats (11% vs. 29%). More than 93% of the victims of Irish violence are Britons. French terrorists focus on the business class (51% vs. 21%) and the police (12% vs. 0.5%). Most of the victims of French terrorism are French. Seven-eighths of French and Irish actions are bombings as compared to one-half for the more media-wise Palestinians and other Middle Eastern terrorists, whose repertoire is more diversified. The modes of operation of Spanish and Armenian terrorists are similar.

In contrast to traditional terrorists, media-oriented terrorists might be expected to emphasize actions that would produce maximum direct publicity. Since the American television networks are the preeminent media organizations in the world, media-oriented terrorists would be expected to seek media recognition by attacking American nationals rather than the citizens of the states with which they are actually in combat.

Palestinian, other Middle Eastern, and Latin American terrorists fit the mold of those who deploy violence to capture direct media attention. On traditional grounds, Palestinians would be expected to target Israelis and Jordanians; PLO territorial claims have been interpreted as involving both countries. But the media advantage of attacking Americans helps explain why more than twice as many Palestinian attacks were directed against Americans as against Israelis (36% vs. 17%) in this period and more than 10 times against Americans as against Jordanians (36% vs. 3%). Similarly, twice as many attacks were made by other Middle Eastern groups against U.S. citizens as against the citizens of Israel (20% vs. 10%). The victims of Palestinian terrorism were more frequently American than Israeli (see Figure 2.12).

Unlike more traditional terrorist groups, the media-motivated Palestinians, Middle Easterners, and Latin Americans did not single out the military, the police, or institutions and did not resort with special frequency to the traditional weapon of the oppressed, the bomb. Middle Easterners and Latin Americans placed somewhat more emphasis on kidnapping while Palestinian terrorists tilted towards attacks on institutions such as embassies.

In terms of brutality, the other Middle Eastern and the Palestinian terrorists were the most severe. Thus, the other Middle Eastern terrorists averaged almost two fatalities per event, the Palestinians almost one (0.92), the Irish somewhat less (0.73), and all other groups less than 0.5 per event.

To this point, we distinguished between two ideal types: *traditionally motivated* and *media–motivated* terrorists. When the traditional quasi-guerrilla terrorist group seeks media attention, it seeks it as a by-product of action; for media-motivated terrorists, publicity is all, or almost all.

The reality of terrorist conduct can be more subtle and less clear. Sometimes one branch of essentially the same movement will be more interested in media recognition than another and/or will be driven by very different doctrinal or tactical goals. Such was the case of Quebec's *Front de Libération du Québec* in October 1970. One analyst has portrayed the twin-celled FLQ as a "two-Headed Monster."[37]

Sometimes the quest for publicity and recognition is driven by jockeying for power within a terrorist coalition. Such internal competition between factions has been a factor among both Irish and Palestinian terrorists.[38] The assassination in 1980 of Lord Louis Mountbatten, war hero and member of the royal family, can be understood in terms of competition for publicity and market share among rivalrous republican groups.

Terrorist activity reflects not only the internal realities of terrorist groups but also the external realities of international politics. For Palestinian terrorist groups, the reality of international politics often means striking alliances with one or more feuding Arab states. For Irish terrorists, the reality of international politics means self-restraint in dealing with Americans. Irish terrorists have looked to supporters in the United States for financial assistance and arms supplies. Given the importance of these supporters and the advantages of keeping the United States as neutral as possible in the terrorists' conflict with Britain, one ought not to be entirely surprised that Irish terrorists have targeted Americans as victims less often than have any other major terrorist group (see Figure 2.12).

37   Ronald D. Crelinsten, "The Internal Dynamics of the FLQ during the October Crisis of 1970," in David C. Rapoport, ed., *Inside Terrorist Organizations* (New York: Columbia University Press, 1988), 78.
38   On the significance of Palestinian factional rivalries, see David T. Schiller, "A Battlegroup Divided: The Palestinian Fedayeen," in Rapoport, ed., *Inside Terrorist Organizations*, 90-108.

Chapter 3

Media-oriented Terrorism

The Theater of Terror

> Let me put forward the proposition that the media, particularly television, and terrorists need one another, that they have what is fundamentally a symbiotic relationship. Without television, terrorism becomes rather like the philosopher's hypothetical tree falling in the forest: no one hears it fall and therefore it has no reason for being. And television without terrorism, while not deprived of all interesting things in the world, is nonetheless deprived of one of the most interesting.[1]
>
> Ted Koppel, ABC anchor

This statement, made by a prominent journalist, may not surprise students of the media or terrorism or the increasingly aware general public. During the early 1970s, academics commented with increasing frequency on the media-directedness of terror. Terror had entailed a mass psychological aspect historically. But contemporary terrorists became exposed to new opportunities for exerting mass psychological impacts as a result of technological advances in communications and transportation.

The most significant technological change was the emergence and widespread diffusion of television broadcasting. Television's impact was strengthened by advances in the communications systems that journalists used to transmit from the field to the head offices. Enhanced air transportation meanwhile enabled reporters to reach distant locations more quickly than previously imagined.

Paralleling the growth in technology-driven opportunities for terrorist action were efforts by terrorists themselves to hone their communications skills. During the 1970s, academic observers remarked increasingly on the theatrical proficiency with which terrorists conducted their operations. Brian Jenkins concluded a study of the subject by observing: "Terrorist attacks are often carefully choreographed to attract the attention of the electronic media and the international press. Taking and holding hostages

---

1   See "Terrorism and the Media: A Discussion," *Harper's* (October 1984), 47.

increases the drama. The hostages themselves often mean nothing to the terrorists....Terrorism is aimed at the people watching, not at the actual victims." As Laqueur put it more simply, "The media are the terrorist's best friend. The terrorist's act by itself is nothing, publicity is all." Commenting on the motivations of terrorists, Bell said: "It has become more alluring for the frantic few to appear on the world stage of television than remain obscure guerrillas of the bush."[2]

Modern terrorism can be understood in terms of the production requirements of theatrical engagements. Terrorists pay attention to script preparation, cast selection, sets, props, role playing, and minute–by–minute stage management. Just like compelling stage plays or ballet performances, the media orientation in terrorism requires a fastidious attention to detail in order to be effective. But the metaphor has its limits.

Terrorists have powers beyond the reach of legitimate producers. Terrorists have coercive influence over who will be in the immediate audience and what the reviewers will say. In the particular cases of hijacking and kidnapping, terrorists can decide which journalists and which hostages will be permitted interviews, from which script the hostages will read, and hence to some extent what will actually be reported. In the extreme instance of a nonobliging journalist, terrorists have means of reprisal that are unthinkable for the mere playwright or Broadway producer.

The Media within the Terrorists' Paradigm

Violence as a means of communication received an impetus with the inception of the mass media. Schmid and de Graaf point to the discovery of dynamite in 1866 and the perfection of the rotary press in the same year—"two inventions that soon started to interact."[3] A headline in the anarchist paper *Truth* declared: "*Truth* is two cents a copy, dynamite is forty cents a pound. Buy them both, read one, use the other."[4]

2   B. Jenkins, *International Terrorism* (Los Angeles: Crescent Publication, 1975), 4; W. Laqueur, "The Futility of Terrorism," *Harper's* (March 1976), 104; J. B. Bell, *Transnational Terror* (Washington, D.C.: American Enterprise Institute, 1975), 89.
3   A. Schmid and J. de Graaf, *Violence as Communication* (Beverly Hills, Calif.: Sage, 1982), 9.
4   See B. Johnpoll, "Terrorism and the Mass Media in the United States," in Y. Alexander and S. M. Finger, eds., *Terrorism: Interdisciplinary Perspectives* (New York: John Jay Press, 1977), 160.

3 Media-oriented Terrorism

Nineteenth-century European anarchists faced the problem of communicating their ideas to the general public, to the masses they wanted to liberate. Their pamphlets had a limited distribution in part because of the difficulty of reaching the illiterate. Anarchists turned to the "propaganda of the deed," using acts of violence in order to win coverage from the national and international press as well as encourage word-of-mouth communication.

According to Laqueur, the late nineteenth century Italian anarchists Malatesta and Cafiero were among the first to postulate the nature of a media-terror nexus. They declared that "the insurrectional fact destined to affirm socialist principles by deeds is the most effective means of propaganda and the only one which...can penetrate the deepest social layers...."[5] Out of this perspective emerged the concept of "propaganda by deed."

During the same period in Russia, Peter Kropotkin expanded similar observations into a theory of terror. "By actions which compel general attention," he noted, "the new idea seeps into people's minds and wins converts. One such act may, in a few days, make more propaganda than a thousand pamphlets."[6] The Narodnaya Volya acted on the theory. A czar and senior officials were executed. The assassinations were neither ends in themselves nor direct means of acquiring power. Victims were selected on the basis of an anticipated propaganda effect.

The potential for a propaganda effect increased as a result of technological innovation in news transmission, printing, and circulation. By the end of the nineteenth century, mass circulation papers could reach one million readers within 12 hours. As Western societies became more literate and consumers more able to purchase daily newspapers, the mass press became a powerful social force. And this power did not go unnoticed.

In 1901, the anarchist who murdered U.S. President William McKinley explained: "A man should not claim so much attention while others receive none." The anarchist who murdered Empress Elizabeth was a collector of news clippings; he said that he wanted to kill "someone important so it gets into the papers."[7]

5   *Bulletin de la Fédération Jurassienne* (Dec. 3, 1876) in W. Laqueur, *Terrorism* (London: Weidenfeld and Nicolson, 1977).

6   Quoted in Z. Iviansky, "Individual Terror: Concept and Typology," *Journal of Contemporary History* 12 (1977), 45.

7   F. Hacker, *Terror, Mythos, Realitat, Analyse* (Reinbeck, Rowohlt), 259, and B. Tuchman, *The Proud Tower* (New York: Bantam Books, 1972), 118.

Empress Elizabeth's executioner expressed naively the complex relationship between terrorism and the media that many twentieth century practitioners would master. Menahem Begin, leader of the Irgun Zvai Leumi or
National Military Organization during the British Palestine Mandate (1920-
1948), wrote about that experience during the 1960s, long after Irgun's
demise and before he would become prime minister of Israel. Irgun's twin
goal was to force a British withdrawal so that a Jewish state could emerge
and to protect Jewish settlements from Arab attack.

Begin remarked upon the attention his organization would secure both
among the local Jewish population and in the world press as a result of
dramatic and/or humiliating acts against the British forces. Irgun's
newspapers, posters, and broadcasts succeeded in gaining an attentive
audience as a result.[8] A special wing of Irgun, the Revolutionary Propaganda Force, "was given the task of disseminating the message of revolt. Our
people expected explanations of our actions and we had to give explanations
in order to secure what we wished to secure: their understanding and their
sympathy."[9]

Irgun learned self-consciously from the experience of underground movements in Europe about the importance of communicating its point of view
and about different ways of doing so. "We were compelled to defend
ourselves," noted the movement's former leader. "One of the most important
means was our radio station. At first we broadcast for only five minutes a
day....Thereafter we broadcast for ten, fifteen or twenty minutes. We were
never silenced."[10]

The target audience for Irgun's propaganda extended beyond the Jewish
community in Palestine. At home, Irgun sought to employ word and deed
to demoralize the British military. Abroad, Irgun sought to enhance support
among both Jews and non-Jews. "We translated our broadcasts," wrote
Begin,

> into foreign languages and distributed them among the foreign newspaper
> correspondents and foreign diplomatic representatives. Our broadcasts
> generally contained factual news and political analysis. As we learnt, they
> received very wide publicity in the world's press, from Sydney to San Francisco.
> This was important in keeping the Eretz Israel problem in the focus of
> international attention. The voice of revolt and of freedom was carried far and
> wide despite the British Government's jamming. If scores of thousands were

8   M. Begin, *The Revolt: Story of the Irgun* (Tel Aviv: Hadar, 1974), 84.
9   Ibid., 80-81. See also 59, 82-83.
10 Ibid., 82-83.

prevented from hearing it, millions heard it, and Eretz Israel continued to hold the world's attention even when the explosives were silent.[11]

The British forces of the time and subsequent commentators termed Begin's group "terrorist," a moniker that he rejected. "The British Press and the British troops continued to call us by that name which, in their General's opinion, suggested bravery on our part and fear on theirs. And yet, we were not terrorists....it all depends on who uses the term. It frequently happens that it is used by both sides in their mutual exchange of compliments."[12]

While Begin was attentive to the propaganda opportunities presented by modern media technology, he was also sensitive to lessons that could be drawn from the historical past. He was anxious not to repeat some of the provocative actions of the Zealots so that Irgun could avoid conflicts in which it would be at a disadvantage. Begin and his lieutenants exercised careful supervision over the distribution of weapons among Irgun followers. Strict control over the selection of targets and the use of munitions were essential in light of the group's considerable dependence on Arabs for its arms supply.

Begin's prime of place as an astute analyst-practitioner would later be ceded to the Brazilian revolutionary Carlos Marighela. Known as the "father of urban guerrilla warfare," Marighela would explore the use of media to reach the urban masses and to goad government into escalation in books and booklets during the late 1960s and early 1970s.[13] His *Minimanual of*

---

11 Ibid., 84.
12 Ibid., 59.
13 John W. Williams highlights the ambiguity and uncertainty associated with the author and revolutionary. "Even the spelling of Marighela's name has been confused." Citing James Nelson Goodsell of the *Christian Science Monitor*, Williams observes that Marighela himself varied both the spelling and pronunciation of his own name. Following Goodsell and Williams, we spell his name with one *l*, not two. See Williams, "Carlos Marighela: The Father of Urban Guerrilla Warfare," *Terrorism* 12 (1989), 1 and 1n.

the Urban Guerrilla became a vital source for terrorist movements around the world. Indeed, it was banned in many countries.[14] Termed "the most celebrated text of twentieth century terrorism," the *Minimanual* consists of 41 chapters prescribing guerrilla operating procedures with respect to organization, logistics, propaganda, and media manipulation.[15] The document was found among the possessions of the Symbionese Liberation Army, known for the kidnapping of heiress Patricia Hearst, as well as in Palestine Liberation Army camps in southern Lebanon.[16]

Marighela sees violence as an essential means of achieving psychological impacts and not as an end in itself. Terrorists should contemplate the widest possible range of options for violence so as to orchestrate the violence for optimum psychological effect:

> The coordination of urban guerrilla action, including each armed action, is the principal way of making propaganda. These actions, carried out with specific and determined objectives, inevitably become propaganda material for the mass communication system. Bank assaults, ambushes, desertion and diverting of arms, the rescue of prisoners, executions, kidnappings, sabotage, terrorism, and the war of nerves are all cases in point. Airplanes diverted in flight, ships and trains assaulted and seized by guerrillas can also be solely for propaganda effects.[17]

An astute political observer, Marighela is alert to the psychological complexity of how individual terrorist actions may be viewed by the mass public. He also sees violence as an essential element of psychological warfare aimed to sow confusion, spur demoralization, and even prompt news censorship. Above all, every choice of target should be made with the view to how it will be portrayed in the mass media and how the portrayal will impact on the general public. For example, he observes that

> to kidnap figures known for their artistic, sporting or other activities who have not expressed any political views may possibly provide a form of propaganda

14   This influential manual has made an appearance in various versions and translations. The original version was published in the *Tricontinental Monthly* (Havana, Jan.-Feb. 1970), 16-56. Unless otherwise indicated, we refer to the original Havana version of the *Minimanual*. On the different editions of Marighela's manual and for a brief biography, see Williams's article, cited in note 13, above.

15   M. Amon, "The Unravelling Myth in Progress," in D. C. Rapoport and Y. Alexander, eds., *The Morality of Terrorism: Religious and Secular Justifications* (New York: Pergamon Press, 1982), 70.

16   F. M. Watson, *Political Terrorism: The Threat and the Response* (New York: Robert B. Luce, 1976), 9-10.

17   *Minimanual of the Urban Guerrilla* (Havana: Tricontinental, 1970), 103.

favourable to the revolutionaries, but should only be done in very special circumstances.[18]

Marighela explores at length the opportunities for revolutionaries that are provided by the mass media:

> Modern mass media, simply by announcing what the revolutionaries are doing, are important instruments of propaganda. However, their existence does not dispense fighters from setting up their own secret presses and having their own copying machines. The war of nerves—or the psychological war—is a fighting technique based on the direct or indirect use of the mass media…. Its purpose is to demoralize the government. By it we can spread false, or contradictory, information [and] sow… anxiety, doubt and uncertainty among the agents of the regime. In psychological warfare the government is at a disadvantage and therefore censors the means of communication. Censorship of course has a boomerang effect, since it leads to unpopularity….[19]

In the wake of his extensive and discursive analysis of media-terror relationships, Marighela himself pinpoints five fundamental principles that should guide terrorist conduct for it to be effective. The five principles are:

- terrorist acts should be aimed at the audience, the general public
- victims should be chosen for their symbolic meaning
- the media are eager to cover terrorist violence
- the media can be activated, directed, and manipulated for propagandistic effect
- governments are at a disadvantage because their only choice is between censorship and letting terrorists make use of the media

18   Marighela, *For the Liberation of Brazil* (Harmondsworth: Pelican, 1971), 87-90.
19   *Minimanual*, 103.

Evidence from Diaries and Interviews

Terrorists' autobiographies, diaries, letters, and interviews can provide some perspective on the ways in which terrorists perceive the role and value of the media. In a recent insightful overview of such documents, Gerrits examined the autobiography of Provisional IRA chief of staff Sean Mac-Stiofain, and that of his erstwhile colleague in arms, Maria McGuire, along with the writings of Gerry Adams, president of the IRA's political wing, Sinn Fein.[20] Gerrits also analyzed the memoirs of German urban guerrillas Michael (Bommi) Baumann and Hans-Joachim Klein and of Palestinian figures Abu Ijad and Leila Khaled.[21]

From a careful analysis of these and other terrorist documents, Gerrits identified various stratagems for achieving publicity:

- designing interventions with news value in mind
- embarking on ancillary propaganda and recruitment efforts
- timing and locating actions in light of their publicity value
- disseminating official statements
- maintaining contacts with journalists and providing interviews
- proclaiming responsibility for terrorist deeds
- communicating to terrorist audiences through the meaning or symbolism of the target or modus operandi.

The memoirs of terrorists reveal their media-mindedness, their sensitivity to media considerations, and their efforts to integrate media considerations into their overall planning. Gerry Adams explained the media rationale

20 Robin P. J. M. Gerrits, "Terrorists' Perspectives: Memoirs," in D. L. Paletz and A. P. Schmid, eds., *Terrorism and the Media* (Newbury Park, Calif.: Sage, 1992), 46. Adams authored *Falls Memories* (Dingle, Ireland: Brandon, 1982) and *The Politics of Irish Freedom* (Dingle, Ireland: Brandon, 1986). McGuire wrote *To Take Arms: A Year with the Provisional IRA* (London: Macmillan, 1973), while MacStiofain's thoughts appeared in his *Revolutionary in Ireland* (Famborough: Gordon Cremonesi, 1975).

21 Gerrits's sources were: Baumann, *How It All Began* (transl.) (Amsterdam: S. Landshoff, 1976), Klein, *Return to Humanity* (transl.) (Reinbek: Rowohlt, 1979), Ijad, *Fatherland or Death* (transl.) (Dusseldorf: Econ, 1979), and Khaled, *My People Shall Live* (London: Hodder and Stoughton, 1973).

succinctly: "The tactics of armed struggle is of primary importance because it provides a vital cutting-edge. Without it the issue of Ireland would never even be an issue. So, in effect the armed struggle becomes armed propaganda."[22] Many terrorists have referred to actions that amounted to *glorious failures* in which publicity achievement compensated for military setback. For example, McGuire refers to the interception in the Netherlands of Czech arms destined for Irish republicans—"a spectacular operation which put the Provisional IRA on the front pages of the world's newspapers—even though the operation ultimately failed."[23]

According to Michael "Bommi" Baumann, the Red Army Faction believed that the "revolution will not be built up by political work, but through headlines, through its appearances in the press, which reports again and again that guerrillas are fighting here in Germany."[24] In retrospect, Baumann expressed concern that his group had been excessively preoccupied with media reaction. "We always immediately looked how the newspapers, especially in Berlin, reacted to our actions, and how they explained them, and thereupon we defined our strategy. But this was wrong."[25] He describes himself as having been on a "media trip." After an operation, his group "would go home and watch it all on the telly. That was great."[26]

The issue of comparative news value prompted many terrorists to contemplate ways of enhancing the newsworthiness of their actions, for example, by victimizing prominent individuals. Hans-Joachim Klein wrote about a proposal to "kidnap the princess of Monaco because in those days in the German magazines a lot was written about Caroline...."[27]

The newsworthiness of an action could also be enhanced by symbolic content. Dramatic impact could be achieved by means of symbolism in the timing or location of actions and in the identity of the victims. German practitioner Michael Baumann reports choosing the anniversary of the key Nazi pogrom of 1938 for its obvious emotive impact: "It was a prize for the

---

22   *The Politics of Irish Freedom*, 64.
23   McGuire, *To Take Arms*, 37.
24   Quoted in Gerrits, "Terrorists' Perspectives: Memoirs" in Paletz and Schmid, eds., *Terrorism and the Media*, 49.
25   Baumann, *How It All Began*, 94., Gerrits' translation, ibid., 48.
26   Baumann, *How It All Began*, 25, Gerrits' translation, in ibid., 57.
27   Klein, *Return to Humanity*, 212.

press, because of all people, it had to be Germans again, who planted a bomb in a Jewish Synagogue on the Kristallnacht."[28] Klein also mentions taking an embassy hostage on its national holiday. After Lord Louis Mountbatten's assassination in 1980, an IRA leader observed that "there was inevitably going to be enormous publicity....we had no hatred for him as a person. It is the society, the military and the political machine he symbolized that we were aiming at."[29]

In its 1972 assault on Israeli athletes at the Munich Olympics, the Palestinian Black September showed an ability to combine symbolic and operational impact. By seizing a dormitory at the worldwide games and killing two athletes at the outset, the group acquired an immediate audience of 800 million viewers. The operation was taking place in Germany, the principal author of the Holocaust, and in Munich, site of Hitler's abortive beer hall putsch in 1923. The terrorist group itself was named in symbolic memory of those who had perished in the September 1970 massacres of Palestinians by King Hussein's security forces. In 1971 in reprisal, Black September assassinated the Jordanian prime minister on a visit to Cairo. But the group's attack on athletes in Munich a year later would achieve far more attention and mark a significant stage in the evolution of the theater of terror.

Several terrorists reported that the psychological climate created by terrorist actions helped to facilitate the undertaking of complementary propaganda and recruitment efforts. Baumann wrote about the necessity of parallel pamphleteering and youth efforts on the one hand and "hit-and-run" actions on the other.[30] Khaled reported on the special effectiveness of propaganda touring in the wake of a high-profile action.[31]

Publicity was achieved, it seems, not only by means of newsworthy actions but also by studied efforts to befriend potentially accommodating journalists. For example, Maria McGuire refers to the many hours of labor necessary to telephone personal invitations to journalists for Provisional IRA press conferences.[32] As Adams notes with a clarity that would appeal to any business communicator, "The media demand special attention

---

28 Ibid., 64.
29 From *An Phoblacht/Republican News*, quoted in Cynthia L. Irvin, "Terrorists' Perspectives: Interviews," in Paletz and Schmid, eds., *Terrorism and the Media*, 77-78.
30 Gerrits, "Terrorists' Perspectives" in Paletz and Schmid, *Terrorism and the Media*, 49.
31 Khaled, *My People Shall Live*, 50-60.
32 McGuire, *To Take Arms* 133.

because of their importance in influencing their audiences' opinion and values."[33]

Weimann had the occasion to interview at length a former terrorist on the subject of communications strategy. The interview was conducted on condition that the former terrorist's identity be protected and that he approve the transcript of the interview. No longer engaged in violence but nonetheless retaining his hopes for revolutionary change, the exterrorist did not want his erstwhile companions to suspect him of betrayal. "D."—his choice of code name—had been active in the German Red Army Faction and Italian Red Brigades until his arrest, conviction, and imprisonment for several years.

When D. was asked about the relationship between the media and terrorism, he replied pointedly that "the mass media are one of the best tools for us, for our cause...." "We want the best for our society," D. went on to say, "and we want...[the public] to know it, to understand it. And this can be done only by using the media."

Asked how this could be done, D. replied:

> We, we give the media what they need: newsworthy events. They cover us, explain our causes and thus, unknowingly, legitimize us....You must understand: the media are very interested in our actions. They look for contacts with us, they try to get information from us and they are eager to report everything we do or say....Take for example the news agencies—within half an hour after calling them and briefing them, which we did quite often, you are in the headlines all over the world....All you need is one phone call, a threat or a declaration....Those [terrorist organizations] I know managed to establish contact and close contact with selected journalists. And the activity is often planned with the media as a central factor. Some actions are planned for the media....You see, in the various organizations, you can find people who are experts in various aspects of psychology, communications, and even propaganda. And they know what should be done. And the timing is crucial: if there is a big event organized by the [political] right, we schedule an act, an attractive act that will overshadow them and attract the media to our message.

When asked which media or public are of greatest interest to terrorists, D. singled out the United States. Capturing the attention of the American media, he noted, had been a problem until the late 1960s. U.S. journalists became more receptive after Washington's involvement in the Vietnam war had brought about intense domestic conflict and prompted the emergence of the New Left. The American media gradually became more cooperative. "And, of course, there was the blackmailing."

33   Adams, *The Politics of Irish Freedom*, 147.

"Blackmailing?" queried the interviewer. "Yes," D. added,

if you don't publish, we kill or bomb...but this is required. We can plan actions that will bring the media to us...the work is done in the Middle East or in a European airport but it is planned by people who know the media, who know how to use them. So they have to report it. And they have to explain it: why all the killings? Why are there bombs? So the public in Europe and the U.S. can hear us, understand our motives and see us as fighters in a social war and not as criminals or lunatics.

D. discussed at length the management of the media by terrorist organizations. For example, during the 1970s some European groups sought to humanize their movement by setting aside ideological discourse and placing more emphasis in interviews on the personalities, backgrounds, and motivations of their leaders. On some occasions, the terrorists themselves became so enthralled with their unprecedented public exposure that they began internecine wars of exposure and ridicule through the media. Individual factions turned on each other, knowing that journalists would welcome stories of betrayal, counterbetrayal, and intimate revelations from the inside.

The management of mass communications was never haphazard, D. was at pains to emphasize:

There is even a division of labour: some are planning, some are executing, and some are monitoring. You see, we can learn from our experience with various media who is reliable, who can be trusted. We learn who should be contacted next time, who should be the first to know or which one is likely to publish what we want. In the organizations there are people with professional background in communication so they know how to do it and how to improve it. There are even journalists and publishers who are members or supporters so their advice and guidance are very helpful.

Cynthia Irvin examined the records of interviews with terrorists, and reached a slightly different conclusion from D.'s. In her view, terrorists often perceive the media as antagonistic and of mixed or moderate value.[34] It is possible for terrorists to be both media-wary and media-wise. The intriguing documentary evidence that Irvin submits in support of a portrait of media-wary terrorists can also be used in support of a portrait of media-wise terrorists. For example, Irvin quotes an internal document of Sinn Fein, the political wing of the IRA, labeling the media as "hostile to our position."

34   Cynthia Irvin, "Terrorists' Perspectives: Interviews," in D. L. Paletz and A. P. Schmid, eds., *Terrorism and the Media* (Newbury Park, Calif.: Sage 1992), 67.

But the same Sinn Fein document identifies a "great benefit if one can build up a personal relationship with journalists."[35] The republican document proceeds to observe that "complaining about bad media coverage is a vital part of the process of getting good media coverage." Complaining vociferously could even "sow seeds of doubt...[to] make...[anti-republican] journalists a bit more careful...."[36] The IRA feels that it must cultivate relations with the press partly because it must contend with a media adversary, the British government, which possesses "a very sophisticated and well financed publicity network, especially internationally...."[37]

In Northern Ireland, the republican movement possesses terrorist wings as well as a political wing in the form of Sinn Fein. Spain's Basque separatist movement likewise produced terrorist groups in the form of the various incarnations of ETA along with a political organization, Herri Batasuna. For such dualistic movements, the challenge is how to parlay episodic violence-induced publicity into ongoing political recognition in the media. A leader of Herri Batasuma has lamented that

> with few exceptions the only time the media want to speak with us is when ETA has carried out an operation. They don't want to hear what we have to say about the environment, about social issues, about our proposals to resolve the conflict, all they want to hear is about what we think about this or that ETA action. So, I would say that media reports of ETA actions, while keeping the public aware that there is a serious political conflict here which won't go away...have a limited impact on our day-to-day political struggle.[38]

How terrorists themselves utilize the media in practice can be illustrated by a consideration of two terrorist incidents, the Hanafi hostage-taking in Washington in March 1977 and the Palestinian seizure of the Italian cruise ship *Achille Lauro* in the Mediterranean in October 1985. Twelve members of the American Muslim sect Hanafi seized 134 hostages at the B'nai B'rith

35   Sinn Fein, "The Needs and Demands of the Struggle," internal briefing document (Dublin, 1986), p. 8, quoted in ibid., 67.
36   Ibid.
37   IRA Headquarters staff position in *An Phloblacht/Republican News* (June 28, 1881) quoted in ibid., 74.
38   Inaki Pinedo, personal communication to Cynthia Irvin, ibid., 75.

International headquarters in the U.S. capital. The Hanafi episode might be classed under international terrorism to the extent that an international edifice is deemed a foreign location. Even if the episode is deemed essentially domestic in character, it is worth retelling because of the lucidity with which the Hanafi leader outlined his media strategy. Overwhelmed by the size of the press contingent, Hamaas Abdul Khaalis peremptorily refused an interview with a Texas radio station: "You are not worth talking to. I don't talk to radio with less than 50,000 watts...."[39] Khaalis's economy of purpose made sense in view of the enormous coverage his group would receive from the networks and major press.[40]

On October 7, 1985, four Palestinian terrorists seized control of the *Achille Lauro* near Alexandria, Egypt. Threatening to kill the passengers, the terrorists forced the crew to sail towards Syria. On the second day of the hijacking, Leon Klinghoffer, a 69-year-old wheelchair-bound New Yorker and Jew, was shot in the head and thrown into the sea.

The terrorists aboard the Italian cruise ship certainly understood how to secure attention. The 50 largest-circulation American newspapers became intensely preoccupied with the event. Hundreds of reports appeared. As many as 43 newspapers editorialized on the issue; only five did not comment editorially; the remaining two dailies were on strike.

Analyzing the Terrorists' Quest for Limelight

We have presented some verbal and nonverbal evidence that the terrorists themselves are acutely aware of the importance of the mass media and design their violent actions with the requirements of the media foremost on their minds. Without media recognition, the terrorists are destined to remain frustrated village thespians, lacking the attention, authority, and funds that accrue to professionals performing before large metropolitan audiences. However skilled a terrorist may be at the violent aspect of his trade, his work cannot be widely known if it is not covered.

---

39 H. Siegel, "Looking at the Media from the Other End of the Gun," in M. Snider, ed., *Media and Terrorism* (Newton, Kans.: Prairie View, 1978), 45-46.

40 The three networks featured the Hanafi story as the lead item for three consecutive nights. NBC assigned 18 camera crews and 100 staff members. Over half its total coverage (53%) was assigned to the story. ABC and CBS devoted 40% and 31%, respectively, of their total news broadcast time to the event. The *Washington Star* and *Post* devoted, respectively, all and most of their front page. H. A. Terry, "Television and Terrorism," *Indiana Law Journal* 53 (1978), 574.

One important question to consider is which village thespians make it to the big city theater and why. More precisely, which of the 500 or so international terrorist groups in the world receive media recognition? And which aspects of their conduct account for their recognition? But, before exploring these somewhat detailed questions, let us consider how much recognition the media accord to international terrorism in general.

One of the first systematic and quantitative studies of this question was conducted by Wurth-Hough in the early 1970s. Her project examined American network news coverage during the approximately three-year period from August 1968 to December 1971. Wurth-Hough found that the three commercial U.S. networks devoted 210 stories to the subject, reporting on about one-fourth of the terrorist activity actually undertaken in that three-year period. Over the time period examined, she found that the networks devoted an increasing amount of attention to terrorism and assigned increasingly important slots on broadcasting timetables.[41]

Delli Carpini and Williams undertook a more extensive analysis.[42] They examined U.S. network coverage of events recorded in a dataset called ITERATE (International Terrorism: Attributes of Terrorist Events) during the years 1969-1980. Their findings added to the growing evidence of internetwork similarity of coverage and pointed to the limited resemblance between patterns of coverage and patterns of actual terrorism. Thus, events in some regions and some terrorist victims were much more likely to be covered than others. Our own work parallels the study by Delli Carpini and Williams in that, like them, we undertake both a cross-sectional and a time series analysis. We also reach similar conclusions about the lack of isomorphism between events and coverage. Our analysis differs insofar as it involves diverse media across several continents as well as more attributes of both the events themselves and of the media treatment of each event.

Several scholars have contributed to an understanding of the media-terrorism nexus through case studies. Nacos, Fan, and Young examined press reports of the 1985 TWA hostage crisis. From their content analysis of the *Washington Post*, *New York Times*, and *Los Angeles Times*, they concluded that "the press facilitated the attention-getting desires of the terrorists very

---

41 S. Wurth-Hough, "Network News Coverage of Terrorism: The Early Years," *Terrorism* 6 (1983), 403-421.

42 M. X. Delli Carpini and B. A. Williams, "Television and Terrorism: Patterns of Presentation and Occurrence, 1969-80," *Western Political Quarterly* 40 (1987), 45-64.

generously. The terrorists were also quite successful in getting their causes and grievances reported while they had only limited success in gaining coverage that might have helped their efforts to gain respectability and legitimacy."[43]

Another case study contrasted U.S. and South Korean coverage of the November 1987 crash of a Korean Airlines (KAL) flight over the Thai-Burma border. North Korean agents had placed a bomb aboard in Dubai during a flight stopover, but this fact was only ascertained and confirmed sometime after the crash itself. Authors Salwen and Lee found that the press in both countries discussed the possibility of sabotage very little before clear evidence emerged, but then placed great stress on the terrorist theme.[44]

A number of scholars have sought to enhance an understanding of the media-terrorist relationship by means of conceptual refinement rather than through empirical analysis alone. Karber portrays terrorism as symbolic behavior:

> As a symbolic act, terrorism can be analyzed much like other media of communication, consisting of four basic components: transmitter (the terrorist), intended recipient (target), message (bombing, ambush) and feedback (reaction of target audience). The terrorist's message of violence necessitates a victim, whether personal or institutional, but the target or intended recipient of the communication may not be the victim.[45]

Dowling recommends that terrorist action be understood as a "rhetorical genre" designed to capture access while Bell suggests that terrorist actions be seen as a special type of "media event" that he terms a "terrorist spectacular."[46]

Altheide has focused on the media side of the media-terrorism relationship. In one study, he compared British and U.S. television coverage of a Hyde Park bombing by the IRA in July 1982. He concluded by making a

43 B. Nacos, D. P. Fan, and J. T. Young, "Terrorism and the Print Media: The 1985 TWA Hostage Crisis," *Terrorism* 12 (1989), 107.

44 M. B. Salwen and J. Lee, "News of Terrorism: A Comparison of the U.S. and South Korean Press," *Terrorism* 11 (1988), 327.

45 P. Karber, "Urban Terrorism: Baseline Data and a Conceptual Framework," *Social Science Quarterly* 52 (1971), 529.

46 R. E. Dowling, "Terrorism and the Media: A Rhetorical Genre," *Journal of Communication* 35 (1986), 12-24, and J. B. Bell, "Terrorist Script and Live-Action Spectaculars," *Columbia Journalism Review* (May-June 1970), 50. See also G. Weimann, "Media Events: The Case of International Terrorism," *Journal of Broadcasting and Electronic Media* 31 (1987), 21-39.

distinction between event-type or news programming and topic-type or public affairs programming:

> Event-type reports tended to focus on terrorism as tactics and aftermath, and to a lesser extent on objectives. On the other hand, topic-type reports more compatible with the documentaries tended to emphasize goals, objectives, and precipitating social conditions. This interpretation suggests that reports cast in the event mold are more ideologically constrained than are reports compatible with the topic form.[47]

Though Altheide concludes that topic-type reports are more open to ideological messages from journalists, it is not clear whether topic-type programming is also more open to the ideological messages of terrorists themselves.

As our contribution to an understanding of the media-terror nexus, we created two content analytic datasets—one on the coverage of terrorist events by the three American commercial networks, the other on such coverage by nine major newspapers around the world. The television and newspaper datasets were then merged with the RAND Corporation data on terrorist events in order to permit a systematic analysis of how these events were covered by the different media.

The two content analytic datasets were created by a combined team of 40 students at Haifa and Carleton Universities. The network datasets were compiled using the records of the Vanderbilt Television News Archive, while the newspaper datasets were compiled directly from microfilm/fiche of the papers in question. The three networks were of course ABC, CBS, and NBC. The newspapers were the *New York Times*, Toronto's *Globe and Mail*, *Times of London*, London's *Daily Telegraph*, *Le Figaro* in Paris, *Frankfurter Allgemeine Zeitung*, *Yediot* in Tel Aviv, Cairo's *Al Aharam*, and the *Pakistan Times*.

Each student coder received training and a list of all the events of international terrorism for a given period. A uniform coding form was used to record whether or not an event was covered, the number of column-lines devoted to it, placement, the inclusion of a photo, reference to the terrorists' motive, and the use of labels to portray the group. Double coding was used. Any resulting discrepancies were checked at source. Because of the simplicity of the variables, the problem of intercoder reliability rarely arose.

The merging of the RAND dataset on terrorist behavior with the content analytic data on news reporting permits comparisons to be made of the

---

47 D. L. Altheide, "Format and Symbols in TV Coverage of Terrorism in the United States and Great Britain," *International Studies Quarterly* 31 (1987), 173.

characteristics of the events themselves with the various ways in which the events were reported in the different media. The content analytic data cover the period 1968-1980.

Figure 3.1 portrays the news coverage given to terrorist events for the years 1968-1980 among the three networks and nine newspapers. Only a small minority of terrorist events are actually reported in the case of each media outlet—less than one-third. Thus, the media exercise a vital *gatekeeping* function, determining which terrorist attacks are reported and which are not. The television networks are especially selective, covering in each instance barely one-seventh of the terrorist events that take place. The highest share of coverage, 33%, appears in the *New York Times*, whose motto is fittingly "All the news that's fit to print." However, even the Yankee paper's 33% score is still far short of "all" or 100% so that it too exercises an important gatekeeping function. The Israeli paper *Yediot* achieves the lowest rate of coverage, 22%. As we shall show below, its coverage tends to be relatively detailed in the cases of those events that it reports.

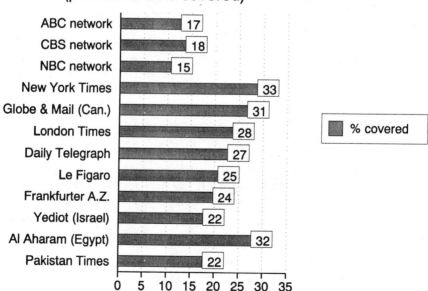

Figure 3.1 Coverage of Terrorist Acts
(percent of acts covered)

Media	% covered
ABC network	17
CBS network	18
NBC network	15
New York Times	33
Globe & Mail (Can.)	31
London Times	28
Daily Telegraph	27
Le Figaro	25
Frankfurter A.Z.	24
Yediot (Israel)	22
Al Aharam (Egypt)	32
Pakistan Times	22

The average terrorist story on television is about two minutes or 120 seconds (see Table 3.1), but this number is only an average. There is considerable random variation among networks and by year in the length of televised reports on terrorist incidents.

Table 3.2 contains comparable information on the volume of coverage provided by the nine newspapers. For each daily paper for each year, the table provides information on the average number of articles devoted to each terrorist event that was actually covered plus an indicator of the average of column-lines devoted to each terrorist event. Terrorist reports are not brief. Among the nine newspapers, stories on terrorist events typically range in size from 60 to 200 column-lines with two or more stories devoted to each event.

Compared to its counterparts, Israel's *Yediot* tends to be more selective in the events it chooses to cover (Figure 3.1) and more voluminous in its coverage of those it does report (Table 3.2). *Yediot*'s articles are more numerous per reported event and longer. The paper averages about five articles per event, each on average in the range of 60 to 100 column-lines. By comparison, London's *Daily Telegraph*, a paper providing middling coverage among the sample of papers, averages about three articles per event, each typically of 21 to 60 column-lines in length. The Israeli paper's pattern and intensity of reporting is explainable in terms of the country's susceptibility to terrorist threat.

Table 3.1

Amount of TV Coverage—1972–1980

Average time per story (seconds)

Year	ABC	CBS	NBC
1972	104.35	117.50	177.93
1973	126.66	141.05	180.00
1974	112.72	85.35	119.94
1975	78.48	82.79	130.27
1976	144.42	154.70	252.10
1977	157.61	127.16	130.40
1978	95.16	92.59	136.68
1979	104.70	102.04	128.57
1980	90.87	83.53	106.31

Table 3.2 Amount of Press Coverage—1972–1980

	NYT		GM		TL		DT	
	SC	NA	SC	NA	SC	NA	SC	NA
1972	2.89	2.17	2.26	1.84	3.00	2.97	2.52	5.26
1973	2.80	2.21	1.85	2.57	2.87	2.23	2.59	3.85
1974	2.90	1.68	2.59	1.83	3.09	1.43	2.96	4.20
1975	2.92	1.70	2.37	1.56	3.30	3.60	1.59	3.37
1976	3.02	2.64	2.25	1.82	3.06	2.67	1.85	2.72
1977	2.43	3.08	2.78	2.12	2.08	2.41	2.39	2.53
1978	3.08	1.98	2.85	1.65	2.88	2.19	2.43	2.23
1979	2.88	3.16	3.07	1.87	2.56	3.39	1.88	1.40
1980	2.60	2.63	2.46	1.79	2.94	2.39	2.31	1.41
Aver.	2.84	2.49	2.02	1.86	2.90	2.73	2.26	2.99

	FI		FR		YD		AA		PK	
	SC	NA	SC	NA	SC	NA	SC	NA	SC	NA
1972	2.28	2.57	2.47	2.62	3.18	8.34	2.60	2.06	2.52	5.26
1973	3.75	3.50	2.29	2.11	3.29	4.56	2.48	2.70	2.51	3.85
1974	2.30	1.59	2.39	1.90	3.53	3.12	1.88	1.63	2.96	4.20
1975	2.04	2.31	3.05	4.55	3.40	4.03	2.19	2.29	1.59	3.37
1976	2.29	1.83	2.10	1.86	3.67	8.35	2.00	2.36	1.83	2.72
1977	2.12	3.45	1.89	4.41	2.26	2.04	1.89	1.51	2.31	2.53
1978	2.00	1.97	2.53	2.04	3.19	3.56	1.73	1.40	2.43	2.23
1979	2.06	1.63	2.19	1.80	3.41	3.98	2.15	1.83	1.88	1.40
1980	2.05	2.08	2.23	1.53	3.11	3.86	1.68	1.75	2.31	1.49
Aver.	2.09	2.31	2.34	2.53	3.19	4.89	1.77	1.78	2.26	2.99

Key: SC=average of space categories: 1=1–20 column lines; 2=21–60 column lines; 3=61–100 column lines; 4=more than 100. NA = number of articles. NYT=New York Times; GM= Globe and Mail; TL=Times of London; DT=Daily Telegraph; FI=Figaro; FR=Frankfurter Allgemeine; YD=Yediot; AA=Al Aharam; PK=Pakistan Times.

Among the remaining papers in the sample, one might expect the most intensive coverage to be found in the *New York Times*, the leading paper from the world's leading state. As discussed earlier, the *New York Times*, the thickest of the papers, does place first in breadth of coverage (Figure 3.1). But the intensity of its coverage places it just below that of the *Times* of London (Table 3.2), itself well below *Yediot*. Given the decline of Great Britain's imperial reach and the decay of its economy, one might not have expected the British paper to have outpaced the American in intensity of coverage. The intensity of the *Times* of London's coverage may be explained by the historically cosmopolitan interests of its audience and the quality of its local newspaper competition.

Toronto's *Globe and Mail* and Cairo's *Al Aharam* both combine high breadth of coverage (Figure 3.1) with low intensity of coverage (Table 3.2), albeit for different reasons. *Al Aharam*'s breadth of coverage reflects the needs of any Middle Eastern state, particularly the Arab leader, to monitor terrorist events. But as the semiofficial organ of an authoritarian regime, the Cairo paper can protect its sensitive position best by sticking to the bare facts and avoiding lengthy and potentially inflammatory analysis.

The *Globe*'s breadth of coverage reflects the Toronto paper's ready access to the world's mainly English language wire services and Canada's special interest in United Nations' peacemaking efforts in trouble spots around the globe. The paper's low intensity of coverage reflects Canada's lack of imperial tradition and overseas investments as well as the ongoing preoccupation of the country's journalists, academics, and opinion leaders with internal constitutional conflict.

To this point, we have shown that terrorists themselves are deeply interested in the limelight, but that less than one-third of all terrorist events are actually reported. Given that only a minority of events are ever covered, it is vital to consider which events are chosen and why. The ensuing pages look at such predictors of coverage as the location of violence, the identity of the victims, and the identity of the perpetrators. Before considering the impact of location and identity upon whether an event is reported, we examine overall patterns of similarity and dissimilarity among the individual media.

Similarity and Dissimilarity: Television vs. the Press

The most important pattern of similarity and dissimilarity in media reporting distinguishes the American television networks from the daily newspapers studied. The networks cover proportionately fewer stories than the press, 15-18% as compared to 22-33% in the case of daily newspapers. Because they inform their audience about only a minority of events, both television and the press exercise powerful gate-setting functions. That television is more selective than the print media betrays an element of irony because it has been widely held that terrorism is virtually "made for TV." Of course, television is apt to be more selective than the press because

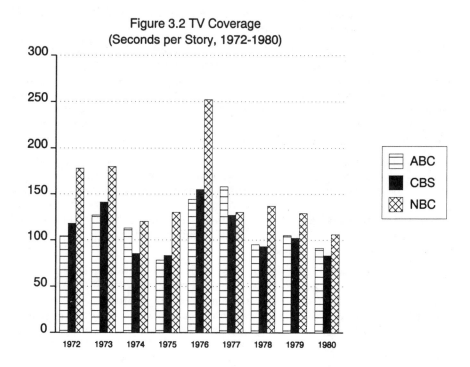

Figure 3.2 TV Coverage
(Seconds per Story, 1972-1980)

television is more constrained in the amount of information that it can convey.

For whatever professional reasons, the networks tend to be homogeneous in their coverage. They tend to assign the same amount of broadcast time to terrorism (see Figure 3.2) and report precisely the same events. The vast majority of events covered by any one broadcasting system are covered by at least one other as well. For example, CBS reports 86% of the stories covered by NBC and 80% of those covered by ABC. Meanwhile the networks leave unmentioned 78% of the terrorist events which take place around the world. As we shall show later, the 78% left unmentioned is not a random selection.

Table 3.3 displays the very high pattern of statistical intercorrelation among the stories carried by the three broadcasting systems. Perfect correlation is 1.00. The intercorrelations among the broadcasters are all close to +.90, a very high indicator of similarity and suggestive of a form of competitive imitation. By contrast, Table 3.4 shows the much more modest correlations among the nine newspapers, thus demonstrating their much greater individuality or differences of approach. Not a single newspaper correlates with another as strongly as do the three networks amongst themselves. The vast majority of the inter-correlations among the newspapers have values lower than +.50. Only one correlation is higher than +.70, that between the *New York Times* and the *Times* of London (+.81).

Although all the correlation coefficients are statistically significant, positive, and high, correlations involving the *New York Times* are particularly noteworthy. Thus, a terrorist story published by the *New York Times* is especially apt to also appear in the world's press, a pattern consistent with the thesis that news is exported from the U.S. media to the rest of the world.

Table 3.3 Correlations in TV Coverage

	ABC	NBC	CBS
time in ABC:	-	.88	.91
time in NBC:	-	-	.89
time in CBS:	-	-	-

Note: All the coefficients generated are statistically significant under the null hypothesis of R=0 with p < .001.

Table 3.4 Correlations in Newspaper Coverage

Number of Articles in:

	GM	TL	DT	FI	FR	Yed	AA	PK
NYT	.63	.81	.35	.44	.32	.67	.24	.27
GM		.56	.45	.48	.31	.53	.34	.33
TL			.41	.46	.34	.65	.23	.27
DT				.40	.48	.53	.27	.28
FI					.53	.44	.21	.21
FR						.42	.21	.23
YD							.36	.34
AA								.34
PK								

Note: All the coefficients generated are statistically significant under the null hypothesis of R=0 with p < .001.

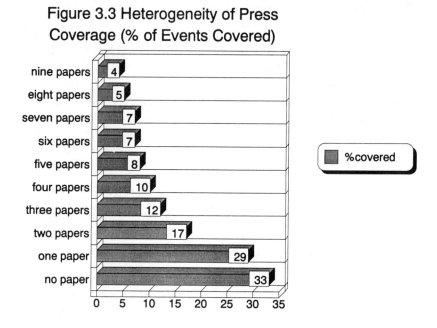

Figure 3.3 Heterogeneity of Press Coverage (% of Events Covered)

Figure 3.3 provides another indication of the diversity of coverage among the print media. As illustrated in this graph, there is very little overlap of coverage. Thus, only 4% of terrorist events are covered in all nine papers while 29% are covered in only one and 17% in only two papers. Of course, all the newspapers are engaged in gatekeeping, but the pattern of gatekeeping is more varied than in the case of the broadcasters.

Table 3.5 portrays the results of a statistical procedure known as factor analysis, which was performed on the correlations in coverage displayed in Table 3.4. The technique of factor analysis can be used to reveal the small number of patterns that underlie a large set of correlations. The results in Table 3.5 show the existence of two underlying factors or patterns—a television pattern and a press pattern. Intriguingly, the pattern of reportage at the *New York Times* is much more similar to that of the eight other newspapers than it is to the networks. Indeed, the American paper correlates with the press factor more than does any other newspaper. Thus, the data support the view that the *New York Times* may be an archetype for when international terrorism is covered by the international press but not for when it is covered by American television.

Table 3.5 Factor Analysis of Coverage

Rotated Factors, All 12 Media

	Factor 1	Factor 2
NBC	0.24	<u>0.86</u>
CBS	0.24	<u>0.87</u>
ABC	0.26	<u>0.85</u>
NYT	<u>0.63</u>	0.31
TL	<u>0.64</u>	0.29
DT	<u>0.60</u>	0.32
FI	<u>0.59</u>	0.20
FR	<u>0.71</u>	0.20
YD	<u>0.69</u>	0.11
AA	<u>0.64</u>	0.21
PK	<u>0.57</u>	0.13
GM	<u>0.52</u>	0.48

Variance explained by each factor:
Factor 1   30.6%
Factor 2   24.1%

Though the factor analysis revealed two factors and though we suggested that the press tend to follow a slightly different pattern of reporting from that of the American television networks, the differences between broadcasting and print should not be exaggerated. Compare, for example, the correlations involving the three networks and the *New York Times*. The correlations among the networks themselves are all very high (approximately +.90), distinctly higher than their correlations with the *Times*. However, the network–*New York Times* correlations are not close to zero; they hover around respectable scores of +.40 and +.50. Most importantly, our ability to make generalizations about differences between TV and the press is constrained by the absence of non-U.S. broadcasters from the sample. Our data are more amenable to generalizations about the press than about television.

Among the nine newspapers, the New York paper may be the most typical while the Egyptian and Pakistani papers may be the least so. The latter two papers have very modest correlations with each of the others and there is little variation in the strength of these modest correlations. *Al Aharam's* highest correlation (+.36) is with *Yediot*. Meanwhile the coverage of the *Pakistan Times* is most correlated with the content of the Israeli and Egyptian papers (both +.34).

The three highest newspaper correlations involve the *New York Times*: first with the *Times* of London (+.81), second with Tel Aviv's *Yediot* (+.67), and third with Toronto's *Globe and Mail* (+.63). The coverage in these four papers tends to be highly intercorrelated, but not, paradoxically, with Britain's *Daily Telegraph*. The *Tele* is virtually as correlated with the French and German press as it is with the Anglo-Saxon and Israeli papers.

Among the North Atlantic dailies, the *Frankfurter Allgemeine Zeitung* displays the most modest average correlations. It is the most apt to follow its own notion of priorities in terrorist reporting. The West German publication's least weak correlations are with *Le Figaro* (+.53) and the *Daily Telegraph* (+.48).

At this point in the chapter, we turn to an examination of the pattern of gatekeeper decisions affecting the dissemination of news on terrorism. These gatekeeper decisions are inferred from the statistical data describing what the media actually cover.

Coverage—A Matter of Location

If the reporting of terrorist events were influenced strictly by the ostensible news value of the individual event, one should expect very little variation from one region of the world to another in the percentage of terrorist events that are reported. In fact, there is a considerable variation in the proportion of events covered, particularly in the case of television news.

Figure 3.4 portrays the proportion of events reported by the three American networks according to the region in which the individual terrorist incidents originated (see also table 3.6). The pattern of geographic selection is very similar across networks but dissimilar across regions. Among the networks as a whole, the likelihood of being mentioned on a television news broadcast varies by a factor of almost 3, ranging from a low of 8.6% and 9.3% in the case of sub-Saharan Africa and Latin America to highs of 22.3% for the Middle East and 23.3% for North America. Thus, fewer than one in 10 terrorist incidents in Latin America or Africa are reported on American television as compared with almost one-quarter of such events taking place in North America and the Middle East.

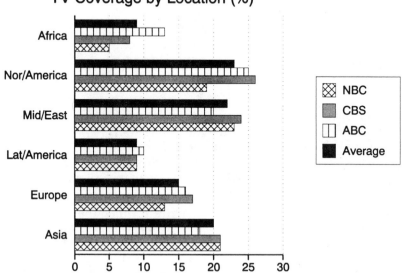

Figure 3.4
TV Coverage by Location (%)

Table 3.6 TV Coverage by Location

Average Rate of Coverage

	NBC		CBS		ABC		aver.
	N	C	N	C	N	C	C
ASIA	79	21	79	21	82	18	20.0
EUROPE	87	13	83	17	84	16	15.3
LAT/AMER	91	9	91	9	90	10	9.3
MID/EAST	77	23	76	24	80	20	22.3
N/AMER	81	19	74	26	75	25	23.3
SUB SAH	95	5	92	8	87	13	8.6

Key: C = covered, N = not covered.

Table 3.7 Press Coverage by Location (percent of events covered)

	NYT	GM	TL	DT	FI	FR	YD	AA	PK	aver
ASIA	43	29	37	26	24	30	22	34	26	30.1
EUROPE	32	33	36	37	32	34	27	40	24	32.8
LAT/AMER	24	27	18	14	20	14	9	16	17	17.6
MID/EAST	41	30	33	26	27	29	40	46	27	33.2
N./AMER	35	32	18	20	16	13	13	30	21	22.0
SUB/SAH	18	29	18	33	20	9	16	24	15	20.2

Latin America is a major source of international terrorism, accounting for almost one-fourth of the world total, and yet terrorism on this continent is the least likely to achieve media attention abroad. Part of the reason for the lesser coverage given to Latin American than, say, Middle Eastern terrorism is the lower lethality of Latin American terrorism, to be discussed in chapter five.

Table 3.7 contains information on the rate at which the nine newspapers in our study report terrorist events in each of six regions. As in the case of television, the press varies in its predisposition to report events from the regions, albeit somewhat less so. The likelihood of a terrorist incident's being mentioned in the press varies regionally by a factor of less than 2 as compared with a factor of almost 3 in the case of broadcasting. As in the case of television, Latin American terrorism is underreported while terrorism in the Middle East is comparatively overreported.

The most important difference between the selectivity of the television networks and the newspapers in our study is the much greater tendency of the press to report events in Europe. European incidents have a 32.8% probability of being covered in the print media as compared to only 15.3% on the three networks. The underreporting of European terrorism on American television is not the result of a disinterest embodied in American political culture. The *New York Times* does not underreport terrorism in Europe in comparison with the eight other papers. The New York paper's rate of coverage is 32%, very close to the average of 32.8% among all the papers.

One plausible explanation for television's underreporting of terrorist incidents in Europe is that television is especially susceptible to media-oriented terrorism but European terrorism is not especially media-oriented. Our previous chapter showed that Irish and French terrorists display traditional rather than media-oriented styles. Unlike Middle Eastern terrorists, the Irish and French tend to target the military, police, and big business rather than diplomats and civilians. Furthermore, attacks by Irish and French groups are directed more often against Europeans rather than Americans and tend to produce fewer fatalities.

Before concluding a discussion of the impact of location on coverage, it may be appropriate to consider the locational proclivities of the individual media outlets. Few differences separate the networks. ABC, CBS, and NBC exhibit virtually the same probability of covering events in the different regions (Figure 3.4). In terms of length of coverage, NBC tends to assign more attention than the other networks to events in Europe, Latin America, and North America, the same in Asia and the Middle East, and appreciably less in sub-Saharan Africa. For example, the average time for an NBC story on terrorism in Latin America is 114 seconds as compared to 86 for CBS and 69 for ABC (Table 3.8). Meanwhile NBC assigns only about 50 seconds to terrorist events in Africa as compared to 115 and 98 at CBS and ABC.

Terrorist incidents are most likely to be mentioned in the *New York Times* and *Al Aharam*, but the substance of coverage will be different. Of the nine papers, the one in Cairo tends to publish the shortest analyses and the fewest articles per event (see Table 3.9). By contrast, the *New York Times* and especially *Yediot* tend to be fulsome in their assessments. In every region except the Middle East itself, the Israeli paper covers proportionately fewer events than the other papers. Yet whatever it covers it analyzes at length. For example, the Tel Aviv paper devotes almost five articles to each event as compared to fewer than two in the case of Toronto's *Globe and Mail* and Cairo's *Al Aharam*. Terrorist events in Europe, the Middle East, or Africa that are covered by *Yediot* are apt to be covered in very great detail. For example, the Israeli paper averages 6.5 articles per European incident as compared to 3.5 in the case of the *New York Times* and fewer still in the case of each of the other newspapers.

Table 3.8 Average TV time / story by location (in seconds)

	NBC	CBS	ABC
ASIA	165.07	167.42	153.33
EUROPE	171.52	119.87	131.73
LAT/AMER	114.31	86.48	69.25
MID/EAST	143.45	111.87	120.01
N./AMER	75.70	48.38	54.52
SUB SAHARA	50.00	115.00	98.00

Table 3.9 Average Number of Articles per Event

	NYT	GM	TL	DT	FI	FR	YD	AA	PK
ASIA	2.14	1.96	2.32	3.85	2.33	2.00	2.54	1.70	1.52
EUROPE	3.47	2.23	3.43	3.36	2.42	3.28	6.49	1.82	1.08
LAT/AMER	1.94	1.78	2.14	3.05	1.87	1.71	1.88	1.17	1.24
MID/EAST	2.48	2.00	2.64	2.61	1.75	2.02	5.30	2.44	1.39
N./AMER	1.62	1.65	1.57	1.50	1.21	1.40	1.57	1.07	1.13
SUB/SAH	2.40	2.68	3.50	5.40	4.50	2.00	4.44	2.91	2.12

Much of the variation in the newspapers' probabilities of covering events in each region is readily explained in terms of their or their countries' traditional geographic preoccupations. The Israeli and Egyptian papers exhibit a high probability of covering events in their region and of devoting a number of articles to each such event. The Canadian and American papers are the most likely to report events on their continent. The British, French, and German papers are more apt to cover terrorist events in Europe than are the Israeli and Pakistani papers. The *Daily Telegraph* emphasizes events in sub-Saharan Africa, reflecting its own and its country's traditional imperial interest on the continent. Whereas the *Tele* covers a third of events in Africa below the Sahara, the Frankfurt paper reports less than a tenth, reflecting Germany's more limited cultural and historical bond with the region.

The *Pakistan Times* departs from the norm in its tendency to underreport events in its own region. Underreporting events in its own region may be an act of self-preservation for a quasi-independent paper operating without strong guarantees of freedom of the press. Indeed, among the sample of nine newspapers, the *Pakistan Times* underreports terrorist violence in its own region the most and devotes the least attention to those incidents that it does report.

Intriguingly, the *New York Times* ranks with the Egyptian and Israeli papers in its probability of covering events in their region. The American paper's preoccupation with the region may reflect the country's geo-strategic stake. Egypt and Israel are the focus of U.S. aid efforts while the United States is the principal nonregional actor in regional conflicts. The American paper's interest in the region may also reflect Judaeophile tendencies rooted in American culture, including traditions of Christian

Zionism in American Protestantism.[48] The paper's geographic focus may also reflect the particular interests of the paper's metropolitan Jewish readership.

The *Globe and Mail* was more apt than other papers in the sample to cover events in Latin America. This pattern is intriguing because Canada has historically considered the countries south of the Rio Grande as a cauldron to be gazed at from a great distance, if at all. In practice, the Toronto paper's frequent coverage of Latin American events presaged the country's later membership in the Organization of American States and its involvement in negotiations over free trade involving Mexico and the United States.

Some Victims Attract More Attention than Others

The victims of international terrorism belong to several dozen different nationalities. As shown in the previous chapter, the citizens of nine countries are especially apt to be targets of terrorist violence. The 12 media outlets were compared according to their probability of reporting terrorist attacks involving citizens of these countries. Figure 3.5 portrays the average rate of coverage across all 12 media outlets of incidents involving citizens of the nine countries in question.

The single most striking and most unambiguous finding is the *media pre–eminence* of Israelis as victims. When Israelis are victims, the attack has virtually a 0.5 probability of being reported (Tables 3.10 and 3.11). Terrorist incidents involving citizens of other nations have no more than a 30% probability of being mentioned in the media, and usually the probability is lower. The rate of coverage of anti–Cuban attacks is a paltry 8.3%. The previous chapter demonstrated that American citizens are the most frequent victims of international terrorism. Yet, the rate of coverage of anti–American violence is a moderate 20.3%, less than half the rate in the case of Israeli victims.

48   For an account of the biblical appeal of Zionism for American Protestants from John Adams to Harry Truman, see Peter Grose, *Israel in the Mind of America* (New York: Alfred A. Knopf, 1983).

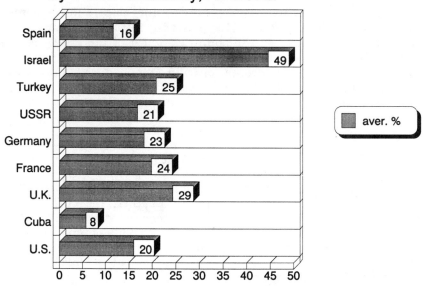

Figure 3.5 Average Coverage in Percent by Victim Nationality, All Media

Table 3.10 Rates of TV Coverage by Nationality of Targets (in percent)

	NBC	CBS	ABC
United States	17.3	20.2	18.2
Cuba	3.9	5.3	5.3
United Kingdom	21.9	25.0	29.2
France	6.9	13.8	13.8
West Germany	17.1	14.6	19.5
USSR	8.1	8.1	8.3
Turkey	7.4	14.8	14.8
Israel	37.8	37.0	35.3
Spain	8.7	2.2	4.3

Table 3.11 Rates of Press Coverage by Nationality of Targets (in percent)

Nation	NYT	GM	TL	DT	FI	FR	YD	AA	PK	aver.
U.S.	32.0	28.1	19.5	20.2	17.9	16.4	12.2	24.0	18.1	20.3
Cuba	15.8	16.8	10.5	7.0	6.3	8.4	3.2	10.6	6.5	8.3
U.K.	41.1	55.8	60.5	66.7	40.3	41.1	24.1	47.9	29.6	28.6
France	22.2	28.9	19.0	26.7	50.0	23.4	15.9	45.7	24.6	24.1
Germany	4.6	21.4	29.0	22.2	28.6	35.7	17.4	18.8	21.4	22.5
USSR	31.5	16.7	31.5	26.7	25.9	25.9	20.4	30.6	28.3	21.1
Turkey	35.6	25.0	30.5	27.1	28.3	35.0	11.9	40.0	31.4	25.1
Israel	59.3	49.7	48.3	43.1	46.2	47.4	77.9	72.8	31.3	48.8
Spain	7.4	22.2	20.4	26.5	33.3	24.1	11.1	15.2	15.7	15.9

Tables 3.10 and 3.11 provide measures of the rate of coverage by 12 media outlets of terrorist attacks against nine nations. The victimization of Israelis elicits the highest rate of coverage among seven media outlets and the second highest rate of coverage among the remaining five. For CBS, NBC, ABC, the *New York Times*, *Frankfurter Allgemeine Zeitung*, and especially *Al Aharam* and *Yediot*, the presence of Israeli victims tends to render a story newsworthy. Among the remaining papers, the fact of Israeli victimization remains an important gatekeeping consideration. At the *Globe and Mail* and *Le Figaro*, events involving Israeli victims are almost as likely to be covered as events involving British and French victims, respectively. At the *Pakistan Times*, primacy is shared among Israeli, Turkish, and British victims.

At the two British papers in the study, attacks against Israelis are the second most likely to be reported. These two papers are the only media outlets in the study to place a distinctly greater emphasis on a national group other than Israelis. For example, the rate of coverage of attacks against Britons in the *Daily Telegraph* is 67.3% as compared to 43.1% in the case of attacks against citizens of the Jewish state.

At least one of the four American outlets might have been expected to accord greater priority to the victimization of Americans. Americans are after all the favorite target of terrorists, and the U.S. journalists might reasonably be expected to emphasize the tragedies confronting their fellow nationals. However, Israeli victims are consistently more newsworthy from the perspective of the American media, particularly television. Indeed, each American TV network is at least twice as likely to report an attack against

Figure 3.6 Average Time per Story on U.S. Television by Perpetrator

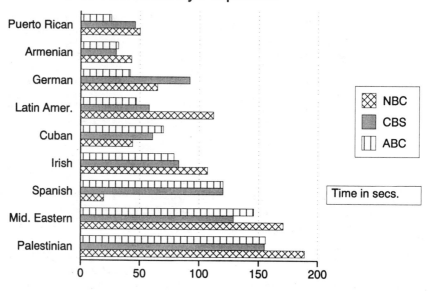

an Israeli than against an American. For example, NBC covers only 17.3% of attacks against American citizens and as much as 37.8% of attacks against Israelis.

Apart from the common Israeli theme, the coverage provided by the media outlets reflects some differences among national political cultures. For example, the English language Canadian paper assigns comparatively more attention to stories involving American and British victims. The *New York Times* is apt to report terrorist attacks against Americans and Soviet citizens. *Le Figaro* pays particular attention to French and Spanish victims. The Cairo paper is most apt to cover tragedies involving the citizens of Israel, Turkey, and Britain, three countries with which Egypt has been vitally linked.

The Significance of the Perpetrators

We turn here to an analysis of the impact on coverage of the identity of
the perpetrators. For purposes of analysis, the hundreds of different
terrorist groups were clustered into national groupings. For example, a
German grouping was composed of the Red Army Faction, Baader–Meinhof,
2nd of June movement, Revolutionary Cells, and others. An Armenian
grouping subsumed the Armenian Secret Army for the Liberation of Armenia, Justice Commandos for the Armenian Genocide, Third of October
Group, New Armenian Resistance, and other factions (see Appendix for
details).

The impact of the perpetrators' identity on coverage was examined in two
ways—by comparing rates of coverage and also by comparing the intensity
or length of coverage of each individual event. Rates of coverage vary
enormously. For example, barely 2% of Spanish terrorist acts are reported
in American television as compared with about two–fifths of Palestinian
terrorist acts (Figure 3.6). The highest rate of coverage belongs to Middle
Eastern groups, Puerto Ricans, and especially to the Irish and Palestinians.

The 12 media outlets tend to vary in their rate of coverage of terrorist
groups according to patterns of national political culture and geopolitical
interest. The ability of terrorists to secure attention in any given outlet
appears to depend on the political interests of the country in which the
outlet operates and the country's cultural affinity for the terrorists, their
victims, or their targets. Consider the following patterns to emerge from
Table 3.12:

- Palestinian and other Middle Eastern terrorists receive
  their greatest rate of coverage in the Egyptian, Tel Aviv,
  and New York papers;
- Germans receive their greatest rate of coverage in their
  indigenous paper and in the papers of their neighbors
  to the west (French and British);
- Irish terrorist events are most apt to be noted in the
  British press and in the paper published in Toronto, a
  longstanding center of Protestant Ulstermen;
- Puerto Rican violence is relatively likely to be reported
  in the two North American papers and in one of the
  British papers, the *Times*;
- Spanish terrorists achieve their greater rate of coverage
  in the papers of their neighbors to the north (French
  and German);

- the North American papers pay particular attention to both Cuban and Latin American terrorist events;
- Armenians receive especially high rates of coverage in the Egyptian paper.

For academics, it may be intriguing to explore which papers cover which terrorists, but for the terrorists themselves the goal is frequently to maximize publicity overall. Palestinians are tied with Puerto Ricans in terms of their ability to capture the immediate attention of the media (see Table 3.12) while they are the clear winners in terms of ability to sustain prolonged attention (Tables 3.13 and 3.14 and Figure 3.6). Palestinian terrorist groups have a 40% probability of being covered on NBC as compared to 36% in the case of Puerto Rican terrorists, 2% for Spanish terrorists, and 6% for Cubans. Once Palestinians gain access to the media, they are apt to remain in the spotlight for prolonged periods. Thus, the average Palestinian terrorist story on NBC lasts for more than three minutes as compared to less than a minute in the case of Puerto Rican, Spanish, Cuban and Armenian terrorists. Other Middle Eastern groups also have higher than normal rates of coverage as well as broadcasts which are substantially longer than normal.

Terrorist incidents are most likely to be mentioned in the *New York Times* and *Al Aharam*, but the substance of coverage will be different. Of the nine papers, the one in Cairo tends to publish the shortest analyses and the fewest articles per event (see Table 3.9). By contrast, the *New York Times* and especially *Yediot* tend to be fulsome in their assessments. In every region except the Middle East itself, the Israeli paper covers proportionately fewer events than the other papers. Yet whatever it covers it analyzes at length. For example, the Tel Aviv paper devotes almost five articles to each event as compared to fewer than two in the case of Toronto's *Globe and Mail* and Cairo's *Al Aharam*. Terrorist events in Europe, the Middle East, or Africa that are covered by *Yediot* are apt to be covered in very great detail. For example, the Israeli paper averages 6.5 articles per European incident as compared to 3.5 in the case of the *New York Times* and fewer still in the case of each of the other newspapers.

The pattern of preference for Palestinian and Middle Eastern stories on the networks extends to the print media. For example, in the *New York Times*, Palestinians have a 59.2% probability of being reported. Furthermore, a single Palestinian terrorist attack is apt to be followed by almost four news stories in the Eastern seaboard paper as compared to barely one in the instance of German, Cuban, Armenian, and Spanish terrorists.

Table 3.12 Rates of Coverage by Perpetrators and Medium

	NBC	CBS	ABC	NYT	GM	TL	DT	FI	FR	YD	AA	PK
Pales.	40.2	39.7	36.2	59.2	47.2	49.8	42.9	38.9	46.5	63.4	63.7	30.9
Ger.	19.0	23.8	23.8	28.0	26.9	36.0	42.3	34.6	50.0	28.0	25.0	0
Irish	31.3	35.8	38.8	53.3	73.3	76.0	82.0	53.3	56.0	30.7	58.8	40.3
Puer	35.9	46.2	46.2	38.5	43.2	40.3	32.4	32.4	2.7	10.8	48.5	33.3
Spa	2.2	2.2	2.2	14.0	22.0	24.0	27.1	48.0	34.0	10.0	26.5	22.0
Cuba	6.2	8.8	6.2	13.6	16.0	9.1	9.2	9.6	7.0	3.2	17.1	7.9
Lat	7.8	13.7	13.7	33.9	30.3	25.5	20.4	25.0	17.8	12.9	20.2	20.4
Arm.	2.5	8.9	7.6	24.1	20.5	34.9	24.1	21.7	25.3	6.0	32.4	27.3
Md/E	17.9	20.3	20.3	44.5	33.3	35.6	28.2	29.3	32.7	39.0	46.8	26.1

Table 3.13 Average TV Time by Perpetrator (in seconds/story)

Perpetrators	NBC	CBS	ABC
Palestinians	188.70	154.60	155.50
Germans	65.00	92.00	42.00
Irish	107.04	83.12	79.23
Puerto Ricans	50.00	46.16	25.50
Spaniards	20.00	120.00	120.00
Cubans	44.28	61.00	70.00
Latin Amer.	112.18	57.92	47.10
Armenians	42.50	30.00	32.16
Mid/East	170.68	129.36	145.76

Table 3.14 Average Number of Press Articles by Perpetrator

Perpetrators	NYT	GM	TL	DT	FI	FR	YD	AA	PK
Palestinians	3.92	3.00	3.81	5.42	3.21	3.54	8.15	2.73	1.57
Germans	1.28	2.14	1.11	1.27	2.11	1.15	1.42	1.66	1.00
Irish	2.30	1.89	4.24	4.43	1.57	2.04	1.69	1.15	1.17
Puerto Ricns	2.00	1.06	2.33	1.00	1.00	1.00	1.00	1.06	1.00
Spaniards	1.42	1.45	1.08	1.00	1.50	1.29	1.80	1.22	1.00
Cubans	1.16	1.30	1.29	1.30	1.22	1.15	1.00	1.00	1.29
Latin Amer.	2.28	2.20	2.55	3.37	2.21	2.04	2.20	1.14	1.39
Armenians	1.05	1.11	1.13	1.05	1.22	1.23	1.20	1.18	1.13
Mid/East	3.11	2.08	3.92	1.83	2.13	2.41	4.40	1.84	1.34

The special attention accorded to the PLO and other Middle Eastern groups by the media is linked inextricably to the attention accorded Israeli victims of terrorism, discussed previously. One factor is the *modus operandi* of Palestinian and other Arab groups. Beginning with the 1972 assault on Israeli athletes in the midst of the globally televised Munich Olympic games, Palestinian and other Middle Eastern terrorist groups have displayed a special understanding of the logistical preparation and dramatic action necessary for accessing the media. Palestinian and other Middle East actions have been characterized by a certain lethality, the communications significance of which will be discussed below in Chapter 5. Nonetheless, the media-minded modus operandi of Palestinian and other Arab terrorists may be only one factor accounting for their success.

Other possible factors accounting for the special attention given Palestinian/Arab terrorists and Israeli victims include

- the sacred nature of the region as the birthplace of Judaism, Christianity and Islam
- oil and the region's geopolitical significance
- the cultural archetype of the suffering Jew in past Christian teachings
- the quasi-sacred resurrection of the Jewish people in modern Israel out of the ashes of the Holocaust

For the *New York Times*, an additional impetus for coverage might be a sizeable Jewish readership and staff. For the U.S. media as a whole, motivations to highlight terrorist stories involving Israelis could include a historical undercurrent of Christian Zionism in American Protestant thought plus a sense of kinship with a reliable, militarily significant and democratic ally.

The *Frankfurter Allgemeine Zeitung* displays a special pattern of terrorist reporting that merits comment. Paradoxically, the German paper devotes a very intensive coverage to those German–led terrorist attacks which it covers (7.15 articles; see Table 3.14). Yet its rate of coverage of events involving German victims is moderate, i.e., 35.7% vs. 41.1% and 47.4% in situations involving British and Israeli victims, respectively (Table 3.11). The apparent limits that the paper places on the coverage of events where fellow nationals are victimized may be understood in terms of West Germany's informal media policies governing the coverage of terrorism, a topic addressed in the concluding chapter.

Like the German paper, *Al Aharam* also displays a special pattern. It provides a high rate of coverage for terrorism in general. It is more apt to report violence by every group of perpetrators except Germans and Latin

Americans than is the voluminous *New York Times*. *Al Aharam*'s reporting of terrorism undoubtedly reflects in part its country's and its region's interest in the phenomenon.

This particular chapter began by considering the importance of media coverage in the minds of terrorists. This was followed by a statistical analysis of the media coverage of terrorist events. In particular, we explored the impact of location, victims' identity, and perpetrators' identity on the likelihood and intensity of coverage. The ensuing chapter explores the characteristics of the terrorist attack which make it a "media event."

Chapter 4

The Terrorist Act as a Media Event

The phenomenon of media-oriented terror, intensified by the opportunities presented by progress in media technology, has stimulated scholarly interest in the media-terrorism nexus. Scholars have begun to explore the communications strategies of modern terrorists, the terrorism strategies of the modern media, and the public affairs consequences of the media-terrorism relationship. However, the growing interest in this area has not been accompanied by the development of a conceptual or theoretical framework.

The central purpose of the book is to describe quantitatively the pattern of international terrorist conduct and the pattern of media reporting, and to explore how the two patterns are linked. This chapter departs somewhat from the empirical emphasis of the book by focusing on conceptual aspects of the communication of terror. The first of two important conceptual questions to ask is what kind of communications phenomenon is modern international terrorism. Our response is that it is frequently a *media event* of the kind delineated by communications scholar Elihu Katz and his colleagues in their classification of the phenomenon.[1] As in the case of other media events, the reporting of terrorist acts is intense and protracted. Political leaders are cast in prominent roles, societal solidarity and conformity are encouraged by symbolic means, and terrorist action is interpreted in such a way as to reinforce the existing order.

If the terrorist act is a media event, the consequent question to ask is what kind of media event it is. Our response is that the terrorist act does not fit neatly into any of the existing three categories in Katz's classification. Katz's three categories are

---

1   E. Katz, "Media Events: The Sense of Occasion," *Studies in Visual Anthropology* 6 (1980), 84-89; E. Katz, D. Dayan, and P. Motyl, "In Defence of Media Events," in R. Haigh, G. Gerbner, and R. Byrne, eds., *Communications in the Twenty-First Century* (New York: John Wiley and Sons, 1981) and "Television Diplomacy: Sadat in Jerusalem," in G. Gerbner and Siefert, eds., *World Communications: A Handbook* (New York: Longman, 1983); E. Katz and D. Dayan, "Media Events: On the Experience of Not Being There," *Religion* 15 (1985), 305-14; D. Dayan and E. Katz, *Media Events* (Cambridge, Mass.: Harvard University Press, 1992).

- coronations—rites of passage such as the British royal wedding or the Kennedy funeral
- conquests—dramatic decisive actions such as the moon landing or Sadat's arrival in Jerusalem
- contests—usually cyclical events such as the Olympic games

The televised terrorist act resembles Katz's existing categories of media events. Televised terrorism elicits intensive coverage, involves major political and social authorities, and entails symbolic and ritual acts of solidarity and conformity. Like other classical media events, televised terrorism is apt to strengthen the existing political order. The essential decency and normalcy of the existing order is reinforced in the public mind. But the violent macabre quality of the terrorist event necessitates its own distinctive category, the *coercive media event* or *coercion*.

The concept of coercion is an amendment to Katz's classification but an amendment that he and his research team may have anticipated. In their wide-ranging discussion on the topic, Dayan and Katz note that media events can be "hijacked":

> By definition, media events attract the attention of the world: the cameras are mounted, the lights are turned on, the ceremony begins. There is no stronger temptation to advocates of some revolutionary case than to turn these lights and cameras on themselves. Such were the Munich Olympics of 1972, when Palestinian terrorists held Israeli athletes hostage and murdered them in cold blood. Such was the 1968 Democratic national convention in Chicago, when students marched on the convention in protest against United States policy on the issues of the '60's. Such was the case in the signing of the Indo-Lanka peace accord, when a Sinhalese navy ensign struck out at Rajiv Gandhi with his rifle as he was reviewing a military unit that had been assigned to the honor guard of the ceremony.[2]

Conceptualizing Media Events

The concept of media event emerged in the work of Elihu Katz and his colleagues as they examined the character of the high holidays of the media. These memorable broadcasts captivated whole nations or even the entire world audience. A list of these emotionally significant televised events would include the first moon landing, John F. Kennedy's funeral, Britain's royal wedding, the pope's first visit to Poland, Anwar Sadat's visit to Jerusalem, the Olympics, U.S. presidential debates, and so forth.

2   Dayan and Katz, *Media Events*, 72.

According to Katz, the high holidays of broadcasting are characterized by seven distinctive attributes:

- They are broadcast live, transporting the audience to where the event is physically taking place.
- Though not initiated by the media, these significant events are organized with the media foremost in mind.
- The event is emotionally significant and dramatic in the eye of the viewer as well as laden with symbolism.
- The audience considers viewing almost obligatory. The admonition, "Stop everything and join in the making of history," is an undercurrent.
- Although the events are preplanned, not all the specific outcomes are fully known; some dramatic uncertainty is retained.
- The events are delimited in time and space; the events are sufficiently focused to sustain the audience's attention.
- Important personalities are at the center of the unfolding drama; each media event involves heroic individuals or teams and occasionally anti-heroes.

The *Terrorist* Media Event

During the 1970s, scholars began to note the emergence of a new form of terrorism—media-oriented terror. One of the leading experts in the field of terrorism, Brian Jenkins, concluded a major study in 1975 with a pointed observation about the significance of mass communication: "Terrorist attacks are [now] often carefully choreographed to attract the attention of the electronic media and the international press. Taking and holding hostages increases the drama....Terrorism is aimed at the people watching, not at the actual victims. Terrorism is a theater."[3]

Scholars commented on the phenomenon of media-motivated terror during the 1970s in part because this was the period during which the phenomenon experienced growth. Weimann's analysis of 6,714 terrorist events during the 1968-1980 period revealed a continual increase in the proportion of events that were sparked by a desire for coverage.[4] Terrorists

---

3   *International Terrorism* (Los Angeles, Calif.: Crescent Publication, 1975), 4.
4   "Mass Mediated Theatre of Terror: Must the Show Go On?" in *Media and Terror* (Ottawa: Carleton University, 1987).

were not only keen to receive media attention, but they were to become increasingly adept at achieving it. As Krauthammer observed in *Harper's,* "Terrorists are rather resourceful about creating new theatrical productions; every year or two they come up with a new variant that captures the media's imagination."[5] With each year, international terrorists seemed to follow ever more obediently Walter Laqueur's principle that "the terrorist act alone is nothing; publicity is all."[6]

Many commentators reached the same conclusion, albeit using different words. As Bell noted, "it became more alluring for the frantic few to appear on the world stage of television than remain obscure guerrillas of the bush."[7] International terrorism became so increasingly motivated by media considerations that it virtually qualified as a pseudo-event. The term pseudo-event was coined by Daniel Boorstin in the early 1960s to identify an act that is undertaken solely for the purpose of creating a particular media-transmitted impression.[8]

Terror is apt to be reported because it satisfies many of the requirements of journalistic convention. In their widely accepted portrayal of journalistic norms, Galtung and Ruge identified six canons of newsworthiness.[9] Together, these canons help to account for the attraction of journalism for terror. They are

- scarcity
- unexpectedness
- hostility to elite people or nations
- violence
- intensity
- unambiguity.

Following the logic of newsworthiness delineated by Galtung and Ruge, terror becomes newsworthy because it does not occur daily; it happens

---

5   C. Krauthammer, "Terrorism and the Media: A Discussion," *Harper's* (October 1984), 47-58.

6   "The Futility of Terrorism," *Harper's* (March 1976), 104.

7   B. Bell, *International Terror* (Washington, D.C.: Institute for Policy Research, 1975), 89.

8   *The Image: A Guide to Pseudo-Events in America* (New York: Athenaeum, 1961).

9   J. Galtung and M. H. Ruge, "The Structure of Foreign News," *Journal of International Peace Research* 1 (1965), 64-80. For empirical applications to broadcast coverage of terrorism, see Tony Atwater, "Network Evening News Coverage of the TWA Hostage Crisis," in *Journalism Quarterly* 64 (1987), 520-525, and Michael X. Delli Carpini and Bruce A. Williams, "Television and Terrorism: Patterns of Presentation and Occurrence, 1969 to 1980," *Western Political Quarterly* 40 (1987), 45-64.

unexpectedly, and it involves violence against elite people such as diplomats or elite nations such as the United States. Terror is also newsworthy because it entails intense drama in which unambiguous terrorists commit unambiguous aggression against innocent, unarmed victims.

If terror satisfies the professional requirements of print journalism, it is an even better match for television. Livingstone, another expert on terrorism, has described at length the especially intimate link between modern terror and television:

> Terrorism, as an extreme form of violence, is particularly newsworthy and well suited to the needs of television, which is a highly visual and compact medium with little time for exposition. Unlike wars and most revolutions, which are usually protracted and highly complex events that are too broad in scope to be grasped readily and easily understood, acts of terrorist violence normally have a beginning and an end, can be encompassed in a few minutes of air time, possess a large degree of drama, invoke participants who are perceived by the viewing public as unambiguous, and are not so complex as to be unintelligible to those who tune in only briefly. It has been said, speciously but with some truth, that terrorism is so ideally suited to television that the medium would have invented the phenomenon if it had not already existed. [10]

The terrorists themselves are intensely aware of the journalistic opportunities for the phenomenon. Over the past generation, terrorists have increasingly planned their operations with journalists in mind. As revealed in our interview, above, with the European terrorist "D.", terrorist groups often make personal contact with supportive journalists. Carefully constructed *photo opportunities* are often provided along with opportunities for intensely dramatic interviews.

The June 1985 hijacking of a TWA aircraft by armed Shi'ite terrorists illustrates the nature of the media event and the symbiosis between journalism and terrorism. On June 14, the civilian passenger plane was commandeered and routed to Beirut and then on to Algiers. It was then forced to return to Beirut, where an American hostage was executed. After a second flight to Algiers and back once again to Beirut, the terrorists freed some of their hostages and demanded from Israel the release of 776 prisoners, mostly Shi'ites. For 16 days, 39 American passengers and crew were held hostage. They were to regain their freedom in Damascus only after the Israelis acquiesced to the hijackers' demands.

---

10   N. C. Livingstone, *The War Against Terrorism* (Lexington, Mass.: Lexington Books, 1982), 62.

The TWA hijacking became a very major news story, covered fully by most of the world's press organizations. As *Time* magazine observed, it was an instance of "prime-time terrorism":

> All week the world was held in dreadful thrall by the spectacle of Americans turned into political pawns in a distant land. Anchormen effortlessly reverted to the vocabulary of the Iran crisis five years ago: "This is day 7 of the hostage crisis." News bulletins flashed by incessantly, often bearing little or no news: experts on terrorism and onetime Government officials droned on in network studios, explaining what they would do if they were President. Around the country, ordinary Americans, buffeted by feelings of outrage and concern, tied yellow ribbons to trees and prayed for the hostages' safe return.[11]

In their coverage of the episode, the U.S. networks displayed their nation's capacity for ingenuity and resourcefulness as well as its enormous ability to mobilize resources in a time of crisis. For example, on the very first day of the hijacking, June 14, CBS not only provided special coverage on its morning and evening news and countless newsbreaks, but it also provided a total of 10 special reports ranging from one to six minutes each as well as a 30-minute-long midnight news special. Not be outdone, the NBC network broadcast nine special reports through the day, delivering more than 38 minutes of extra coverage beyond its regular news bulletins.

The networks responded to a situation that was inherently dramatic. In turn, by the intensity of their response they heightened the dramatic tension. CBS's Dan Rather, ABC's Peter Jennings, and NBC's Tom Brokaw, all major television personalities, were rushed to Beirut. Special reports were provided not only from the Lebanese capital but also from London, Washington, Jerusalem, New York, and Damascus. Maudlin interviews were conducted with distraught family members and friends of the hostages. The networks even provided interviews with the hostage-takers and willingly participated in a press conference organized by the Shi'ites. Sandwiched among the countless foreign reports and emotional interviews were station break promotions and teases (e.g., "Are positions hardening? Details later tonight.").

11   *Time* (July 1, 1985), 10-11.

The networks rescheduled their routines in order to make possible the intensive coverage required of a major media event. The magazine programs and morning shows joined the regular evening news bulletins in covering the hijacking. ABC's "Nightline," which had originally been created during the Iranian hostage-taking, examined the story every night for two weeks. Altogether, almost 60% of air time during the event was devoted to the hostages and closely related stories.[12] Given the inherent drama of the story and the enormous supplementary drama provided by the networks themselves, the TWA hijacking soon became a media celebration of tension, anger, grief, and, finally, release.

Terrorism and the Attributes of a Media Event

As mentioned above, Katz and his colleagues identified seven key attributes of media events. This section explores these attributes from the perspective of the concept of the theater of terror, using the TWA hijacking as an illustration.

The Live Broadcast

In many terrorist episodes, large American and international audiences are afforded the opportunity to watch live coverage of every macabre detail of a terrorist operation: the initial takeover, stages of negotiation, rescue attempts, and the eventual denouement. Thanks to the media, Western viewers live an ersatz experience of being kidnapped and taken hostage.

A content analysis of American network coverage during the period when the TWA flight was commandeered demonstrated that American viewers could not help but experience vicariously the entire series of events unless they lived the life of hermits, cut off from urban-originating broadcasting and mass communication.[13] During the 16 days of the crisis, the ABC network devoted 68% of nightly news broadcasts to the hijacking.

---

12   For the results of a content analysis conducted by the News Study Group at New York University, see *TV Guide* (September 21, 1985), 6-13. From his content analysis of network news during the period, Atwater concludes that the hostage crisis was the "dominant" news event, but one that generated very little historical or other background analysis. The "extensive" coverage was "dramatic [and] reactive" rather than analytic or reflective. Tony Atwater, "Network Evening News Coverage of the TWA Hostage Crisis," *Journalism Quarterly* 64 (1987), 525.

13   The content analysis was conducted by W. C. Adams at George Washington University and reported in *Near East Report* (October 21, 1985), 168. See also Tony Atwater, "Network Evening News Coverage of the TWA Hostage Crisis," *Journalism Quarterly* 64 (1987), 520-25.

Meanwhile CBS allotted 62% of its evening news to the story; NBC allotted 63%. In terms of volume alone, the TWA hijacking qualified as a media event. Furthermore, a high proportion of the coverage was "live." Thus, live interviews were broadcast with the hostages, Nabih Berri and other Shi'ites, the terrorists themselves, and U.S. government officials. The Shi'ite press conference was covered live.

Preplanning

Katz stresses the importance of a preplanned schedule as a requirement of a media event. Terrorist events meet this requirement even if the fact of preplanning is not fully appreciated by the audience. The terrorists themselves give considerable forethought to the role of the media. Brazilian revolutionary Carlos Marighela's *Minimanual* examines dispassionately how to extract the biggest benefits from media coverage. Revolutionaries are exhorted to pay close attention to the media implications relating to the timing, choice of victims, location, and type of action. We quoted Marighela, above, on the potential propaganda benefits to be drawn from kidnapping a prominent but politically neutral artistic or sporting figure. More generally, Marighela notes that all terrorist activity may "become [potential] propaganda material for the mass communication system...planes diverted in flight by revolutionary action, moving ships and trains assaulted and sieged by guerillas, can also be used for propaganda effects."[14]

The media do not normally know precisely when a terrorist action is apt to be undertaken. But the terrorist action is rarely totally unexpected. Whether or not journalists are taken by complete surprise, they do possess routine procedures for responding to the apparently unexpected so long as the unexpected falls into one of the various conceptual categories reserved for the ostensibly unexpected. The media are able to respond quickly to terrorist events because they already possess frames of reference and organizational routines for conceptualizing new terrorist events as they emerge and for devoting the necessary resources to their coverage.[15]

In the instance of the TWA hijacking, journalists demonstrated their organizational skills. Several months earlier, in late 1984, American reporters had retreated from Lebanon in the face of threats of assassination. But the networks and the press had had the foresight to retain skeleton operations in place. Once the fact of the hijacking became apparent, these skeleton operations were activated so as to provide an infrastructure for a

14   C. Marighela, *Urban Guerrilla Minimanual* (Vancouver: Pulp Press, 1974), 103.
15   See G. Tuchman, "Making News by Doing Work: Routinizing the Unexpected," *American Journal of Sociology* 79 (1974), 110-31.

rapid influx of personnel. ABC soon had 40 professionals in Beirut as compared to 25 in the case of NBC and 20 for CBS. Satellite channels were promptly opened.

The networks encountered little difficulty resorting to the routines that they had previously established for covering such events. The families of the hostages were located. Experts in terrorism were interviewed. Archival videotape on the Shi'ites was assembled. Acknowledging that he and his colleagues encountered few insurmountable barriers to providing intensive coverage of the hijacking, NBC correspondent Henry Champ said simply: "We knew the players."[16] He might also have said: "We knew the routine."

The terrorists too were well organized. They arranged interviews, meetings, press conferences, and live direct broadcasts. Displaying a fastidiousness for detail, the terrorists even edited the American networks' tapes, deleting the comments of hostages whose remarks were unpleasing. The terrorists determined the plot line, wrote the script, selected the actors, and supervised the production. Although terrorists and journalists had not concerted their actions beforehand, their mutual demeanor conformed to previously set and well-understood norms. With biting sarcasm, *Newsweek* observed: "The networks fought bitterly for the honor of being manipulated"(July 15, 1985).

Drama
Through the ages, successful theater has managed to involve audiences in the great personal passions and moral dilemmas affecting the characters on stage. Riveted to their seats, audiences are transported by an intense identification with the characters as the characters confront a struggle of good against evil and experience horrendous sorrow vicariously. Audiences are particularly awestruck by tragedy, in which a noble protagonist is engaged in a majestic moral struggle that brings him profound disappointment. The protagonist's sadness is attenuated only by its ultimately greater meaning.

Few hijackings of modern jumbo jet aircraft entail the profound moral dilemmas that face the protagonists in serious literature. And yet the modern hijacking does retain some of the elements of dramatic theater and classical tragedy. As in theatrical tragedy, the television audiences in hijackings may come to identify passionately with the innocent protagonists. The members of the television audiences may experience immense vicarious fear as well as secret relief that they are not actually on

16   *TV Guide* (September 21, 1985), 16.

the aircraft in question. This joy may be tempered by concern—some psychologists might say, guilt—as the viewer learns more about the victims and comes to identify with their plight. As the tragedy unfolds, the viewer may privately reflect on how he or she might have coped in a like situation. Would he have opted for escape, resistance, acquiescence, or collaboration?

The classical tragedy involves profound sorrow whose ultimate meaning has nonetheless a positive element. Sorrow has an ultimately positive meaning in terrorism as well. For the conventional Western viewer, who adheres to liberal democracy as both a system and a set of values, the death of innocent victims is not entirely senseless. The killing is a reminder of the moral superiority of the democratic system, which reveres human life, unlike its enemies. Furthermore, paralleling the motif of religious sacrifice, the death of innocents makes possible the continuing vitality of the remaining community. Whether or not the sacrifice is necessary for the greater good, the loss of innocent fellow nationals is a symbolic reminder of collective obligation, courage, and loyalty. The idea that senseless death may not be entirely without purpose is strengthened ironically when terrorists single out military men for punishment among a group of civilian hostages. For the Western audience, it is in some sense reassuring that military men are sacrificed for the common good because that is their duty.

For the minority of the Western audience that experiences a vicarious *Stockholm effect* or for some other reason comes to identify with the terrorists, the terrorist killing also possesses an element of classical tragedy. The innocence of the victims may be fully acknowledged. And yet their fate may be considered justifiable on the grounds that the death of a few apparently innocent people is a small price to pay for the ultimate liberation of the many. Thus, sorrow once again acquires a positive meaning.

Whatever the ultimate meaning of sorrow, a hijacking will capture an audience's immediate attention if the possibility of violence is made clear from the outset. In the case of TWA flight 847, the networks conveyed to their audiences the possibility of death with dramatic urgency. On the very first report of the hijacking on the three American networks, the story began with an extraordinary audio clip. The voice of the pilot is heard, beseeching the Beirut control tower to let him land: "They are beating the passengers!...They are threatening to kill them now." Each successive report makes the audience ever more aware of the frightening situation. One passenger is slain. His body is dumped onto the tarmac. Passengers with ostensibly "Jewish-sounding names" are singled out. Passengers and crew are divided up into groups and removed to various unknown locations in Beirut.

Adhering to their routine for dealing with situations of this kind, the broadcasters expanded their reports on the TWA hijacking to include interviews with terrorists, hostages, and families at home. The networks speculated, perhaps dangerously, on the nature and purposes of U.S. military maneuvers, including the ostensible movements of the counterterrorist Delta Force. ABC commentator George Will, a political and moral philosopher with a traditionalist bent, was outraged by what he considered to be the irresponsible character of the media reporting. He termed the networks' conduct "the pornography of grief."[17]

As if to emphasize the moral character of the terrorist action, the networks portrayed the conflict as a struggle between evil and American decency. Sample headlines emphasized the collective angst: "America Held Hostage" and "America under the Gun." On the 12th day of the attack, NBC's John Chancellor addressed his audience on the broader significance of the hijacking: "The fanatics want America in agony. They want public displays of grief, America brought to its knees. Let's not play into their hands."

In a society where prominent television anchors may be more trusted than a president, the meaning provided by the anchor has great significance. The patriotic motif highlighted by Chancellor found many symbolic manifestations in the reporting of his own and the other networks—flags, ribbons, grave sites, families united in grief, and presidential leadership.

Obligatory Viewing

Not all tragedies are viewable or viewed. To compel an audience's attention, the broadcaster must be able to convey the underlying dramatic theme using theatrical paradigms that are readily understood by the viewer. The networks do succeed. As Livingstone notes, "perhaps nowhere is McLuhan's global village concept better illustrated than in the matter of international terrorism."[18]

During the TWA hijacking the broadcasters' extensive coverage attracted enormous audiences. Ted Turner's Cable News Network, which covered every *breaking* event as it unfolded, set a ratings record on the weekend of

---

17 On the dramatic, reactive character of broadcast coverage, see Tony Atwater, "Network Evening News Coverage of the TWA Hostage Crisis," in *Journalism Quarterly* 64 (1987), 520-525. For a detailed study of crisis reporting, see Dan Nimmo and James E. Combs, *Nightly Horrors* (Knoxville: University of Tennessee Press, 1985).
18 Livingstone, *The War Against Terrorism*, 57.

the hostages' release. Audiences began to grow from the outset of the commandeering. During the very first week of the crisis, CBS increased its viewership for the "Evening News" by more than a full rating point. Each rating point represented about 850,000 television-viewing households.[19]

Terrorist events are not portrayed in the media as if they were strictly abstract phenomena or sociological processes. To the contrary, the events are presented in a highly personalized manner. Schmid and de Graaf have noted that the media have a predilection for describing terrorist events using a dramaturgical paradigm consisting of the "good," the "bad," and the "spectacular."[20] Villains are pitted against heroes while superstars contribute supplementary dramatic interest. Terrorists are normally treated as villainous. Victims and their families constitute heroic sufferers while counterterrorist squads are heroic activists. Celebrities complete the cast of characters, playing the role of superstars.

In the TWA hijacking, the cruel, masked terrorists held the exclusive claim to being villainous. The pilot and U.S. Navy diver who became the first victims were from the outset heroic sufferers. The plane's manifest fortuitously included an artistic celebrity in the person of Demis Roussos, a popular Greek singer who happened to be a passenger. President Reagan and Israeli Prime Minister Peres were celebrities before the terrorist attack but their celebrity status was renewed by the intensive coverage. The hijacking itself created two new celebrities, Nabih Berri, the Shia Amal leader, and hostage spokesman Allyn Conwell, who became a virtual on-scene anchor for the American networks.

Though the networks did resort to a simple paradigm of good, bad, and heroic, the paradigm was often subordinated to the networks' desire for personalization. Suffering families, suffering hostages, and angry Shia were each presented with great intimacy. A revealing example of the quest for personalized reporting was David Hartman's interview with Shia leader Nabih Berri, hostage spokesman Allyn Conwell and Conwell's spouse, Olga. The setting was ABC's "Good Morning America." Hartman asked the Amal leader: "Any final words to President Reagan this morning?" Berri replied, "I want him to deal with this affair like a brother, not like a President." Hartman then invited the hostage and wife to exchange words. They spoke to each other with warmth and fondness, after which Olga Conwell received Berri's assurance, "I will take care of your husband."

19   On television viewership during the crisis, see New York Times (July 6, 1985), 42.
20   A. Schmid and J. de Graaf, Violence as Communication (London: Sage, 1982), 75.

The Priestly Role of Journalists

In media events, suggested Elihu Katz, journalists fulfill a role that is priestly in part. That journalists should be compared to priests during media events is understandable because media events normally involve human circumstances that, in private life and on a smaller scale, would call for a priestly role. A royal wedding remains nonetheless a wedding; Kennedy's assassination involves death; the landing on the moon contains an element of the supernatural.

In ordinary private life, the clergy continue to perform the valuable function of giving meaning to the social system and human existence. At weddings, the clergy employ religious ritual and symbolism to strengthen the sense of matrimonial bond and familial obligation. At funerals, they explain the meaning of death and thus give to the living a sense of continuing purpose. In a wide range of conflictual relationships, from spouses in dispute to relationships between jailers and inmates, clergy have traditionally acted as mediators and interlocutors. The clergy continue to perform priestly functions for private individuals in the increasingly secular and pluralistic societies of the liberal democracies. But the clergy is less able to fulfil these functions for the entire society than it once was.

The priestly function is increasingly shared with journalists in the case of media events, those mediated situations that affect entire societies. In the particular case of mediated international terrorism, the priestly role is almost entirely filled by journalists. Journalists become the mediators. Reporters are permitted to speak with hostages, relay messages from their families, and transmit offers and counteroffers between terrorists and national governments. Like the clergy whose traditional role they are supplanting, journalists define for their audience the ultimate meaning of the conflict and explain the broader significance of sadness and death. Journalists help their flock with their travails.

Just as the pope seeks to mediate international conflict and bring peace to the planet, so too do the network journalists practice diplomacy. The journalists do more than report the news; they create and shape it. David Hartman's question to Shi'ite Nabih Berri ("Any final words to President Reagan this morning?") is an example of a journalist's initiative known as *TV diplomacy*. In the TWA incident, the special priestly diplomatic role of the media was reflected in journalists' efforts to mediate among Shi'ites, Syrians, Israelis, and Americans. Like true clergy, the journalists were also available to fill important roles during the mourning for victims and the celebration of freedom.

The Impact

Because of their intensity, duration, and salience, media events almost inevitably produce societal effects. These effects can be classified according to type of recipient as well as type of psychological effect. A classification of recipients would include

- the direct victims of terrorism
- the terrorists themselves
- the general broadcasting audience
- journalists
- governments

The media effects themselves can be classified according to whether they are primary or secondary in nature. Primary effects consist of immediate psychological changes in the recipient. Secondary effects are those psychological changes wrought on one class of recipients by changes in the behavior of another class of recipients. Apart from being primary or secondary in nature, media effects can also be classified according to whether they are essentially emotive or cognitive.

Most studies of the impact of media events have focused on primary emotive or cognitive effects upon one class of recipients, the general audience. Studies of the early American presidential debates, of John F. Kennedy's funeral, and of other media events revealed that the general audience experiences both emotive and cognitive changes. Members of the general audience undergo the psychological experience of a "sense of occasion," aware that virtually everyone else in their national community was swept up in the same momentous event. Media events provide an occasion for the release of intense collective emotion—grief in the mourning of the loss of JFK, wonder at a vision of the moon landing, euphoria in the wake of Sadat's extraordinary arrival in Jerusalem, patriotic pride released by the coronation of Elizabeth II.

Major terrorist events appear to unleash a common pattern of emotional display—the initial thrill of danger, the tension of anticipation, fear, anger, grief, and finally relief and mass-mediated celebration once the episode comes to an end. This pattern of emotional experience was shared by millions during the 1972 massacre at the Munich Olympics, the 1979 seizure of the United States embassy in Teheran, and, of course, during the TWA hijacking to Beirut in July 1985.

The cognitive effects can be far-reaching. Israeli and indeed North Atlantic attitudes towards Egypt became decidedly more favorable in the wake of Sadat's surprising arrival in Jerusalem. Israeli willingness to return the

Sinai along with the oil fields they had discovered and their willingness to dismantle Israeli settlements were made possible by the Egyptian leader's dramatic action. The change in Israeli and Western attitudes was also made possible by the extraordinary importance attributed to the visit as a result of its being treated as a media event.

During the 1940s, Lazarsfeld and Merton introduced the concept of *status conferral* to describe the prestige and significance that the media are able to bestow on a subject or actor as a result of their coverage of it.[21] Since the media normally select important rather than unimportant subjects to cover, the public is predisposed to assume that any televised event is necessarily important. For terrorists, the phenomenon of status conferral constitutes an incentive to stage a media event. The mere fact of media coverage of a terrorist act confers importance on the terrorists and hence their apparent motives. Indeed, the goals of terrorists may be limited to simply gaining attention and public awareness.

Because terrorism is newsworthy and high on the media agenda, the policy issues that ostensibly motivate terrorists may acquire a priority in the public mind and/or in government decision-making agendas. In practice, publics may become immune to the concerns of terrorists in some circumstances, in spite of intensive media coverage. But governments may act on the assumption that public interest in the concerns of terrorists automatically follows news coverage of these concerns.

The actual cognitive effect on the general public may depend on the precise content of media reporting. A study by Weimann on the public opinion effect of press coverage of terrorist events showed that attitudes towards the terrorists depend on the evaluative language used in published reports.[22] In an earlier study, Paletz and his colleagues examined the nature and effects of American coverage of terrorist groups. American press coverage, they concluded, reflected officialdom's paradigm of terrorism *qua* evil, resulting in a reinforcement of the general public's repudiation of terrorists and their concerns.[23]

---

21   P. Lazarsfeld and R. K. Merton, "Mass Communication, Popular Taste and Organized Social Action," in Bryson Lyman, ed., *The Communication of Ideas* (New York: Institute for Religious and Social Studies, 1948).

22   "The Theatre of Terror: Effects of Press Coverage," *Journal of Communication* (Winter 1983), 38-45, and Weimann, "Redefinition of Image: The Impact of Mass-Mediated Terrorism," *International Journal of Public Opinion Research* (1992), 16-29.

23   D. Paletz, P. Fozzard, and J. Ayanian, "The IRA, the Red Brigades, and the FALN in the New York Times," *Journal of Communication* (Spring 1982), 162-63.

Journalists are increasingly aware of and sensitive to their role in the unfolding of terrorist events. The media are proud to be "the narrators of live history." "Media events give broadcasters," say Katz and Dayan, "the assurance that they are inside, not outside, the establishment."[24] Terrorist events provide the media as a whole as well as individual journalists with optimal opportunities to witness history as it happens, to represent or ameliorate the social order, to influence the course of events, and to bring about a peaceful resolution of conflict. The media can cultivate a profound sense of occasion by abruptly changing schedules, canceling regular programs, introducing newsbreaks, and utilizing visual and oral cues to transmit to audiences a sense of the magnitude of the historical event being observed.

While journalists are proud of the positive role they play as narrators of history, they are also sensitive to the possibility of being manipulated. In the TWA hijacking case as in other instances, the termination of the episode led to a wave of self-criticism. After the hijacking came to an end, many of the headlines in the press revealed journalists' sensibilities about ghoulish excess and being manipulated by the terrorists—"Prime Time Terrorism" (*Time*, July 1, 1985), "The Networks Fight Fiercely on Hostages" (*New York Times*, June 30, 1985), "The Network Circus" (*Newsweek*, July 15, 1985), "TV in the Hostage Crisis: Reporter or Participant?" (*New York Times*, July 2, 1985), "TV Examines Its Excesses" (*Time*, July 22, 1985), "The Bottom Line: How to Do It Right the Next Time" (*TV Guide*, September 21, 1985), and ABC's special, aired on July 30, 1985, entitled "Reporting under the Gun."

Mass-mediated terrorism may produce sundry effects on the terrorists themselves. Sensing the special atmosphere of a media event, the terrorists may realize that they are performing on the largest of world stages. Terrorists are capable of learning from past experiences as well as adjusting their conduct during the unfolding of mediated terrorist events. Realizing the vast impact on publics and governments of their appearance on television, some terrorist groups may even decide to eschew violence. When some terrorist acts seem particularly effective at inducing intense media coverage, these acts are apt to be repeated. In a kind of contagion effect, successful acts of terror tend to be followed by a rash of identical acts.

24   Katz and Dayan, "Media Events," 310.

Comparing Media Events and Their Attributes

In their delineation and classification of media events, Katz and Dayan identify eight theatrical and other attributes by which media events can be compared:

- periodic or cyclical character
- dramatic character
- attitude toward rules and law
- nature of conflict
- attitude toward conflict resolution
- moral lesson or message
- role of performers
- analogue of TV genres [25]

Table 4.1 outlines the differences among the three original media events and our proposed coercive media event with respect to the six attributes. Unlike the other media events, *contests* occur according to a regular periodic cycle. Rules of conflict are agreed to and observed; indeed the moral message is that rules are supreme. Dramatic tension is supplied by uncertainty about the outcome of conflict, namely who will win. As a television genre, *contests* are akin to quiz shows.

As TV genres, *conquests* are similar to westerns while *coronations* are analogous to soap operas. Conquests are predictable events, albeit not on a fixed calendar. The dramatic intensity is provided by uncertainty about whether the main protagonist will win. Coronations neither follow fixed periodical schedules nor are predictable, but they are recurrent. Action is essentially symbolic. Dramatic tension is provided by uncertainty over whether the ceremonial rite will produce success for both the individuals directly involved and the society they embody.

Unlike the other media events, *coercions* have no fixed or expected timing; indeed surprise and shock are essential ingredients in mediated terrorism. Journalists willingly cover other media events, sometimes fulfilling a role that is almost priestly. By contrast, journalists are perceived as being forced against their will to cover coercive events only because of the newsworthiness of these events.

25   "Media Events."

Table 4.1 Categories and Characteristics of Media Events

Characteristics	Contests	Conquests	Coronations	Coercions
periodicity	fixed, cyclical	not fixed predictable	not fixed current	not fixed surprise
drama	who will win?	will he or she win?	will ritual succeed?	at what price?
rules	agreed rules	no rules	ritual rules	against rules
conflict	person vs. person (symbolic)	person vs. nature or society	culture, society vs. nature	person vs. person, society, & culture
conflict resolution	fixed symbolic resolution	invites identification	reflexive recalls basic values of society	condemnation and identifica-tion
message	rules are supreme; victory & defeat are reversible	giant leap for humankind	continuity is assured	violence leads nowhere
time orientation	present	future	past	present
role of performers	demonstrate character	demonstrate charisma	ritual performance	demonstrate power
analogue to TV genres	quiz	western	soap opera	crime series

Source: Based on Dayan and Katz, *Media Events*, 34-35, and Weimann, "Media Events: The Case of International Terrorism," *Journal of Broadcasting and Electronic Media* (1987), 21-39.

As a TV genre, coercions belong to the category of crime series. As in the case of crime series, mediated terrorist events carry a moral message in support of the existing lawful social order. NBC's John Chancellor ex-emplified this ethos when he intoned that "the fanatics want America in agony...America brought to its knees....Let's not play into their hands."

CBS's Dan Rather raged against the TWA hijackers, who "took somebody's son...beat the hell out of him and shot him to death." Once the hostages were released, similar indignation was expressed by government officials, the president, and even the freed hostages.

The persistence of authoritative messages reinforcing the existing moral order during the course of terrorist events has prompted leftwing analysts such as Herman to decry the media treatment of international terrorism.[26] For Herman and others, mediated terrorism has provided the governments of the Western capitalist democracies with opportunities to preach moral virtue and reinforce the existing political and economic order. Indeed, the attention given by the media to international terrorism by nonstate terrorist groups has enabled Western governments, asserts Herman, to distract the public's attention from the allegedly more serious state-sponsored terrorism practiced by the Western governments and their third world allies.

It is possible to reconcile the leftwing argument that mediated terrorism reinforces the existing social order with the evidence that media reports can confer status on terrorist groups and their causes. Compare for a moment the possible effects of international terrorism with the known domestic effects of violence on television. In the wake of the enormous empirical research on the effects of violence on television that was spurred by U.S. presidential interest in the subject during the 1960s, it is now virtually axiomatic that violence on television contributes in a measurable, if modest, way to violent behavior among members of the audience. It is also known that television violence leads to exaggerated fear of violence in real life and engenders increased respect for established governmental authorities as defenders of order. As Gerbner said of TV violence,

> Ritualized displays of violence...may cultivate exaggerated assumptions about the extent of threat and danger in the world and lead to demands for protection. A heightened sense of risk and insecurity is more likely to increase acquiescence to and dependence upon established authority, and to legitimize its use of force, than it is to threaten the social order.[27]

By the same token, mediated terrorism may simultaneously increase the authority of Western governments in the minds of Western publics while increasing the salience of the terrorists themselves and the causes that they claim to speak for.

26 E. S. Herman, *The Real Terror Network* (Boston: South End Press, 1982) and E. S. Herman and G. O'Sullivan, *The "Terrorism Industry"* (New York: Pantheon Books, 1989).

27 G. Gerbner and L. Gross, "Living with Television: The Violence Profile," *Journal of Communication* 26 (1976), 194.

An important but as yet unanswered question is whether terrorists' theatrical efforts ultimately bear fruit. The history of modern international media-motivated terror is not yet long enough to permit a confident conclusion to be reached. Furthermore, international terrorists' objectives can be multiple, complex, ambiguous, and even contradictory, making it difficult to evaluate the degree to which their objectives are achieved.

Terrorists' formally stated ultimate objectives may entail a fundamental change of regime or national boundaries and/or a transfer of population. Measuring terrorists' success requires an assessment of whether these ultimate objectives are considered by the group to be vital ends in themselves. Terrorists' apparently ultimate objectives can in fact be a mere bargaining position, a means of securing popular support, a means of contributing to organizational survival in the terrorists' marketplace, and/or a means of gaining publicity.

If gaining political power is the ultimate objective, then one must conclude that international terrorists are not hugely successful. Few of the hundreds of such groups have genuine prospects for acquiring political power. On the other hand, a definite minority have demonstrated considerable success in acquiring media attention and hence in gaining name recognition and even some understanding among politically active publics in advanced industrial societies.

The case of the comparatively successful PLO illustrates the complexity of attempting to assess whether or not terrorists are successful. The terror of the media-wise PLO may have helped highlight the Palestinian agenda. It may have contributed to a certain esprit de corps, and it may have sown some fear among politicians and journalists. But PLO terrorism became less effective than, even counterproductive compared to, the early intifada.

Like terrorism, the intifada entailed a careful scripting and coordination with the media in order to maximize news value. But for the repellant cruelty of terrorism, the intifada substituted a quasi-biblical motif of stone-throwing women and children battling a heavily armed Goliath. Terrorist raids and intra-Palestinian violence subsequent to the onset of the intifada served to detract from the international public and governmental goodwill that civilian street action had begun to obtain.

Chapter 5

Factors Predicting Media Coverage

In the theater of terror, the mass media provide a stage that is often worldwide in dimensions. The actor-directors are the gate-keeper journalists who determine if, when, and how theatrical opportunities are provided to would-be thespians. The journalists who are empowered to control these opportunities are often subjected to a searing scrutiny from outside their profession. For some critics, journalists may amount to handmaidens of terrorism. In the words of Frederick Hacker,

> The mass media willingly or unwittingly are the spokesmen of the terrorists, the transmitters of the terroristic message, the instrument through which terroristic deeds with all their excitement, drama and significance become known to a world audience.[1]

The role of journalists in communicating news of terrorist events is sometimes unwitting. Some journalists may be motivated by merely a naive curiosity, as Hacker implies, or even by a kind of voyeurism. Some journalists may also be motivated by an ideological affinity with particular terrorist groups, as Hacker also implies. But the factors in journalistic decisions to cover terrorism are broader than either of these two single considerations.

The professional factors that affect coverage of terrorism are particularly complex. Such professional considerations include the editorial norms for what is newsworthy, the administrative routines governing how news is gathered, the self-image and role conceptions of the newsperson, the procedures of news selection within newsrooms, and the competitive ethos in the news industry. Journalists are influenced not only by peer pressure and occupational norms, but also by what the public thinks is newsworthy. Journalists are in turn affected by how they perceive their peers' perceptions of public expectations.

---

1 "Contagion and Attraction of Terror and Terrorism," in Y. Alexander and J. M. Gleason, eds., *Behavioral and Quantitative Perspectives on Terrorism* (New York: Pergamon, 1981), 77.

The national culture of a particular society within which journalists live and work may also exercise an influence.[2] The previous chapter provided evidence from the content analysis of media reporting that national cultures propel individual newspapers to single out terrorist events in some regions of the world but not in others. Thus, the *Times* of London and the *Telegraph* place considerable emphasis on terrorism in Africa, particularly southern Africa, as a reflection of the British colonial heritage on that continent.

Of all the professional and nonprofessional considerations that affect coverage of terrorism, none may be as stark as the threat of reprisal against journalists whose coverage is inadequate in the eyes of the terrorists themselves. Thus, media coverage of terrorism can be understood not only in terms of sundry professional motivations and in terms of societal factors such as national culture, but media coverage can also be seen against a background of inchoate or anticipated hostage-taking in which the journalist is the implicit hostage.

Coercion

Terrorists do not normally resort to threats against journalists in order to produce media coverage. Rather, they count on the media to oblige their desire for attention under the normal conditions of press freedom that prevail in liberal democracies. As Carlos Marighela observed from personal experience in domestic terrorism, the media are "important instruments of propaganda" for the simple reason that they find terrorist actions newsworthy.[3]

In Marighela's native Brazil during the 1960s, terrorists found that journalists were eager to provide coverage. As one member of the Vanguarda Popular Revolucionaria quipped, the press is "ever greedy for news that increases the sale of its papers."[4] Once the government intervened to forestall coverage, the press's ostensibly pecuniary motives were no longer sufficient to guarantee headlines.

Brazilian terrorists adjusted to the situation by seizing radio and television facilities. Broadcasters were forced at gunpoint to diffuse manifestos, messages, and speeches, including Marighela's own. In 1969,

2   David L. Altheide, "Format and Symbols in TV Coverage of Terrorism in the United States and Great Britain," in *International Studies Quarterly* (1987) 31, 161-76.
3   *Minimanual of the Urban Guerrilla* (Havana: Tricontinental, n.d.).
4   Joao Quartim, "Leninism or Militarism," in J. Kohl and J. Litt, eds., *Urban Guerrilla Warfare in Latin America* (Cambridge: M.I.T. Press), 151.

Brazil's National Liberation Action combined with MR-8 (Revolutionary Movement of the Eight) to kidnap U.S. Ambassador Charles Burke, demanding air time as a condition of his release. The innovation was enormously successful. Masses of people all over the country took to the streets, turning their portable radios to the terrorists' manifesto, which detailed the cruelties committed by the country's military regime.

A similar media-terrorist relationship unfolded in neighboring Uruguay. After staging sundry events to attract media attention during the early 1960s, the Tupamaros found that their access to mass communication was blocked by new government regulations, adopted when the president declared a national state of siege. The guerrillas responded by installing pirate radio transmitters, which operated independently of established broadcasters and which sometimes interrupted the regularly scheduled programming of the authorized stations.

In Argentina, the ERP (People's Revolutionary Army) was less subtle and more brutal. In 1973, the ERP kidnapped an executive of the paper *Clarin*, forcing the paper to publish a front-page advertisement on behalf of the group as well as two inside pages urging the electorate to support Peron in the forthcoming balloting. In 1975, another terrorist group kidnapped the director of the country's Mercedes Benz plant. The victim was released only after his company complied with the terrorists' edict to publish large advertisements in major North Atlantic newspapers denouncing the economic imperialism of multinational companies operating in the third world.

Argentinean terrorists supplemented their kidnapping of corporate officials with widespread attacks on journalists, a pattern that was to spread across the continent. By the end of 1978, a total of 162 Latin American journalists had been abducted, many of them murdered; 89 of these were Argentineans. That same year the Sandinistas seized the radio station in Managua so that they could broadcast their views to much of Nicaragua. In nearby El Salvador, the FARN (Armed Revolutionary National Forces) forced the daily press to publish their manifesto as a condition for the release of kidnapped foreign businessmen. Meanwhile, terrorists persuaded a neighboring Dutch language radio station to broadcast into El Salvador as a condition of freeing a hostage who was a director of the Phillips conglomerate.

Cases of media coercion took place in North America as well. In October 1970, Britain's trade commissioner in Montreal, James Cross, was kidnapped by the FLQ (Front de Libération du Quebec), the terrorist wing of the Quebec separatist movement. An anonymous telephone call to a radio station led to a mailbox containing a ransom note that ordered, among other demands, the publication of the FLQ's manifesto on the front page of the province's main newspapers as well as its broadcast on prime time television. In the days ahead, the FLQ position softened as the terrorists prepared to negotiate with authorities. But the demand for broadcast time remained unchanged. The government of Canada relented, instructing the state-owned broadcaster to comply. Experts in communications later judged the manifesto to have been "effective propaganda,"[5] couched in ordinary language and appealing to deeply felt grievances against English-Canada rather than sounding a purely cerebral call for secession from Canada. The terrorists themselves were convinced that they had scored a victory. When the kidnappers and murderers of Cross departed for refuge in Cuba, they left behind tape recordings in which they gloated that the forced broadcast of their manifesto had elicited considerable sympathy: "For the first time, patriots of the Front managed to express themselves by entering every home, through Radio Canada...by making them read our manifesto."

Many of the more extraordinary examples of media coercion were to take place, perhaps fittingly, in the United States, the media center of the world. In September 1976 five Croatians hijacked a TWA flight. Ultimata were issued for the publication of a 3,500-word manifesto demanding the liberation of Croatia from Yugoslav control. The manifesto was duly published as required in the *New York Times*, *Los Angeles Times*, and *Chicago Tribune*. In subsequent announcements, the Croatians demanded that their pamphlets be dropped over Montreal, New York, and Chicago and, then, over London and Paris. The terrorists eventually surrendered in France's capital. In a marvelous example of self-mocking and parody, one of the departing Croatians turned to the cameras and intoned: "That's showbiz!"

Showbiz was certainly a major element of the widely publicized terrorist kidnapping of Patricia Hearst two years earlier. Although an example of domestic rather than international terrorism, the event justifies a reference because of its multiple media entanglements.

In February 1974 the Symbionese Liberation Army seized the teenage heiress to the Hearst media conglomerate. The 12 member army rushed a letter to a local San Francisco radio station, threatening the safety of the hostage if their communications were not fully distributed by the media.

---

5   Anthony Westell, *Paradox: Trudeau as Prime Minister* (Scarborough, Ont.: Prentice-Hall, 1972).

Both the Hearst-owned *San Francisco Chronicle* and the *Oakland Tribune* complied, publishing the terrorists' manifestos and press releases in full.

The emerging symbiotic relation between the Symbionese and the media was replete with irony. The SLA was soon shocked to realize that it did not have to threaten harm to receive copious attention. The members of the fledgling SLA were virtually hounded for news copy, earning seven cover stories in *Newsweek*. The identity of the victim made fascinating reading—the youthful and innocent scion of a wealthy family, her transformation from victim to terrorist, and her ironic descendance from Randolph Hearst, who built his media empire on histrionic, hyperbolic, and intrusive reporting known as *yellow journalism*.

The Hanafi episode showed that terrorists could achieve not only publicity but the right of censorship as well. In March 1977, a black Muslim sect known as Hanafi seized 134 hostages at the International B'nai B'rith headquarters Washington, D.C., holding them captive for 39 hours. They demanded that a recently released film, *Mohammed, Messenger of God*, be proscribed from American theaters. The motion picture's producers, United Artists, complied, and the $17 million film was withdrawn from circulation.

Western European terrorist groups have undertaken a wide range of coercive actions against the media. The Irish Republican Army, the Basque Separatist Movement (Euskadi ta Askatasuna), the Italian Red Brigades, and the West German Red Army Faction have each murdered, injured, and/or threatened reporters.[6] When the well-being and even the lives of journalists are threatened and when news of these threats is submerged or even suppressed, it is possible to speculate about, but difficult to demonstrate, the impact on reportage.

It is easier to demonstrate the effect on reportage of terrorist acts when the victim's right to life is made conditional on media cooperation. In February 1975, a group of Red Army terrorists named *The June 2nd Movement* kidnapped the West Berlin politician and mayoral candidate Peter Lorenz. As a requirement for his release, the terrorists made a successful demand for the broadcasting of their declarations as well as the live transmission of the release of six prisoners whose liberation they had sought. German television was "hijacked," as one television executive commented later:

> For 72 hours we just lost control of the medium. It was theirs, not ours....We shifted shows in order to meet their time-table. Our cameras had to be in

6   For details, see A. Schmid and J. de Graaf, *Violence as Communication* (Beverly Hills, Calif.: Sage, 1982), 42-53.

position to record each of the released prisoners as they boarded the plane to freedom, and our news coverage had to include prepared statements at their dictates....It was the gangsters who wrote the script and program the mass media. We preferred to think that we were being "flexible", but actually we were just helpless....Surely it must be the first recorded case of how to hijack a national TV network.[7]

The Italian Red Brigades were at least as media conscious as their West German collaborators. The Italian terrorists kidnapped a director of Fiat, knowing that the automaker and industrial conglomerate owned the mass circulation *La Stampa* and hence was in a position to accommodate ultimata for the publication of terrorist manifestos. In some instances, the Red Brigades resorted to the most direct approach of all: they simply seized private radio stations by force of arms in order to ensure the broadcast of their messages.

Perhaps the strongest indication of terrorist coercion against journalists involves the PLO and its allies. In his book *Double Vision*, Ze'ev Chafets documents scores of cases in which Western journalists were executed, tortured, kidnapped, or merely assaulted by Palestinian and Arab terrorists.[8] Chafets concludes:

> Over a period of some seven years, Reuters, *Time*, *Newsweek*, the *N.Y. Times*, the *Washington Post*, CBS, ABC, and the Associated Press—to name only some—played an active part in hiding from the public many of the facts about what was happening in Lebanon in general and, in particular, the way in which their newsmen were being subjected to intimidation and violence there.

The journalists' inclination to silence about violence against members of their own profession deserves a thoughtful consideration. An uncharitable interpretation is that the media do not wish their audience to be aware of the constraints and moral ambiguity associated with their reporting of terrorism. By contrast, a charitable interpretation is that the media simply wish to downplay violence against journalists in order not to give such violence undue encouragement. Of course, this charitable interpretation has a morally ambiguous aspect. If it is desirable to downplay terrorist violence against journalists, it is equally desirable to downplay terrorist violence against nonjournalists.

---

7   Cited in Melvin J. Lasky, "Ulrike Meinhof and the Baader-Meinhof Gang," *Encounter* 44 (1975) 6, 15.

8   *Double Vision: How America's Free Press Distorts Our View of the Middle East* (New York: Morrow, 1984). See also Gabriel Weimann, "Who Is After the Media in Lebanon," *Middle East Focus* 8 (1985), 4.

Whether or not the conduct and motives of journalists should be interpreted charitably, it is reasonably evident that journalists are not viewed charitably by either the terrorists on the one hand or by their innocent victims on the other. David Hubbard, a psychiatrist who has interviewed scores of terrorists, cites the views of one terrorist as typical of most: "Television is a whore. Any man who wants her full favours can have them in five minutes with a pistol."[9]

One of the hostages in the Hanafi incident expressed an equally uncharitable view, albeit less flamboyantly and more thoughtfully:

> As hostages, many of us felt that the Hanafi takeover was a happening, a guerrilla theatre, a high impact exercise program for the TV screen, and secondarily for the front pages of newspapers around the world....Beneath the resentment and the anger of my fellow hostages toward the press is a conviction gained...that the news media and terrorism feed on each other, that the news media and particularly TV, create thirst for fame and recognition.[10]

To this point in the book, we have shown that modern terrorists harbor a strong desire for media exposure and that journalists are eager to satisfy that desire. One reason for journalistic accommodation is the threat of violence against journalists themselves. Anticipated violence against journalists may sometimes affect the magnitude and content of coverage of terrorism. But in most locations and on most occasions, journalists cover terrorism not because they live in fear but because they judge terrorist actions to be newsworthy. Hence, to understand the coverage of terrorism, it is essential to understand the general character of what is newsworthy as well as the newsworthiness of terrorism in particular.

The Newsworthiness of Terrorism

"Everyone needs news. In everyday life, news tells us what we do not experience directly and thus renders otherwise remote happenings observable and meaningful," observe Molotch and Lester in their sociological analysis of the media.[11] Given the axiom that mediated news is prized by all those whose horizons are wider than their hamlet or village, the question

---

9   Cited in Neil Hickey, "Terrorism and Television," *TV Guide* 24 (31)(1976), 6.

10   Cited in A. Schmid and J. de Graaf, *Violence as Communication*, 42.

11   H. Molotch and M. Lester, "News as Purposive Behavior: On the Strategic Use of Routine Events, Accidents, and Scandals," *American Sociological Review* 39 (1974), 101.

to consider is why some events are deemed newsworthy while others are communicated by word of mouth only.

The media's relegation of an event to word-of-mouth status or promotion to newsworthy status can be understood as a kind of political process. According to communications sociologist Herbert Gans, deciding what is news is a matter of pressure and counter-pressure: "Story selection is a power struggle over what messages enter the symbolic arena."[12] News organizations are surrounded by individuals and groups wanting to get their messages into the arena with a maximum of helpful and a minimum of harmful publicity.

The power struggle among successful and would-be newsmakers is an unequal one. Some actors possess "habitual access" to the media while others, lacking it, make use of "disruptive access."[13] In most societies, habitual access is accorded to government officials, major corporate figures, and individuals who, according to the particular national culture, are deemed potent, glamorous, or otherwise worthy of attention. Those who lack habitual access to the media can compensate for their weakness by making news, by generating surprise or shock and thereby crashing through the ongoing routines of newsgathering.

Media-motivated terrorism is an obvious example of such disruptive access. The actual or anticipated use of violence are normally sufficient to assure access. This is a point well understood by the terrorists themselves. Hans Joachim Klein, a German terrorist, confided to *Der Spiegel*: "We...asked ourselves...what would be an action that no one can disregard, that everyone must talk about in the media and report on. We found it: a bomb. Even though the bomb did not explode, this story went halfway around the world."

Of course, bombs are not the only instrument of violence, and violence is not the only factor affecting newsworthiness. Our own quantitative analysis of media coverage, presented later in this chapter, shows that bombing is in fact a less effective means of gaining coverage than kidnapping and other forms of violence.

Before narrowing our focus to consider only the newsworthiness of different forms of violence, it is appropriate to undertake a broader overview of the factors that render newsworthy any international event, violent or otherwise. In their well-known analysis of the structure of international

12   *Deciding What's News* (New York: Pantheon, 1979), 249.
13   H. Molotch and M. Lester, "News as Purposive Behavior," 108.

news, Galtung and Ruge pinpointed 13 features of an event that determine whether or not the event is reported. These 13 attributes include the timing and cyclical nature of the event, its unambiguous character, and its negative meaning. The passages that follow enumerate the requirements for newsworthiness identified by Galtung and Ruge and explore how well terrorist events satisfy these requirements.[14]

Frequency

Events are apt to become newsworthy if their frequency is compatible with the frequency of news production. Thus, the media are not likely to provide much coverage of slowly unfolding events or processes. But the media are apt to report events that are daily in occurrence and can be recorded between the manufacture of two successive issues of a daily newspaper or daily news program. Terrorist events fulfill the timing requirements of news production because they are normally short in duration and intense.

The compatibility of terrorist events with the media's production requirements is often taken into consideration when terrorists undertake their initial planning. Media-wise terrorists may organize their activities around the deadlines, schedules, and programming constraints of the journalists whose attention they desire. Schmid and de Graaf make the following observation in this regard:

> How sophisticated the media strategy of the Red Brigades is can be inferred from the fact that they choose Wednesdays and Saturdays as their preferred communication days, knowing that on Thursdays and Sundays papers are thicker and have higher circulation figures. By placing their communiques just before the evening deadlines for the morning papers, as they frequently do, they give the editors very little time to tailor their messages. In their anonymous telephonic communications they simultaneously call several papers and broadcasting stations in various towns so that the media compete against each other. In this way they have been able to induce papers to bring special editions to the streets and [to induce] radio and television stations to interrupt their regular programs.[15]

Threshold

Galtung and Ruge observe that events must surpass a threshold of emotionally significant meaning to be covered by the media. Terrorist events normally encounter little difficulty in achieving the required level of significance for coverage. When in doubt, terrorists can program their actions

14   J. Galtung and M. H. Ruge, "The Structure of Foreign News," *Journal of International Peace Research* 1 (1965), 64-80.
15   Schmid and de Graaf, *Violence as Communication*, 51.

for a sufficient level of injuries, death, and international involvement to assure coverage.

The media have a strong preference for events that exhibit considerable dramatic intensity. Intense events are easier to analyze, easier to place within the format of news production, and easier to employ as a means of capturing audience attention. Terrorist events are normally very intense: they are typically brief, dramatic occurrences that involve a specific location (e.g., hijacked aircraft or embassy under siege) and well-defined actors (i.e., terrorists, victims, police, etc.). When the intensity of a situation appears to be abating, terrorists can reestablish a sense of crisis by introducing deadlines for compliance with their wishes and by making threats in the event of noncompliance.

Unambiguity

Galtung and Ruge emphasize journalists' preferences for events that are uncomplicated—easily understood and easily reported. The less ambiguity, the greater the likelihood an event will be noticed and covered. The political, economic, religious, social, and other processes that give rise to terrorism are difficult to report because they may be complex, protracted, ambiguous, and subject to conflicting interpretations. But the terrorist act itself is usually clear and easy to grasp. Indeed, Livingstone points to the special simplicity and clarity of terrorism in comparison with other types of violent phenomena:

> Unlike wars and most revolutions, which are usually protracted and highly complex events that are too broad in scope to be grasped readily and easily understood, acts of terrorist violence normally have a beginning and an end, can be encompassed in a few minutes of air time, possess a large degree of drama, invoke participants who are perceived by the viewing public as unambiguous, and are not so complex as to be unintelligible to those who tune in only briefly.[16]

Meaningfulness

For it to have a good chance of being reported, an event should not only be clear and unambiguous but it should also be meaningful within the cultural framework of the audience. The media pay particular attention to phenomena that are familiar and culturally proximate. Just as journalists are more apt to report traffic accidents occurring locally or involving local inhabitants, in international news the media are more apt to report events involving fellow nationals or taking place on national soil.

16 N. C. Livingstone, *The War Against Terrorism* (Lexington, Mass.: Lexington Books, 1982), 62.

International terrorists are certainly cognizant of the predilection of the media for that which is culturally meaningful. Although modern terrorism is carried out largely by non-Western organizations, terrorist acts take place disproportionately on Western soil and are targeted primarily against citizens of Western countries. During the 1968-1980 period, nearly half of all incidents of international terrorism occurred in Western nations while North Americans and Western Europeans provided 60% of its victims.[17] The nationals of the countries of the Soviet bloc are virtually immune from all such attacks.

Meaningfulness and Relevance

For an international event to be newsworthy in the eyes of a national community of journalists, the event should not only be culturally meaningful or understandable but it should also involve a manifest link and relevance to the nation in question. In the wake of a generation of modern media-oriented terrorism, attacks on aircraft, ships, and passenger terminals are almost instantly meaningful to large portions of the world audience for the mass media. A *local news angle* provides any particular journalism community with added relevance. A terrorist attack is apt to become relevant to a multitude of journalistic communities if the character of the targets, victims, and terrorist networks is heterogeneous. The Palestinian seizure of the *Achille Lauro* in October 1985 carried relevance for various national journalistic fraternities because of the multinational character of the event: a Spanish crew aboard an Italian ship with German and American passengers sailing to Syrian and Lebanese coasts after being hijacked en route from Egypt to Israel. Given its multinational relevance, it is not surprising that the episode became a media event.

Unexpectedness

To be newsworthy, Galtung and Ruge point out, an event should be unexpected rather than predictable, and relatively unique rather than repetitive. Although journalists require professional routines for the processing of news, the events themselves should not be excessively routine. By its very nature, international terrorism embodies surprise. Its constant battle with security forces necessitates secrecy and unexpectedness. When terrorists become bureaucratic, they risk capture. When terrorists lose their fear of capture by civil authorities, as they have in Lebanon, and their actions become routinized, these actions tend to recede from the headlines.

---

17   Based on "Patterns of International Terrorism," U.S. Central Intelligence Agency, National Foreign Assessment Center (June 1981).

Scarcity

Rarity supplements unexpectedness as a source of newsworthiness. Events should be infrequent; scarcity alone contributes a strong element of drama. The necessity of scarcity does not go unnoticed by the media-oriented terrorists. Krauthammer and others have observed terrorists' resourcefulness in creating new theatrical productions.[18] For periods of a year or two at a time, the world experiences waves of hijackings or other types of terrorism. Then, as if recognizing the need to forestall the boredom of routinized violence, the terrorists themselves abruptly change their pattern of action. Thus, the hijacking of aircraft may make way for the hijacking of trains while the kidnapping of individuals may be succeeded by the theft of corpses, a Latin American innovation.

Continuity

Galtung and Ruge suggest that once an event of a type has been defined as news and earned headline status, other events of the same type will continue to be defined as newsworthy even if their dramatic intensity or *amplitude* is much lower. Thus, once a single event of a given kind is accorded attention, similar events in a series tend to benefit from reflected status. The disposition of journalists to confer recognition on succeeding examples of the same kind of phenomenon is explained partly by inertia, partly by a desire to justify the initial news decision, and partly by the journalists' expectation that their audience will encounter little difficulty processing the information.

Galtung and Ruge's axiom of continuity is compatible with our finding of a contagion effect, discussed below in Chapter 8. The fact that a successful mass-mediated terrorist action is followed by a wave of similar acts suits the media's need for continuity, at least for the short term, and therefore helps fulfill the terrorists' needs for attention. The journalists' sense of continuity is reflected not only in their predisposition to cover like events in a series but also in the content of their headlines, viz. "another case of a car bomb" or "one more car bombing."

Personification

Events are more likely to be reported if they can be personified, explained in terms of the actions of individuals rather than in terms of the confluence of social processes. Personification is one of the strongest requirements for news production because it fulfills so many of the professional requirements of the newsroom:

18   C. Krauthammer, "Terrorism and the Media: A Discussion," *Harper's* (October 1984), 50.

- Events are more easily portrayed in terms of people than in terms of social forces;
- The audience can identify more easily with human actors than with social forces;
- The personification of events eases the journalists' task of making sense of events, reducing the journalists' requirement for a specialized knowledge of history, culture, and society;
- The personification of events facilitates the physical production of news because it is easier, for example, to prepare video footage of individuals than of social forces;
- Portraying an event in terms of individual human beings makes it easier to interpret the event as a morality play pitting *good* characters against the *bad* and thus to incorporate dramatic content;
- Emphasizing the role of individuals rather than social forces makes it easier for journalists to highlight audience-catching histrionics—cruelty, determination, mercy, heroism, grief, and altruism.
- Finally, the personification of events is congruous with the human-centered paradigm of Western civilization, namely that man is the master of his own destiny and not the victim of forces beyond his control or comprehension.

Reference to Elite Nations

By its nature news is elite-centered; it focuses on elite nations and elite individuals. News is elite-centered partly on account of the objective consideration that elites are influential and hence their actions justify monitoring. News is also elite-centered for the subjective reason that the mass media are controlled by elites, who utilize their control over the media to flatter, legitimate, and learn about themselves. The important mass media are essentially American and Western European.[19] For this reason alone, one might expect the flow of news to be from the North Atlantic region to the rest of the world. Indeed, the global production of news is so concentrated in the Western world that third world countries often find that

19 J. Tunstall, *The Media Are American* (London: Constable, 1977); H. Schiller, *Mass Communication and the American Empire* (New York: Augustus M. Kelley, 1969); T. Varis, "Global Traffic in Television," *Journal of Communication* 24 (1974), 102-109; A. Wells, *Picture Tube Imperialism?* (New York: Orbis Books, 1972).

they must await broadcasts emanating from New York, London, or Paris in order to learn about events in their own region.

The marked elite-centeredness of the media helps to account for the focus of modern terrorism on Western societies. Media-oriented terrorists appreciate that they are more apt to attract attention if they design their actions with Western locales and/or Western victims in mind. Hence, the most preferred targets of international terrorism are the United States, France, Germany, Israel, Britain, Italy, and other elite nations.

Reference to Elite Individuals

We quoted earlier Marighela's dictum that "to kidnap figures known for their artistic, sporting or other activities who have not expressed any political views may possibly provide a form of propaganda favourable to the revolutionaries."[20] In his observation, the Brazilian revolutionary articulated clearly the media's predilection for news about important personages. Their understanding of media behavior leads terrorists to chose victims who possess very high media profiles or are visibly associated with individuals who do. This explains the range of targets selected by terrorists. The following sample illustrates the point:

- the IRA's attempted bombing of Prime Minister Margaret Thatcher and her cabinet assembled for a party convention in Brighton, England;
- the Palestinians' kidnapping of ministers attending a Vienna meeting of the Organization of Oil Exporting Countries in 1975;
- the June 2nd Movement's kidnapping of prominent West German politician Peter Lorenz that same year;
- the same movement's intended kidnapping of Pope Paul VI the following year;
- the Red Brigades' execution of Italy's Christian Democratic leader Aldo Moro;
- Black September's attack on Israeli athletes at the Munich Olympics in 1972.

To this sample of targets could be readily added a long list of film actors, political leaders, senior civil servants, corporate executives, and diplomats.

20 Carlos Marighela, *Minimanual of the Urban Guerrilla* (Havana: Tricontinental, n.d.), 103.

Destructive Events

It has been axiomatic in the news industry that negative events are much more likely to be reported and to receive extensive coverage than events that embody pro-social, humanitarian, or constructive values. Galtung and Ruge account for this pattern in several ways. For example, negative events are better able to fulfill the frequency criterion for newsworthiness because negative events are briefer in duration and simpler to portray. Compare the length of time and complexity associated with building a house with the brevity and simplicity of destroying it by fire. Likewise compare the time needed to create a functioning human being with the time required to extinguish a life.

Negative events are comparatively unambiguous. Positive events may be complex—positive in some respects to some people, positive in other respects to other people, and negative in still other respects to still other people. By contrast, negative events are rarely perceived in shades of gray.

The simplicity of negative events is attractive to journalists in their search for professional criteria of news selection as a guard against the introduction of personal ideological considerations. Most journalists in the liberal democracies make serious attempts to "leave their conscious personal values at home," to borrow the words of media observer Herbert Gans.[21] Journalists submerge their personal or political values in a kind of professional ideology of newsworthiness. Gans terms the professional outlook of journalists a "paraideology" while the journalists themselves speak of "objectivity." Objectivity in the realm of journalism entails the use of predetermined standards of selection and reporting, personal detachment, and a disregard for the ramifications of whether and how an event is reported.

Journalistic objectivity requires choosing news not on the basis of whom it will help or harm but rather on the basis of the kinds of impersonal criteria of newsworthiness that Galtung and Ruge identified and are being enumerated in these passages. Logically, objective news reporting must necessarily sometimes do harm. Thus, in a kind of perverse way the apparently occasional harmfulness of news reporting constitutes indirect evidence of the possibility that the reporting may be strictly objective.

The professional culture and organization of journalism reinforces professional conceptions of objectivity. Reporters are rotated in order to impede the development of feelings of attachment. Journalists are dis-

---

21   See his *Deciding What's News* (New York: Pantheon, 1979), 182-202.

couraged from contemplating the implications of news reporting. They are also discouraged from acquiring much specialized expertise. Indeed the profession has often lagged behind others in the importance it attaches to higher education, language acquisition, and specialized skills. The rotation of reporters and the low value placed on knowledge and education sometimes arise from the commercial motives of media owners; personnel costs can more easily be controlled.

Yet, journalism's quest for objectivity is also motivated by high ideals including the goal of contributing to a better informed, more civic-minded liberal democracy. At the beginning of the twentieth century, Pulitzer in the United States looked to journalism education as a means of imparting this altruistic and impartial sense of mission.[22] By the end of the twentieth century, several liberal democracies seemed to acknowledge the benefits of some degree of fairmindedness and impartiality in reporting. France saw a socialist government transform a governmental broadcasting system into a mixed public-private system on the Canadian model in an effort to provide long-term conditions for pluralism, if not impartiality. Britain saw the emergence of the comparatively nonpartisan and impartial *Independent* daily newspaper.

Whatever the reasons for Western journalists' commitment to their conception of professional objectivity, one should not be surprised that their commitment to objectivity leads to an eagerness to cover terrorism and thus for a major role for the media in the theater of terror.

The Aldo Moro Case

In 1978, the Italian Red Brigades or Brigate Rosse kidnapped and murdered ex-Prime Minister Aldo Moro along with five bodyguards. Although the Red Brigades were essentially a case of domestic terrorists, they possessed well-developed international links with their German counterparts, with Libyan authorities, and with other foreign organizations. The two-month-long saga would build a large domestic and foreign audience, illustrating well the potential symbiosis between journalism and terror.

---

22   See Theodore Peterson, "The Social Responsibility Theory of the Press," in Fred S. Siebert, Theodore Peterson, and Wilbur Schramm, *Four Theories of the Press* (Urbana: University of Illinois Press, 1956), 83.

The unfolding crisis satisfied well most of the Galtung-Ruge attributes of newsworthiness. The conflict was a culturally meaningful drama, complete with martyred victims, terrorist lions, governmental Caesars, and media tribunes.[23] As Italy's likely next president, Moro was an elite individual, kidnapped in a prominent place. The carefully organized action was an unexpected, swift, dramatic, and unambiguous assault on the regime. The assault on the regime was timed to coincide with Moro's anticipated unifying compromise among the Christian Democratic, Socialist, and Communist parties. During the ordeal, the release of Brigade communiqués and letters from Moro were timed for maximum impact, including publication in the newspaper editions with the widest circulation. Dramatic tension and magnitude of coverage were enhanced by calculated delays of execution. The terrorists' final dramatic act was the symbolic placement of the former prime minister's dead body in the center of Rome on a street linking two party headquarters.

The terrorists acquired a potent, albeit temporary, recognition. They received direct appeals from the pope and UN secretary-general along with massive attention from the domestic and international media. For their part, Italy's principal newspapers experienced circulation increases of 56-89%.[24]

Predicting Coverage—An Empirical Analysis

To this point in the chapter, we analyzed without the benefit of quantitative data many of the professional considerations that might affect what is deemed newsworthy. We also looked at several extraprofessional considerations such as terrorists' threats against the life and limbs of journalists themselves. Here we turn to an empirical examination of the kinds of terrorist events that are actually covered and why.

The tables below contain numerical information on television and press coverage of terrorist events according to the various characteristics of these events—for example, the lethality of the event, the kind of target selected, the nationality of the victims, and the nationality of the perpetrators. Chapter 3 on media-oriented terrorism, above, explored the impact on news coverage of the identity of the perpetrators and victims. We return to this theme here, casting a wider net for possible predictors of coverage. For

---

23   R. F. Farnen, "Terrorism and the Mass Media: A Systemic Analysis of a Symbiotic Process, *Terrorism* (1990), 116.
24   Farnen, "Terrorism and the Mass Media," *Terrorism*, 117.

example, we look at the impact of the particular character of the terrorist action, for example the number of people killed or injured and the mode of attack.

Companion Tables 5.1 and 5.2 present data on the percentages of various kinds of terrorist events that achieve coverage among the twelve media in the study. Table 5.1 pertains to the press, table 5.0 to television. Both Tables report the incidence of reporting according to the location, mode of action, occupation and nationality of target, extent of fatalities and injuries, and claimed responsibility for each action.

For the press, the most efficient coverage-yielding location is the Middle East, where actions gain attention 34% of the time. Europe occupies second place (32%), while Latin America is in distant last position (18%). With respect to mode of action, hijacking is the most powerful predictor with an average success rate of 43%. Airlines are the choice targets from a communications perspective because 40% of actions against airlines gain publicity in the print media. Ordinary citizens follow in second place with a rate of 34%. The incidence of press coverage is lower for attacks against police and security forces (25%), who, being militarily significant, are more traditional targets.

. Doing physical harm is a potent predictor. The presence of injuries doubles the prospects for attention in print and more than doubles the prospects in the case of television. When no one dies, the probability of print coverage is only 22%. But this jumps to 48% when at least one person is murdered. The presence of one or more fatalities is one of the very highest predictors for both types of media. The conjuncture of low coverage for nonviolent actions and high coverage for violent ones constitutes an almost inexorable publicity incentive for violent actions.

Both newspapers and television accord more attention if the identity of the perpetrators is claimed than if responsibility is unknown. When responsibility is claimed as opposed to unknown, the prospects for print coverage rise by a factor of 4, for television by a factor of 10. Thus, the media are more apt to provide coverage when they can identify the perpetrators.

Overall, the data in Tables 5.1 and 5.2 reveal evidence of three levels of explanation for what renders terrorism newsworthy. At the highest level of consensus, all 12 outlets are much more apt to report an action if injury, death, a hijacking, an airline, and/or claimed responsibility are involved. At a middle level of consensus, a large majority of the twelve media are more apt to report an action if it is located outside Latin America and is aimed at British or Israeli targets by Irish or Palestinian perpetrators.

Table 5.1 Terrorist Conduct and Press Reporting Threshold

Percent of Various Types of Events Covered in Each Paper

	NYT	GM	TL	DT	FI	FR	YD	AA	PK	aver.
Location of terrorist action										
Europe	32	34	36	37	29	33	27	40	24	32
L/Amer.	24	27	18	15	20	13	19	16	18	18
M/East	41	31	33	29	26	30	40	46	28	34
N/Amer.	34	34	18	21	16	13	13	30	21	22
Afr/Asia	34	25	30	20	37	28	20	18	20	26
Mode of terrorist action										
Kidnap	36	37	38	26	29	23	21	22	16	27
Attack inst	24	18	18	16	18	17	18	25	12	18
Hijack	40	33	39	57	40	37	39	48	52	43
Bomb	23	20	19	22	19	17	15	28	17	20
Occupation of target										
Diplomat	27	24	24	20	23	20	16	29	21	23
Business	23	22	19	22	19	16	10	22	17	19
Milit/police	28	25	28	30	19	20	16	25	12	25
Airline	47	52	36	41	34	34	34	42	41	40
Citizen	40	33	38	29	32	30	41	43	21	34
Fatalities										
None	26	26	22	21	21	18	17	28	20	22
One or more	61	52	52	49	43	47	46	52	34	48
Injuries										
None	28	27	23	22	21	19	18	29	20	23
One or more	51	48	49	44	43	42	41	50	33	45
Responsibility										
Known	57	63	42	47	40	39	40	49	46	47
Claimed	35	29	30	26	27	24	24	35	20	28
Unknown	12	12	9	14	9	10	7	17	12	11
Nationality of target										
U.S.A.	32	32	20	20	16	12	12	30	20	22
L/Amer	21	26	14	14	21	15	10	15	19	17
U.K.	41	32	61	80	42	57	24	58	41	48
European	25	29	27	31	31	31	18	37	21	2

Israeli Perpetrators	59	44	48	40	47	43	78	75	29	51
Palest	59	47	51	43	39	47	64	64	31	49
Italian	14	14	5	36	7	21	6	17	8	14
German	28	27	36	42	35	50	28	25	0	30
Irish	53	73	76	82	53	56	31	59	40	58
L/Amer	28	24	22	15	18	13	11	19	15	18

At the lowest levels of explanation, individual outlets or groups of outlets reflect the apparent national preoccupations of their own personnel and audiences. Thus, not surprisingly, the North American media give priority to terrorism in North America, the British media to actions against Britons, the *Frankfurter Allgemeine Zeitung* to terrorism by German groups, and the Middle Eastern media to the Middle East. For example, the *New York Times* and *Globe and Mail* each reserve their highest rate of coverage for terrorist acts on their continent, 34%, which compares with a rate of 22% among the nine newspapers as a whole. The *Times* of London covers 80% of actions against British targets, a rate that is 60% higher than the average coverage of such actions among the nine newspapers and 400% higher than the *Times*'s coverage of actions against U.S. targets.

Several apparently idiosyncratic patterns of coverage are explainable. The higher than average reporting of Italian terrorism by the Frankfurt paper may derive from the strong ties between the German Red Army Faction and the Italian Red Brigades. The supranormal coverage of Irish terrorism by the *Globe and Mail* and of Palestinian terrorism by the *New York Times* may reflect past and present cultural affinities for Great Britain and Israel.

The succeeding tables analyze essentially the same data but in a different way, using correlation and regression analysis. For example, Table 5.3 presents a series of zero-order bivariate correlations between the various characteristics of terrorist events and whether or not these events are covered on each of the 12 media outlets. For example, the table shows that the number of fatalities involved is a moderate predictor of coverage on NBC news; the correlation is +.24. Another predictor of NBC coverage is whether the event was a bombing, for which the correlation is a negative, -.16. Compared to other kinds of actions, bombings are slightly *less* likely to be covered.

Table 5.2 Terrorist Conduct and TV Coverage Threshold

Percent of Various Types of Events Covered on Each Network

	ABC	CBS	NBC	aver.
Location of terrorist action				
Europe	16	17	13	15
L/Amer.	9	9	9	9
M/East	20	24	23	22
N/Amer.	25	26	19	22
Afr/Asia	16	16	15	16
Mode of terrorist action				
Kidnap	13	10	10	11
Attack inst.	14	12	12	12
Hijack	44	50	47	47
Bomb	12	13	10	12
Occupation of target				
Diplomat	15	15	13	14
Business	9	10	8	9
Milit/police	18	20	20	19
Airline	26	30	27	28
Citizen	22	24	25	23
Fatalities				
None	14	14	12	13
One or more	27	32	29	30
Injuries				
None	3	14	11	13
One or more	31	31	29	30
Responsibility				
Known	1	43	42	42
Claimed	17	17	13	16
Unknown	3	5	5	4
Nationality of target				
U.S.A.	18	20	17	19
L/Amer	10	9	7	9
U.K.	9	25	22	25
European	12	11	10	11
African	0	3	0	1
Israeli	35	37	38	37
Perpetrators				
Unknown	3	6	5	5
Palest	36	40	40	39
Italian	7	8	2	6
German	24	24	19	22
Irish	39	36	31	35
L/Amer	14	15	10	13

Table 5.3 Terrorist Conduct and Magnitude of Coverage:

Correlations between Selected Attributes of Terrorist Events and
Television Coverage Time or Newspaper Reporting Space

Dependent variables	Positive correlates	Negative correlates
NBC	fatalities (.24) known responsib. (.23) injuries (.22) Palest terrorists (.21)	bombing (-.16) unknown responsib. (-.10)
CBS	fatalities (.24) injuries (.23) known responsib. (.32) Palest terrorists (.19)	bombing (-.15)
ABC	known responsib. (.24) injuries (.22) fatalities (.21)	bombing (-.15) unknown terrorists (-.10) unknown responsib. (-.10)
N.Y. Times	Palest terrorists (.24) injuries (.23) known responsib. (.22) Israeli targets (.19) fatalities (.18) hijacking (.18)	unknown responsib. (-.23) bombing (-.22) Lat/Amer locus (-.12)
Globe and Mail	known responsib. (29) injuries (.23) fatalities (.18) airline target (.20) Palest terrorists (.16) Irish terrorists (.16)	bombing (-.24) unknown responsib. (-.21) unknown terrorists (-.21)
Times	Irish terrorists (.24) U.K. targets (.22) injuries (.21) Palest terrorists (.20) fatalities (.18)	unknown responsib. (-.12) unknown terrorists (-.20) bombing (-.17)
Telegraph	Irish terrorists (.33) U.K. targets (.22) injuries (.21) Palest terrorists (.20) fatalities (.18)	unknown responsib. (-.21) unknown terrorists (-.20) bombing (-.17)
Le Figaro	injuries (.20) fatalities (.18)	unknown responsib. (-.18) unknown terrorists (-.18)

	known responsib. (.18)	bombing (-.17)
	Palest terrorists (.18)	
Frankfurter A.Z.	injuries (.25)	unknown responsib. (-.17)
	fatalities (.23)	bombing (-.16)
	Palest terrorists (.23)	unknown terrorists (-.16)
	Eur. locus (.17)	
	claimed responsib. (16)	
Yediot	Israeli target (.45)	Lat/Amer locus (-.17)
	Palest terrorists (.44)	unknown responsib. (-.18)
	injuries (.29)	unknown perpetrator (-.18)
	M/East locus (.25)	bombing (-.16)
	fatalities (.17)	
	claimed responsib. (.15)	
Al Aharam	Palest terrorists (.35)	L/Amer terrorists (-.19)
	Israeli target (.27)	unknown responsib. (-.18)
	M/East locus (.26)	L/Amer locus (-.18)
	injuries (.26)	unknown perpetrat. (-.16)
	fatalities (.20)	
	known responsib. (.18)	
Pak. Times	Known responsib. (.26)	bombing (-.15)
	hijacking (.24)	unknown responsib. (-.13)
	airline target (.22)	unknown perpetrat. (-.13)
	fatalities (.18)	
	injuries (.15)	
	Palest perpetrat. (.14)	

Note: The above linear correlation coefficients are statistically significant at the .000 level under the null hypothesis of no correlation.

Patterns of Terrorist Conduct

In light of the professional criteria for newsworthiness, one might expect news coverage to be affected by the way in which terrorists conduct their actions. For example, compared to bombings, greater media attention might be given to kidnappings and especially hijackings because these two actions involve intense personal drama. Photo and interview opportunities are particularly available in the case of hijackings. The data in Table 5.1 show that our newspapers are most apt to report hijackings and second most apt to report kidnappings; they are much less apt to report either bombings or attacks on installations such as embassies. For the sample as a whole, 43% of hijackings are deemed newsworthy as compared to only 18% of attacks on installations (see rightmost column of Table 5.1, section entitled "Mode of terrorist action"). Hijackings receive even more privileged treatment on television, where they are four times more likely to be reported than any of the three other modes of terrorist action (see Table 5.2).

Terrorists can not only provide themselves with greater assurance if they undertake hijackings, but they can also increase the probability of coverage by planning to maim or murder during the course of their hijacking. The press are almost twice as likely to report an event involving injuries and more than twice as likely if fatalities are involved (22% vs. 48% for the press; 13% vs. 30% for TV).

A violent hijacking scores highly on a scale of newsworthiness because it meets the dramatic, personalized, timely, and other requirements of newsworthiness explored earlier in this chapter. Following the logic of Galtung and Ruge, discussed above, one would expect the media to accord much more attention to terrorist acts whose authors claim the responsibility. Indeed, when responsibility for an event is known, the event is 4 times more likely to be reported by the press (47% vs. 11%) and 10 times more likely to be reported by television (4% vs. 42%).

Table 5.3 presents bivariate correlations between a series of attributes of terrorist events and the magnitude of coverage provided by the 12 media in the study. For every media outlet, coverage of a terrorist act is predicted by the magnitude of fatalities and/or injuries and by whether or not responsibility for the act is known. The mode of terrorist attack is a factor for 11 of 12 media. With the exception of the Egyptian newspaper, bombings tend to be under-reported compared to kidnappings and hijackings.

Location and Occupation as Factors

As noted in a preliminary fashion in Chapter 3, the location of a terrorist event may affect its coverage. For our sample of papers, events are more likely to be reported if they occurred in Europe or the Middle East but less likely if they took place in Latin America (see Table 5.1). Terrorist events are almost twice as likely to be deemed newsworthy if they occur in the Middle East as opposed to Latin America. In the case of the three American networks, terrorism in the Middle East is 2 1/2 times more likely to be covered than if it occurred in Latin America (table 5.2; see also the correlations in table 5.3).

There is a certain consensus among the nine newspapers in the sample about the newsworthiness of different locations, but this consensus has its limits. Some of the moderate departures from the consensus are easily understood. Thus, their own location in North America may explain the relative propensity of the *Globe and Mail*, *New York Times*, and the three networks to report terrorism on this continent. The comparative emphasis of the Egyptian and Israeli papers on terrorist events within the Middle East and the comparative emphasis of the North American papers on terror in Latin America can be understood in a similar vein.

Terrorism in Africa and Asia has a middling likelihood of being reported by the newspapers and broadcasters in our sample. *Le Figaro* is the most apt to cover events in this composite region, perhaps as a legacy of France's substantial colonial presence on the two continents. The *New York Times* provides better than average coverage of terrorism in Afro-Asia as it does for all the other continents except Europe, for which its coverage is average. One could speculate that the comparatively lower attention devoted by the U.S. paper may reflect the American legacy of alienation from Europe dating to the country's origins.

Apart from the location of an action, the occupation or profession of the chosen victims may impact upon whether the event receives media attention. An earlier chapter contrasted traditional terrorist groups, which targeted governmental authorities and institutions, and modern media-oriented terrorists, who assault civilians and other nonmilitary targets in the expectation of greater media attention. Tables 5.1 and 5.2 show that non-military targets such as ordinary civilians and airline personnel do in fact produce more media attention. Thus, from a rational calculus perspective, terrorists are right to emphasize innocent victims. Table 5.1 shows that attacks against airlines are 60% more apt to be reported by the nine newspapers in the sample than attacks against the military or police (40% vs. 25%) and 74% more apt to be reported than attacks against diplomats (40% vs. 23%). Table 5.2 shows that the U.S. television networks are almost 50% more likely to report attacks on airlines as on the military or police and twice as likely as attacks on diplomats.

Providing a Comprehensive Explanation of Coverage

The remaining challenge for this chapter is to summarize with reasonable parsimony the factors that affect coverage of terrorism. One approach is to erect a summary measure of coverage. In place of 12 different measures of coverage corresponding to the 12 media outlets in the study, a small number of composite measures of coverage are provided. Four such composite measures of coverage are

- total television coverage
- total press coverage
- total media coverage (i.e., magnitude of TV plus press coverage)
- total media threshold (i.e., number of media providing any coverage)

Table 5.4 lists those attributes of terrorist acts that are positively and negatively correlated with each composite measure of coverage. In the case of *total television coverage*, the macabre attributes of fatalities and injuries are the best predictors of coverage (correlations of +.24 and +.23, respectively). An event is also apt to be reported if responsibility for the event is known and if the perpetrator is Palestinian. Turning to the negative correlates of total television coverage, one can see that bombings are less likely to be deemed newsworthy than other modes of violence.

With respect to *total press coverage*, the magnitude of fatalities and injuries is also a factor. The press as a whole are also more likely to report a terrorist act if responsibility is known, if the event entails a hijacking or attacks on airlines, if the event occurs in the Middle East but not in Latin America, if the intended victims are not Latin Americans, and if a bombing is not entailed.

Total media coverage is a composite variable reflecting the magnitude of coverage by both press and television. As shown in Table 5.4, this composite measure is affected most of all by the number of victims injured in a terrorist action. It is also affected by the number of fatalities, whether responsibility for the crime is known, and if the attack involved a bombing. *Total media exposure* is a measure of the number of media in the sample that provided coverage of any given event. This dependent variable is predicted by a large number of attributes. Altogether, the sample of nine papers and three networks are more likely to report a terrorist event if one or more of the following conditions are met:

- responsibility is known
- the perpetrators are Palestinian
- there are many injured victims
- the number of fatalities is high
- the perpetrators are Irish
- the targets are Israelis
- the targets are not Latin American
- the mode of action is a hijacking
- the locus of the attack is not Latin America

Table 5.4 *Correlations between Attributes of Events and*
Composite Measures of Coverage

Dependent var.	Positive correlates	Negative correlates
total TV coverage	fatalities (.24)	bombing (.-16)
	injuries (.23)	unknown perpetrat (-.12)
	known responsib (.23)	unknown responsib (.-11)
	Palest perpetrat (.20)	
total press space	known responsib (.35)	unknown responsib (-.24)
	injuries (.35)	bombing (-.24)
	fatalities (.30)	L/Amer target (-.18)
	hijacking (.23)	L/Amer locus (-.17)
	M/East locus (.21)	
	airline target (.18)	
total media	injuries (.30)	bombing (-.18)
coverage	fatalities (.30)	unknown responsib (-.15)
	known responsib (.27)	
total media	known responsib (.35)	unknown responsib (-.27)
threshold	Palestin perpetrat (.34)	unknown perpetrat (-.27)
	injuries (.34)	bombing (-.23)
	fatalities (.25)	L/Amer target (-.19)
	Israeli target (.25)	L/Amer locus (-.18)
	Irish perpetrat (.25)	
	hijacking (.25)	

Note: The above linear correlation coefficients are statistically significant at the .000 level under the null hypothesis of no correlation.

Table 5.5 *Multiple Correlations between Combinations of*
Attributes and Measures of Media Coverage

Depend. Variables	Regression variables	Correl.
ABC	fatalities, injuries, known responsib, bombing	.58
CBS	same	.52
NBC	same	.52
All TV	same	.54
NYT	same plus unknown responsib, hijacking, L/Amer locus	.52
GM	fatalities, injuries, known responsib, Irish perpetrat bombing, unknown responsib, Palestin perpetrat	.50
TL	fatalities, injuries, known responsib, Palestin perpetrat bombing, unknown responsib, Irish perpetrat	.48
DT	fatalities, injuries, known responsib, Palestin perpetrat bombing, Eur. locus	.51
FI	fatalities, injuries, known responsib, unknown perpetrat bombing, Eur. locus	.47
FR	fatalities, injuries, known responsib, Palestin perpetrat bombing, Eur. locus	.48
YD	fatalities, injuries, known responsib, Palestin perpetrat bombing, unknown responsib, hijacking, L/Amer locus	.59
AA	fatalities, injuries, known responsib, Palestin perpetrat L/Amer target, L/Amer locus	.53
PK	fatalities, injuries, known responsib, Palestin perpetrat Irish perpetrat, bombing, L/Amer target	.42
All press	fatalities, injuries, known responsib, Palestin perpetrat, bombing, unknown responsib, hijacking, L/Amer locus	.61

Tables 5.5 and 5.6 present the fruits of the analysis of the predictors of coverage using multiple correlation and regression. The first of the two tables shows multiple correlations of approximately .50 using slightly different regression models for each dependent variable. The models capable of partly accounting for coverage tend to be more parsimonious in the case of television than in the case of the press. For example, coverage on all three television networks, i.e. total TV, is partly explained by five attributes—fatalities, injuries, known responsibility, Palestinian perpetrators, and bombing. Thus, television coverage rises as fatalities and injuries rise, when responsibility for the terrorist act is known, when the PLO or other Palestinian groups are involved, and when the terrorists resort to modes of action other than bombing.

Compared to television coverage, press coverage entails a more complex explanation. Each of the regression models that emerged from the data analysis involves more variables in the case of print journalism than television (see Tables 5.5 and 5.6). For example, the equation that predicts television coverage contains a total of five variables, as mentioned above. By contrast, the equation that predicts press coverage contains a total of eight variables—the same variables used to account for TV coverage plus three more. The three additional variables are unknown responsibility, hijackings, and Latin American location. Thus, the variables that contribute to an understanding of television coverage also impact on the press. In addition, newspapers are more likely to report an event which involves a hijacking and are less likely to report the event if responsibility is unknown and/or if the event occurred in Latin America.

Compared to television coverage, the factors affecting press coverage are not only more complex but they are also more heterogeneous. The regression models are similar in the case of the networks while varying somewhat among the different newspapers. The same variables account for coverage among the three networks and they do so with approximately equal impact. By contrast, the coverage by individual newspapers is not always influenced by the same characteristics of terrorist events or to the same degree. For example, the *New York Times* is more apt to cover a Palestinian attack while Toronto's *Globe and Mail* assigns priority to Irish acts of terrorism. By contrast, *Le Figaro* does not deem Palestinian or Irish acts of terrorism to be more newsworthy than other such acts.

It is tempting to speculate that the greater heterogeneity among our newspapers is simply a sampling accident: our sample of media contains geographically and culturally diverse newspapers but not television systems. However, if geographical and cultural diversity were paramount predictors of coverage, network coverage ought to be very similar to that of the *New York Times*, which after all is located in the same city. Yet, *New York Times* coverage is more similar to that of the foreign newspapers in the sample than it is to the indigenous television networks. Also, if geography and nationality were paramount, one would expect coverage in the *Times* of London and *Daily Telegraph* to be as similar to each other as is coverage among the ABC, CBS, and NBC networks. Yet, a glance at Tables 5.5 and 5.6 will show that coverage by the two British papers is affected by a somewhat different set of factors.

Table 5.6 The Effects of Event Attributes on Coverage in Metric and Standardized Beta Coefficients

Dependent		fatal	injr	known	Pales	bomb	hij	unkn	L/Am	C
ABC	metric	2.30	2.01	49.9	15.2	-12.9				10.5
	stdzd.	.16	.18	.20	.05	-.07				
CBS	metric	2.56	1.93	39.8	21.1	-14.0				12.0
	stdzd.	.18	.18	.16	.08	-.08				
NBC	metric	2.96	2.07	51.8	30.2	-16.8				13.0
	stdzd.	.17	.16	.18	.10	-.08				
TV	metric	7.83	6.01	14.2	67.5	-44.2				35.9
	stdzd.	.18	.18	.19	.08	-.08				
NYT	metric	.03	.03	.41	.59	-.47	.15	-.42	-.31	1.0
	stdzd.	.11	.17	.10	.13	-.16	.03	-.11	-.09	
GM	metric	.02	.03	.68	.22	-.37	.14	-.31	-.12	1.1
	stdzd.	.08	.06	.14	.10	-.08	.15	-.06	-.07	
TL	metric	.02	.02			-.49		-.41		1.3
	stdzd.	.10	.13		.14	-.17		-.12		
DT	metric	.02	.02	.32	.28	-.19	.22	-.15	-.18	1.0
	stdzd.	.07	.06	.15	.14	-.12	.16	-.08	-.08	
FI	metric	.02	.02	.39	.22	-.32		-.28		1.1
	stdzd.	.06	.05	.16	.09	-.19		-.17		1.1
FR	metric	.03	.03	.55	.41	-.27		-.19	-.22	1.0
	stdzd.	.07	.05	.18	.12	.10		.12	.16	
YD	metric	.02	.02	.34	.54	-.41			-.36	1.6
	stdzd.	.07	.13	.09	.20	-.14			-.12	
AA	metric	.03	.02	.37	.86	-.17		-.10	-.34	1.0
	stdzd.	.05	.02	.12	.20	-.12		-.05	-.16	
PK	metric	.03	.02	.30	.20		.32	-.09		1.5
	stdzd.	.10	.06	.19	.12		.14	-.11		
Press.	metric	.21	.26	5.89	4.63	-2.06	.65	-1.90	-2.42	1.0
	stdzd.	.05	.04	.12	.10	-.09	.26	-.16	-.10	

Note: The respective variables are: fatalities, injuries, known responsibility, bombing, hijacking, unknown responsibility, and Latin American locus. C stands for a constant. The dependent variables TV and press are composites.

The greater homogeneity of television coverage reflects in part the communications limitations of television as a technology. When verbatim transcripts of news programs are set to type and compared with newspaper coverage, it becomes readily apparent that the electronic media provide but a fraction of the verbal coverage of which print is capable. Under the constraints of 22 minutes of broadcast time, U.S. evening news programs cannot easily report on the range of issues of which print is capable. Thus, the relative homogeneity of television news is partly a reflection of the greater time and space constraints of the electronic medium.

The relative homogeneity of television news is also a reflection of the constraints imposed by audience tastes. Audiences have grown accustomed to drama and excitement in both entertainment and news shows. To the extent that viewer preferences are important to the viability of networks as businesses, news executives will be drawn to high production value, action-packed camera footage as a means of drawing viewers. For television gatekeepers, the availability of dramatic or action-packed footage hence becomes an important criterion for news selection. For print gatekeepers, no single criterion acquires such apparent primacy, thus explaining print's apparently greater heterogeneity.

The chapter began by quoting Frederick Hacker to the effect that "the mass media willingly or unwittingly are the spokesmen of the terrorists...." The chapter explored the ways in which journalists are coerced or manipulated in order to deliver coverage as well as the professional considerations that prompt journalists to become eager collaborators in the terrorists' quest for attention. The role of journalists in transmitting terrorists' messages is controversial in part because of a fear that the terrorists' mediated messages will have a significant impact on the general public. A major issue is then public opinion and public reaction, the topic to which we turn in the next chapter.

Chapter 6

Mass-mediated Terrorism, Public Opinion, and the Political Process

Terrorists' Purposes and Actual Media Effects

Those practitioners of terror who seek media exposure can take comfort from the evidence of media response. At least a third of all terrorist acts are actually reported by the television networks and the press outlets studied in our project. The actions of the more media-wise terrorist organizations are almost assured attention. By capturing the media agenda for days or weeks, such groups can hope to (a) increase their profile and amplify their message, (b) enhance their relative moral legitimacy, and (c) improve their organizational effectiveness.

Terrorist groups can increase their profile and amplify their message by

- obliging mass audiences to witness fearful situations
- forcing governments and publics to hear and contemplate terrorist demands
- maintaining themselves in the news through stretching out or repeating violent events
- encouraging others to imitate in a contagion effect

Terrorists can hope to enhance their own moral legitimacy and/or diminish their opponents' by

- obtaining recognition
- disseminating the group's raison d'être
- distributing forced confessions and statements by compliant hostages
- gaining journalists' acquiescence through intimidation
- demonstrating their opponents' ineffectiveness
- provoking opponents into unpopular actions
- stimulating public pressure for concessions by the authorities

Terrorists' organizational effectiveness can be improved to the extent that the media coverage of violent action

- boosts morale relative to opposing authorities or other subgroups within a terrorist coalition
- wins converts
- yields information about security forces' capabilities, modus operandi, and compliance with terrorist demands
- yields information about public and elite attitudes
- provides ideas for potential terrorist tactics
- allows the use of journalists for the dissemination of news, negotiation with authorities, and as insurance against reprisal [1]

Terrorists' media success does not automatically assure achievement in the court of public opinion or in the policy process. A vital factor in gaining access to the media, lethality, can sow the seeds of a terrorist group's own destruction. Terrorist groups can experience an irremediable backlash, even among supporters, as a result of doing injury to innocents.

For this reason and others, members of the scholarly community and the informed public are deeply divided in their estimates of the ultimate impact of terrorism coverage on public opinion and governmental policy. It is a controversial subject. As in the case of other controversial subjects, at least some of the division of opinion arises because the policy stakes are high. Ostensible debates about the facts or ethics of media practice are often camouflaged conflicts about the merits or demerits of the purported causes of the terrorist groups whose coverage is being assessed. Thus, concern about media effects sometimes stems from concern about public policy. Concern about public policy is manifested as a concern about media effects because of an assumption that certain kinds of coverage of terrorism may engender public sympathies for the terrorists and that these new public sympathies are translated into a government policy more favorable to the terrorists' causes.

The true relationship between public opinion and public policy is complex and not yet well understood. Polls are only one of many instruments that political leaders use to gauge public opinion. Politicians rely upon letters, telephone calls, personal conversations and other sources of information in addition to polls. Furthermore, in the absence of polls politicians frequently attempt to predict changes in public opinion on the basis of their

---

1   Our outline of terrorist motives is adapted from the appendix to Alex P. Schmid, "Editors' Perspectives," in D. L. Paletz and A. P. Schmid, eds., *Terrorism and the Media* (Newbury Park, Calif.: Sage, 1992), 131-33.

own judgments of how the general public would respond to any given news story on prime time television.

Politicians are often mistaken in their portraits of public opinion; indeed, if they never erred, incumbents would probably never be defeated. A common error among politicians is to overestimate the impact on general public opinion of any given series of news events. Public reactions to mediated traumatic events are sometimes intense but only momentary, *one day wonders*, as they are sometimes called by the media advisors to politicians. Political leaders may misjudge the state of public opinion when confronted with pressure from energetic minorities, whose enthusiasm does not accurately reflect the views of the public at large.

Our own study of the greatly publicized hate trials in Canada yielded evidence of a complex misperception of the state of public opinion. Both the political elites and the public at large concluded from the fact of the extensive media coverage given to two neo-Nazis on trial that the neo-nazis were winning the battle for public opinion. Referring to his success at securing media exposure, one of the defendants declared that he had won one million dollars of free publicity. He accordingly embarked on the marketing of instructional tapes on how to manipulate the media. Canada's political elites were concerned that the fledgling Nazi movement was gaining adherents. In fact, public opinion research revealed that Canadians were repelled by the hate-mongers and the more so as they became exposed to their mediated messages.[2]

This present book on media and terrorism is not concerned with elite perceptions of public opinion but rather with public opinion itself. Even the narrower subject of media effects on public opinion entails considerable complexity and uncertainty. Traditional scholarship on the subject has been divided between a paradigm arguing major media effects and a paradigm that holds that media effects are minimal. Hundreds and, in some cases, thousands of very good research studies have been undertaken without closing the debate.

The debate may never be resolved in part because of the enormous public policy stakes in the matter. Critics of government policy in a given area cannot be expected to be content with media reporting so long as the content of media reporting coincides with the basic directions of government action. Thus the critics' assertion that the media have major effects on society can be a stratagem for bringing about change as well as an

---

2   Gabriel Weimann and Conrad Winn, *Hate on Trial: The Zundel Affair, the Media and Public Opinion in Canada* (Oakville, Ont.: Mosaic Press, 1986).

explanation or alibi for why government policy is the way it is. Debates about media effects are bound to contain an ideological element when the stakes are worth caring about.

Nonetheless, debates about media impact involve more than strictly ideological conundra; they also entail some difficult empirical questions. In the extreme, media effects may take the form of a transformation of attitudes. Short of an attitudinal change, media effects may take the form of *agenda setting*, influencing the choice of issues people deem important, or *priming*, influencing the criteria by which people evaluate issues.

The agenda setting, priming, or attitudinal effects of the media may be influenced not only by what the media do but also by the prior attitudes, knowledge, and expectations of the audience. The mixed evidence of media impacts may well require researchers to undertake far more detailed inquiry of specific media impacts. Indeed it may become axiomatic that audiences are more influenced by the media on subjects about which they know little than about those upon about which they know a great deal. Hence a careful assessment of media effects might require a separate examination of the question of effect for each of a wide number of different themes and subjects. It is with this reasoning in mind that the present chapter reports the results of experimental research on the impact of terrorist reports on attitudes toward terrorist groups. Because of the increasing evidence that media effects may be issue- and audience-specific, it is vital to have direct evidence of the impact of mediated terrorism rather than speculate about the media effects of terrorism coverage from evidence unrelated to terrorism. But before reporting the results of this effort, we explore the traditional debate about major versus minimal effects as well as the different ways in which media effects could emerge.

The Debate about the Power of the Media

Early empirical research on the effectiveness of the media was dominated by the image of media that were powerful and of a mass society that was defenseless. Society was believed to consist of atomized individuals, unconnected to each other and vulnerable to the suggestions, if not the dictates, of omnipotent media. As Katz observes, "The assumption was that the media would operate totally (on every eye and ear), directly (without interference), and immediately (evoking collective reaction, as if from one man)."[3] To the growing puzzlement of researchers, proof of media impact proved difficult to secure while the burden of findings suggested that the media might be overrated in importance.

Klapper summarized the emerging evidence of minimal effect in his 1960 book, *The Effects of Mass Communication.*[4] That book became a virtual sacred text for the adherents of the minimal effects school of thought as well as a point of departure for scholars on both sides of the argument. As Crigler et al. observe, it became "fashionable to begin one's research study with reference to Joseph Klapper's minimal effects notion and then proceed to declare that the new data at hand will now settle the issue once and for all."[5]

Thirty years later, an enormous quantity of primary research has been completed along with some synthetic analyses, but without any true resolution of the debate. Two recent and thoughtful summaries of evidence should be quoted at length to illustrate the lack of resolution of this debate. In 1986, McGuire completed a comprehensive propositional inventory of the scientific literature on the subject. His aptly entitled "The Myth of Massive Media Impact" reached the following conclusion:

> We have reviewed and evaluated the evidence regarding the dozen types of media effects that have received most attention and most study, six having to do with intended effects and six with unintended effects of the media. For each of the dozen areas of purported effects we concluded that the demonstrated impacts are surprisingly slight. Even in the areas with the most impressive results, including frequent statistically significant effects in methodologically adequate studies, the size of the impacts are so small as to raise questions about their practical significance and cost effectiveness. [6]

In 1987, Iyengar and Kinder published an equally important and vital study of media impact, this one largely based on carefully structured experimental research. Their conclusion, completely incompatible with McGuire's, needs to be quoted at length for that reason:

> Americans' views of their society and nation are powerfully shaped by the stories that appear on the evening news. We found that people who are shown network broadcasts edited to draw attention to a particular problem assigned

---

3   Elihu Katz, "On Conceptualizing Media Effects," *Studies in Communications*, vol. 1 (1980), 119-41.
4   Joseph T. Klapper, *The Effects of Mass Communication* (New York: The Free Press, 1960).
5   "Understanding Issues in the News," paper presented at the Annual Conference of the American Association for Public Opinion Research, May 2, 1988.
6   In George Comstock, ed., *Public Communication and Behavior* (New York: Academic Press, 1986), 233.

ɹ that problem—greater importance than they themselves
.eriment began, and greater importance than did people
ɔl conditions that emphasised different problems. Our sub-
.ne target problem as more important for the country, cared
., believed the government should do more about it, reported
ɹngs about it, and were much more likely to identify it as one of
.y's most important problems. Such differences were apparent
.ely after conclusion of the broadcasts, one day later, and one week
ɹore over, these experimental results were generally corroborated by
oₓ ɹalysis of trends in network news coverage and national public opinion.
That we found essentially the same result using different methods strengthens
our conclusion that television news shapes the relative importance Americans
attach to various national problems.[7]

In spite of their clear-cut argument about the power of the media over agenda setting, Iyengar and Kinder do not actually refute the minimal effects argument. Indeed, they acknowledge the essential validity of the minimal effects argument as it applies to sympathies. For Iyengar and Kinder, the evidence is overwhelming that the media possess enormous power to influence what the public deems important but much more limited power to influence the preferences of the public because the public has so many other sources of values and sympathies. In order to understand the impact of the media on public preferences, the two authors emphasize the vital importance of distinguishing among different thematic areas, for example between a subject close to home as opposed to one that is distant from the experience of the audience.

Iyengar and Kinder conceive of media effect largely in terms of a hierarchy ranging from mere agenda setting to attitude change with priming in between. Priming refers to the ability of the media to influence the criteria employed by the public in reaching political judgments. While the media, acknowledge the authors, may have only a limited direct impact on attitude change, they exercise considerable influence with respect to both agenda setting and priming.

Iyengar and Kinder's desire to distinguish among different kinds of effects within each of many different areas of human experience is consistent with one of the earliest traditions in communications research. As early as 1949, in a summary of the field of mass communications as it then existed, Bernard Berelson pointedly noted the heterogeneous effects of the media. As he put it, "some kinds of communication on some kinds of issues,

7   Shanto Iyengar and Donald R. Kinder, *News That Matters* (Chicago: University of Chicago Press, 1987), 112-13.

brought to the attention of some kinds of people under some kinds of conditions, have some kinds of effects."[8]

With the passage of years, scholars increasingly directed their research efforts to understanding the limits of media influence. Two factors loomed on the horizon: audience selectivity and interpersonal relations. No longer viewed as strictly atomistic, viewers of television, listeners of radio, and readers of the press were increasingly understood to have the autonomy to avoid, resist, and/or twist messages that challenge their preconceptions and understandings. For over a generation it has now been axiomatic that audiences perceive information and recall it in such a way as to avoid a state of *cognitive dissonance* between new information and old understandings. More recently, research points to the desire of audiences not merely to screen out information that runs counter to their worldview but also to screen out information about events about which the viewer feels powerless.[9]

Along with selectivity, interpersonal influence has long been understood as a factor limiting media impact. Interpersonal networks and opinion leaders have been seen as filters of mass-mediated information, contributing to reinforcement rather than change in audience opinions. Together, selectivity and interpersonal networks have been held to undermine the conception of an atomized mass society and of the media as omnipotent. As a more complex portrait of media effects gradually evolved in the minds of scholars, research began to focus on more specific media effects and especially on those that are not apt to trigger the defense mechanisms of selectivity and personal influence. Evidence began to emerge of agenda-setting effects and even attitudinal effects in specific aspects of social life—with respect to violence, socialization, knowledge, and so forth.

Knowledge and Information— Their Transmission

At a minimum, the mass media are engaged in transmitting information and knowledge whether or not these transmissions exercise any agenda-setting or attitudinal effects. Indeed the mass public views the media

8   "Communications and Public Opinion," in W. Schramm, ed., *Process and Effects of Mass Communication* (Urbana: University of Illinois Press, 1954), 345.
9   Doris Graber, *Processing the News* (New York: Longman, 1984), passim.

substantially as a source of information. When the Roper organization asked a sample of American adults where they obtained most of their information about *What's going on in the world*, more than 95 percent responded in terms of the mass media.[10] Audiences in the liberal democratic and indeed even among the pre-*glasnost* Communist states have found themselves increasingly dependent on the media for information relevant to their daily lives. De Fleur and Ball-Rokeach have proposed what they term a *dependence theory*, according to which systems of mass communications become ever more important as societies become more technologically advanced: "Dependency on media information is a ubiquitous condition in modern society....As societies grow more complex, and as the quality of media technology improves, the media take on more and more unique information-delivery functions."[11]

Most studies have found a positive relationship between knowledge and media use for all sectors of society. Irrespective of the audience's level of formal education, their knowledge of the world increases with media use. The media become an especially vital source of information and interpretation when alternative or competing sources are unavailable, as is normally the case in national and international affairs events, and, of course, terrorism. In the case of terrorism, the media's decision to cover or not may be the crucial determinant of the public's knowledge of an event and its background. One does not require an elaborately structured piece of experimental research to be persuaded that very few people in mass media societies would know about the Croatian call for independence, the Palestinian problem, the South Moluccans, or the Armenian desire for recognition of its holocaust if these phenomena were not reported, analyzed, and explained at length by the media, often in the wake of terrorist events.

Noncoverage may sometimes be as important as coverage because the absence of reporting may engender ignorance and even denial. In *The Real Terror Network*, Herman asserts that the western media ignore those terrorist activities that are initiated or directed by U.S. government agencies, with the result that the concern of the informed Western public is diverted from what he calls "American Terror in the Third World."[12]

Clearly not all terror is covered and Western-sponsored terror is sometimes ignored. However, inequalities in coverage are not necessarily the

10   Roper, "Changing Public Attitudes towards Television and other Media" (New York, 1977).
11   Melvin de Fleur and Sandra Ball-Rokeach, *Theories of Mass Communication* (New York: McKay, 1975), 3rd ed., 261-62.
12   See Edward Herman, *The Real Terror Network* (Boston: South End Press, 1982).

result of purposeful journalistic decisions. Some inequalities in the coverage of terror stem from inequalities in the desire or the ability of perpetrators to conceal their murderous doings. A generation ago Zolberg analyzed two apparently contrasting West African states, Guinea and the Ivory Coast. The former was far more widely known for its government-initiated terror than the latter. But Zolberg showed that the Ivory Coast's more pacific image had much to do with the more devious way in which its government eliminated adversaries, principally by the use of rivers at night rather than hangings in midday.[13]

International terror is more apt to be reported than state terror because international terrorist groups increasingly seek terror maximization while terrorist states pursue policies of terror optimization. For the nonstate groups, the more publicity, the better. But for states practicing fear-inducing violence, the goal is to disseminate enough awareness to arouse trepidation among target groups but not enough to cause revulsion among the publics of the liberal democracies.

Libya's Qaddafi, a practitioner of state terrorism, has been an exception to this pattern as a result of his thirst for media recognition of his enthusiasm for violent action. But he paid a price for proceeding beyond terror optimization. Libya became the target of a U.S. military strike in 1986 at least in part because Qaddafi's grandstanding helped to create a public mood in the West that would find such a raid acceptable. Libya was not necessarily the preeminent state sponsor of terrorism from the Middle East even if it was the foremost publicity seeker.

Status Conferral

Much of the power of the media is thought to arise from its ability to ascribe importance to an actor or an event by the mere act of reporting. The idea that the mass media confers status or respect upon the people whose activities are reported is predicated upon a quasi-tautology about how audiences perceive mediated information. According to this quasi-circular belief, people who matter are at the focus of mass attention so that people who are not at the focus of mass attention must not really matter. In the words of Lazarsfeld and Merton, "The mass media bestow prestige

13   Aristide Zolberg, *Creating Political Order* (Chicago: Rand McNally, 1966), passim.

and enhance the authority of individuals and groups by legitimizing their status. Recognition by the press, radio or news reels testifies that one has arrived, that one is important enough to have been singled out from the large enormous mass, that one's behavior and opinions are significant enough to demand the public's notice."[14]

Following this logic, the coverage of a terrorist event constitutes a recognition of the importance of the terrorists themselves as well as of their actions and the causes of their actions. Consequently, terrorists may benefit from news coverage irrespective of the tone of the coverage. The mere allocation of valuable time and space may suffice as evidence that the terrorists should be regarded as important and noteworthy. Given that coverage of terrorist events should be broad enough to encompass the various causes that apparently motivate the terrorist as well as their demands for redress, the phenomenon of status conferral extends beyond the terrorists alone to include the political, social, and/or religious movements associated with their actions.

Agenda Setting and Priming

Both studies of agenda setting, whose pedigree dates from the work of McCombs in 1972, and more recent studies of priming seek to reconceptualize media effects by exploring impacts on the audience that fall short of an actual opinion change. The quest for evidence that the media have changed public preferences has been supplanted by the quest for evidence that the media have changed what the public thinks about and how the public proceeds to think about these matters.

Methodologically, research in this tradition has sought to compare the agendas of the media with the agendas of the general public, matching and dating the two respective agendas. Rosengren cites evidence from a number of studies to show that public agendas are closely attuned to media agendas; public rankings of the relative importance of various issues coincide more closely with media rankings than with governmental rankings.[15]

14   Paul Lazarsfeld and Robert Merton, "Mass Communication, Popular Taste and Organized Social Action," in W. Schramm and D. Roberts, eds., *The Process and Effects of Mass Communication* (Urbana: University of Illinois Press, 1971), 561.

15   K. E. Rosengren, "Mass Media and Social Change: Some Current Approaches," in E. Katz and T. Szecsko, eds., *Mass Media and Social Change* (London: Sage, 1981).

There is a general consensus among scholars that the media do produce agenda-setting effects. But there is little consensus about the magnitude of these effects. Thus there is a diversity of opinion ranging *from* a weak portrait predicting only a general overlap among media and public agendas with little regard to the ordering of issues *to* a strong portrait that posits parallel weightings of issues across agendas. At least a part of the differences among the views of academics about the agenda-setting impact of the media is an artifact of methodological differences. For example, media agendas have sometimes been measured in terms of simple counts of the number of articles concerning various issues. Sometimes media agendas are based only on articles on issues that were identified as salient by respondents. On other occasions, media agendas have been measured using formulas weighted by air time or column-inches over varying periods of time.

Time is itself an important methodological variation. Media agendas have been examined in terms of a single short-term event such as a presidential debate or over long periods of time such as an extended election campaign. This lack of methodological uniformity has also plagued studies of the public agenda.

Even if all researchers resorted to precisely the same procedures, certain methodological conundra would nonetheless remain. One particular problem is the direction of causality. It is generally assumed that the direction of causality is from the media agenda to the public agenda, but there are alternative possibilities. The causal relation could be reciprocal, with the media responding to the public agenda as well as vice versa. Alternatively, both the public agenda and the media agenda could reflect autonomous responses to the environmental reality.

To help resolve the question of causal direction, time-lagged correlations and other statistical controls have been used. The main burden of the evidence remains in support of the media agenda as the cause of the public agenda rather than vice versa. For the field of terrorism, the view that the media agenda determines the public agenda implies that the public learns to assign importance to terrorism and to terrorists' behaviors and motivations as a consequence of the newsworthy treatment extended to terrorism by the media. Policymakers' agendas may likewise be influenced. Policymakers are normally attuned to or sensitive about public agendas. Whether or not they have objective evidence that the public has indeed followed the media agenda, policy-makers would normally estimate the position of the public agenda from their knowledge of the media agenda.

The notion that governments act on perceived public preferences is supported strongly by both democratic theory and empirical research. Page and Shapiro undertook large-scale research on poll results and government policy actions in the United States during the period 1935-1979. Their quantitative analysis yielded abundant evidence that policy initiatives and changes of direction complied with measured public preferences. The greater the degree of public preference, the more likely the conformity of public policy to public desires. The more unambiguous the meaning of the government's policy initiatives within a given issue domain, the greater the evidence of unambiguous congruousness between public opinion and government action.[16]

Attitudes—Formation and Reinforcement

While there exists only modest evidence of the media's power to actually change preexisting attitudes, there remains stronger evidence of the media impact on attitudes that have not been fully formed. De Fleur and Ball-Rokeach draw attention to the role of journalism in shaping attitudes in situations where the audience is particularly dependent upon the media for information:

> During any year or decade in recent history, numerous instances of media-in-itiated attitude formation can be found. Publics have formed new attitudes about such events as speed limits, environmental problems, energy crises, specific wars, and political corruption. Modern society presents a constant parade of new political figures, religious leaders, sports personalities, scientists, and artists. There is also a seemingly endless variety of social movement towards which orientations must be worked out. The media portray a never-ending flow of such events, issues, objects, and persons into public attention.[17]

Media coverage of terrorist events has an especially powerful potential influence because media coverage is frequently the only source of information on an issue available to the audience. Media coverage is not only frequently a unique source of information but it may also be a unique source of interpretation. In particular, the general public is apt to rely to an enormous degree on media accounts for an understanding of terrorists' motives, the implications of their actions, and the essential character of the

---

16   Benjamin I. Page and Robert Y. Shapiro, "Effects of Public Opinion on Policy," *American Political Science Review* 77 (1983), 175-90. See also Page and Shapiro, "Changes in Americans' Policy Preferences, 1935-79," *Public Opinion Quarterly* 46 (1982), 24-42, and A. D. Monroe, "Consistency between Public Preferences and National Policy Decisions," *American Politics Quarterly* 7 (1979), 3-19.
17   De Fleur and Ball-Rokeach, *Theories of Mass Communication*, 266-67.

situation. For example, when Armenian terrorists attack Turkish officials in western Europe or North America, most Europeans and North Americans can depend only on the media for assistance in forming an assessment of the Armenian cause. Lacking a previous conception of the issue or even previous information of an elementary nature, the public is apt to absorb the views transmitted by the media.

In a number of instances, the media may conduct themselves so as to provide effective support on behalf of the terrorists' cause. After the Armenian attack on the Turkish Embassy in Ottawa on March 12, 1985, a prominent Canadian columnist drew attention to this odd ménage. Lynch noted that

> the act of terrorism took second place to explanations of the Armenian cause, going back to the Turkish atrocities of 70 years ago. Suddenly more was said and written about the starving Armenians than had been heard in Canada in the whole of the second period. Explanations and backgrounders filled the columns and the broadcast hours....The Turks, and not the Armenians, were presented as the defendant, the aggressors.[18]

Indeed, more than one Canadian journalist provided the Armenian terrorists with supportive coverage, reporting not only the event itself but also the historical background that the Armenian terrorists were purportedly motivated by. Three days after the event, which involved the execution of a Canadian guard, a newspaper columnist wrote:

> The massacre of Armenians in 1915...is a well authenticated historical fact, as well authenticated a historical fact as the massacre of the Jews in Hitler's time. A parallel can be drawn between Turkey and Germany...the trouble with the Armenians is kept alive partly by Turkey's own refusal to acknowledge one of the facts of history.[19]

Canadian television networks transmitted documentaries containing emotive footage of the massacre of Armenians, coverage that may well have had an impact beyond simple agenda setting. The *Globe and Mail*, the country's most prominent newspaper, not only brought the issue to the forefront of Canada's public agenda through its editorials but went so far as to advocate that the government of Canada embrace a number of the terrorists' goals:

> If the Canadian government decided the Armenian community has a legitimate political grievance, then Canadian approaches can be made via diplomacy, to

18   Charles Lynch, "Undue Publicity Helps the Terrorists' Cause," *Citizen* (Ottawa, March 14th, 1985), 4.
19   Don McGillivary in the *Citizen* (Ottawa, March 15, 1985), 8.

the Turkish government with a view of settling the issue. These might range from acknowledgment of the 1915 massacre and regretting its occurrence, to some form of reparations....the Canadian diplomatic establishment is more than adequate for any such moves.[20]

The particular case of the Armenian attack on the Turkish embassy in Ottawa illustrates the enormous potential influence of terrorists on the media. But the case also illustrates the very real limits of the media's influence on governments which are faced with other kinds of pressure. In spite of the attention given by the media to the issue, the journalists' obvious empathy for the Armenians, and the explicit plea of the influential Globe and Mail, there is no evidence that the federal government acted as an interlocutor on behalf of Armenian rights. To the contrary, only two years after the intensely emotive and highly reported attack on the Turkish diplomats, the federal government actually embraced the official Turkish view of the massacres.

The local school board in Canada's capital was about to adopt a new policy for the teaching of the Holocaust and other genocidal events when a senior official of the Department of External Affairs made an unsuccessful last-moment effort to block inclusion of the Armenian massacres in the curriculum. The government of Canada submission to the Ottawa Board of Education claimed that there are two sides to the interpretation of the episode in question and that, whatever actually transpired, the events did not constitute genocide because the concept of genocide was not adumbrated until many years later. The government was concerned that other local school boards would follow the Ottawa example and that the government of Turkey would be enraged at a time that it was contemplating the purchase of a Canadian subway system.[21]

The federal submission to the school board eventually found its way to the press and House of Commons, causing the government some embarrassment. The minister of external affairs felt obliged to criticize his official for interfering in educational matters, which were beyond the constitutional authority of the federal government. Yet the minister insisted that the main outlines of the submission were consistent with his department's long-standing views of Turkey's treatment of its Armenian inhabitants. The

20   Peter St. John, "Why Armenian Terror in Canada?" Globe and Mail (April 1, 1985), 7.
21   Turkish officials apparently told the visiting Canadian minister of transport that purchase of a Canadian subway system would not be considered unless the federal government could ensure that the history of the massacres was not taught to Canadian school children. Source: confidential conversation with federal official, summer 1988.

government's willingness to overstep its constitutional authority in educational matters and risk public embarrassment from disclosure of its act of sophistry suggest that governments do not view the media as omnipotent. In the minds of Canadian officials, the exigencies of an export opportunity were more important than *Globe and Mail* editorials and public passions associated with a now distant terrorist *media event*. On the other hand, subsequent to the Ottawa education board incident, there is no evidence that the Canadian government sustained a campaign of persuasion on behalf of Turkey.

This section on attitude formation began with a virtual axiom that the media have their greatest impact in subject areas remote from the opinion-holder's experience and on opinions that are not fully formed. By the same token, media influence should be low on issues "close to home" in a geographic and psychological sense. By this logic, the ability of the media to affect public attitudes toward, say, a German terrorist group ought to be far greater in Canada or Australia than in Germany itself or among its proximate neighbors.

Hewitt undertook a time-series comparison of public attitudes toward indigenous terrorist groups within each of five countries. Although his research did not involve a consideration of media influence, some of his findings may nonetheless be germane. Public support for nationalist-motivated terrorists such as the IRA and Basque ETA, relatively high at the outset, appeared to be unaffected by changes in the levels of violence. By contrast, public support for revolutionary-motivated terrorists such as Baader-Meinhoff and Uruguay's Tupamaros, lower at the outset, was susceptible to backlash in the wake of violent actions deemed criminal by the public. Thus, strong, emotionally driven support for nationalist terrorism was immune to signs of increasing violence while intellectually motivated support for revolutionary terrorism, often among the upper strata, was susceptible.[22]

The Contagion Effect

To this point in the chapter, we discussed the impact of the media agenda on the mass public's agenda as well on the policymakers' agenda. Another impact of the media agenda can be on the terrorists' own agenda as a result

---

22   Christopher Hewitt, "Terrorism and Public Opinion: A Five Country Comparison," *Terrorism and Political Violence* (1989), 144-70.

of a *contagion effect*. Livingstone has argued that a heavy emphasis on the violent acts committed by terrorists may stimulate other terrorists to repeat the same crimes. In his view, the evidence suggests that detailed coverage of a terrorist act is apt to lead to a rash of similar acts.[23]

We asserted, above, that policymakers may infer changes in the public agenda from changes in the media agenda. Policymakers may decide to change their own policy agendas in anticipation of changes in public opinion that they anticipate from the changes in the media agenda that they perceive. Using the same kind of reasoning, terrorists may infer changes in either the public or policymakers' agenda as a result of changes in media agendas and may decide to adjust their own behavior accordingly. The phenomenon of contagion among terrorist events needs to be considered within a broader context of violent contagion. Growing evidence suggests that violent television programs and film may prompt criminals to commit similar acts in real life. Meanwhile televised violence appears to bring about considerable fearfulness among heavy TV viewers. Berkowitz and Macaulay report that violent crimes increased substantially in the United States following certain well-publicized mass murders. Meanwhile Phillips presents evidence that rates of suicide have increased dramatically following media coverage of suicide cases. Evidence of contagiousness has emerged in relation to a rather wide range of violent behavior, including racial disturbances as well as international terrorism.[24]

The phenomenon of contagion takes form as a result of the transmission of new knowledge and/or new attitudes. Three specific subeffects of contagion have been identified:

---

23   Neil Livingstone, *The War Against Terrorism* (Lexington: Lexington Books, 1982), 63.
24   L. Berkowitz and J. Macaulay, "The Contagion of Criminal Violence," *Psychometry* 34 (1971), 238-60; D. P. Phillips, "Suicide, Motor Vehicle Fatalities, and Mass Media," *American Journal of Sociology* 84 (1979), 1150-74; C. S. Spilerman, "The Causes of Racial Disturbances," *American Sociological Review* 35 (1970), 627-49; and L. C. Hamilton, "Dynamics of Terrorism," *International Studies Quarterly* 27 (1983), 39-54. See also Phillips, "The Impact of Mass Media Violence on U.S. Homicides," *American Sociological Review* 48 (1983), 560-68, and K. A. Bollen and D. P. Phillips, "Initiative Suicides: A National Study of the Effects of Television News Stories," *American Sociological Review* 47 (1982), 802-9.

- the unlearning of inhibitions against the use of violence that were acquired during childhood or early adulthood socialization
- the acquisition of "know-how" relating to the practical uses and applications of violence
- motivations to act violently

Scholars have devoted considerable research to the importance of imitation as an explanation for airplane hijacking, sometimes termed "the sky-jack virus" and at other times merely a "fad."[25] Holden developed a mathematical model of contagion to account for the pattern of hijacking within the United States between 1968 and 1972. His analysis demonstrated that successful hijackings lead to additional hijacking attempts of the same type:

> Each successful extortion hijacking in the United States generated an average of 2.014 additional attempts, with a median delay of 44.8 days. The (contagion) effect explained about 85 percent of the total rate of U.S. extortion hijacking attempts. Even though it was not possible to show statistically that media coverage was responsible for the stimulating effects, the results tend to support the common belief that hijacking spreads as a result of publicity.[26]

Chapter 8, below, measures the contagiousness of various kinds of mediated as opposed to nonmediated terrorism.

To this point in the present chapter we described the unresolved debate about maximal or minimal media effects on public opinion and/or the political process. Confronted with the difficulty of finding a great deal of unequivocal evidence of the role of the media in attitudinal change or in the political process in general, many scholars have explored media impacts that fall short of actually transforming attitudes. Most of this research has contented itself with agenda setting but priming has become an increasing theme. Bernard Berelson's observation of 30 years ago, quoted above, still holds true, namely that "some kinds of communication on some kinds of issues, brought to the attention of some kinds of people under some kinds of conditions, have some kinds of effects."[27]

---

25 E. Rich, *Flying Scared* (New York: Stein and Day, 1972); C. Whelton, *Skyjack* (New York: Belmont, 1972); D. Phillips, *Skyjack: The Story of Air Piracy* (London: Harrap, 1973); R. Chauncey, "Deterrency: Certainty, Severity, and Skyjacking," *Criminology* 12 (1975), 447-73; W. W. Minor, "Skyjacking Crime Control Models," *Journal of Criminal Law and Criminology* 66 (1975), 94-105; and R. T. Holden, "The Contagiousness of Aircraft Hijacking," *American Journal of Sociology* 91 (1986), 874-904.
26 Holden "The Contagiousness of Aircraft Hijacking."
27 Berelson, "Communications and Public Opinion."

Given the need to examine media effects under specific circumstances, it makes sense to explore the impact on the general public of terrorist reporting in particular. Given the virtual axiom that media reporting may be especially potent when the general public lacks prior information, preconception, or attitudes, it is reasonable to hypothesize that media reporting of terrorism could have especially striking effects.

To test various possible hypotheses about the effects of media coverage, Weimann undertook an experimental design for the purpose of exploring the validity of the maximal effects thesis in the particular case of terrorist reporting.

Measuring the Effects on Public Opinion— Evidence from a Case Study

Experimental research designs are often the preferred solution for solving problems of identifying true causality. Experimental designs are particularly well suited to media research because of their ability to control or eliminate the influence of external factors when exploring the precise sequence of coverage–exposure–change.

For this present work, Weimann expanded the use of an experimental design first reported in 1991.[28] The attitudes of subjects in the experiment were assessed both before and after the subjects were exposed to media coverage describing two separate terrorist incidents. Their changed attitudes were then compared with those of a control group consisting of subjects matched to the subjects in the experimental group but not exposed to the media coverage. Hence, any changes in the attitudes of the two groups could be compared and the differences in the changes attributed to the impact of the media reports upon the experimental group.

Weimann's research for this book differed from his earlier effort in that the sample was enlarged, the media coverage was enriched, and the impact upon the experimental group was measured on more dimensions than merely evaluative attitudes. Specifically, the research effort explored the impact of media coverage with respect to status conferral, agenda setting, level of information, and affective attitudes.

---

28 Gabriel Weimann, "The Theater of Terror: Effects of Press Coverage," *Journal of Communication* 33 (1991), 38-45.

A random sample of 300 Israelis, all adult Jews living in urban areas, completed seven Likert-scaled items constituting a general scale of attitudes toward terrorism. The questions explored the conditions under which terrorism might be regarded as justifiable. Scale scores were employed to pair subjects so that they could be randomly distributed between the experimental and control groups. The criteria for matching included variables such as age and education as well as general attitudes toward terrorism.

The matching procedure was repeated six times in order to yield six experimental groups, each with 25 subjects, and six matched control groups, each also with 25 subjects. Each one of the experimental groups was then exposed to one medium (press, radio, or television) along with its coverage of one of two specific terrorist events. These terrorist events were:

- *A South Moluccan train seizure.* On December 2, 1975, a group of South Moluccans seized a train near Beilen, the Netherlands in pursuance of its goal of wresting an independent republic from Indonesia. The event involved the killing of three people and the subsequent triggering of an attack by sympathizers, who stormed the Indonesian Consulate in Amsterdam. Ultimately, the terrorists received heavy prison sentences.
- *A Croatian hijacking.* On September 10, 1976, a group of Croatians seized control of a TWA jet en route from New York to Canada, redirecting it to Europe. The aircraft made bombing runs over London and Paris, dropping leaflets and seeking maximum attention for the terrorists' quest for an independent Croatian homeland. Prior to departure, they had placed a bomb in New York, which exploded, killing a policeman. The media event came to an end in Paris, where the terrorists surrendered to authorities.

These particular events were selected so that they would be remote in time, location, and experience from the subjects in question. The two events were not selected in order to be in any way representative of the full range and character of international terrorist events. They were selected because of their suitability for testing the impact of the media on the general public in situations where the public has little prior knowledge or sentiment.

Following the design for the experiment, each of the six experimental groups was exposed to coverage of one of the two incidents by one of the three media. Thus, one experimental group was asked to read a full set of clipping on the South Moluccan case as drawn from Israel's leading daily newspaper, *Yediot*, while another experimental group was exposed to a comparable full set of clippings relating to the Croatian case. The sets of clippings were neither censored nor deliberately constructed in any particular fashion; they were a full set representing everyday coverage of the sequence of events in each instance. The two corresponding control groups were presented with randomly selected press clippings from the same newspaper but concerning events unrelated to terrorism.

Following the same kind of logic, the research team invited two experimental groups to view the actual televised coverage of the two events as recorded on videotape while their corresponding control groups were exposed to videotaped television news programs containing no reference to terrorism in any form. An analogous procedure was applied to the remaining experimental groups, who were invited to listen to radio reports.

Osgood's semantic differential scales were utilized to measure attitudes and attitude changes. Particular use was made of Osgood's evaluative dimension, notably scales that possessed high *loadings* and were vital to his first rotated factor. Subjects were provided with a list of evaluative adjectives on a 7-point scale, including such pairs as kind-cruel, just-unjust, and brave-cowardly. The postexposure questionnaire was designed to measure a relatively full range of media effects, including

- status conferral
- agenda setting
- change of awareness
- change of information
- priming

Thus, the questionnaire contained questions about the importance of the problem at issue, the need to solve it, the need to report it in the media, self-reported changes in interest and knowledge, and other indices of awareness and information.

The before and after scores on the various evaluative scales were compared. If hypothetically the control groups and their corresponding experimental groups experienced the same changes in attitudes from the first measurement to the second, then the changes could not be attributed to media exposure. On the other hand, in the simplest of situations, if the experimental groups underwent attitudinal change but their corresponding control group did not, the changes among the experimental groups could properly be attributed to the exposure.

Table 6.1 Changes in Evaluative Attitudes toward Two
Terrorist Groups after Exposure to Press Coverage

	South Moluccan case			Croatian case		
	Averages before	Averages after	Matched t-test	Averages before	Averages after	Matched t-test
Good - Bad						
Experimental	2.03	3.14	2.21*	2.17	3.09	2.09*
Control	2.12	2.21		2.23	2.19	
Just - Unjust						
Experimental	2.19	3.32	2.99**	2.74	3.48	2.78*
Control	2.22	2.17		2.76	2.80	
Kind - Cruel						
Experimental	1.85	1.87	n.s.	1.78	1.73	n.s.
Control	1.87	1.79	1.82	1.85		
Fair - Unfair						
Experimental	1.87	2.88	2.83**	1.96	2.73	2.16*
Control	1.83	1.94	2.02	1.98		
Honest - Dishonest						
Experimental	1.57	2.07	2.08*	1.76	2.32	2.10*
Control	1.65	1.68	1.98	2.09		
Valuable - Worthless						
Experimental	1.53	1.77	n.s.	1.87	1.66	n.s.
Control	1.65	1.70	1.72	1.59		
Brave - Cowardly						
Experimental	2.02	4.43	3.76***	2.43	3.97	3.51**
Control	2.16	2.28	2.35	2.24		

Note: Scales range from a negative perception of 1 to a positive perception of 7. * < .05 (two tailed). ** < .01 (two tailed). *** < .001 (two tailed).

Before-after comparisons were undertaken separately for each of the experimental groups because each involved a different medium and terrorist event. Table 6.1 presents the groups' means before and after exposure. Since the principle of statistical normality could not be assumed and the computation involved controlling the variable of prior predisposition toward terrorism, a t-test for matched pairs was used to assess the difference between before and after differences, calculated for each pair of groups for each scale. Average scores are computed from 7 point scales where *1* represents the negative extreme of the semantic differential (e.g., bad, unfair, etc.) and *7* is the positive extreme (good, fair).

The comparison of scores before and after press exposure reveals that exposure does tend to change a certain aspect of the image held of terrorists. The evaluation made by control groups changed little, but most of the experimental groups' scores changed significantly and in some instances substantially. The experimental groups' evaluations remained largely negative, but they moved in the direction of an improvement in the terrorists' image on most of the evaluative scales. The predominant image remained one of disapproval, but terrorists were disapproved of less after exposure than before.

This image-improving effect is more salient for certain evaluative dimensions, namely: brave-cowardly, just-unjust, good-bad, fair-unfair, and honest-dishonest, but not on other scales (i.e., kind-cruel and valuable-worthless). Altogether, terrorist groups exposed to the subjects through the press were less likely to be viewed as cowardly, unjust, bad, unfair, and dishonest but just as apt to be viewed as cruel and worthless as they were before media exposure.

The image-improving effect was similar for both events even if the two events involved rather different actions, motivations, and outcomes. The magnitude of image improvements was almost identical for the two cases.

The next stage of the research effort was to study the impact of exposure to the press upon agenda setting, status conferral, and self-reported levels of information. Table 6.2 contains the responses by the experimental and control groups in the two terrorist situations to a series of questions intended to measure status conferral, agenda setting, and related matters. The observed differences between the experimental and control groups in terms of agenda setting and status conferral are consistent with the differences, already reported, with respect to their evaluation of the terrorist groups. Thus, subjects who were exposed to the media coverage tended to see the issue as more important, to believe that international solutions were desirable, and to hold that media coverage and public attention were merited.

The changes in viewpoint of the experimental groups provide abundant evidence, in this particular experiment, for the status conferral function of media coverage. The fact of press reference to an incident is sufficient for an audience to begin to consider the incident and its background to be of importance. Press exposure creates both awareness and interest: the experimental subjects, those exposed to press reports, were more likely to report an interest in and knowledge of the subjects in question. Experimental subjects were more apt to attribute importance to the issue, thereby providing evidence of agenda setting. Intriguingly, the experiment yielded no statistically significant evidence that individuals exposed to press coverage were as a result more apt to raise the issue in question with their friends. Thus the experiment provides some evidence of changes in image, attitudes, level of information, interest, attributed importance but not change in patterns of interpersonal communication.

Compared to press coverage, television coverage provides a somewhat different impact. Indeed, television coverage yields slightly different attitudinal changes depending upon the story, a fact that, we shall argue, conforms with the idea that the actual content of the story counts as much as whether or not the terrorist event is reported. Table 6.3 presents the results of the measurement of attitudes among the experimental and control groups before and after exposure of the experimental groups to television reports. Exposure to televised reports had a significant impact on certain aspects of the terrorists' image. Terrorists continued on balance to be seen as unjust, dishonest, and otherwise unfavorable. But these unfavorable images became less unfavorable after exposure.

Table 6.2 The Impact of Press Coverage on Public Perceptions of South Moluccan and Croatian cases in Experiments

Percent agreeing with the statement

	South Moluccan		Croatian	
	expt	control	expt	control
"the problem which caused the event is important"	48	16***	44	21***
"the problem should have been reported by the media"	53	21***	47	25***
"the problem should be solved by international institutions"	43	26**	46	24**
"people should know about this event and its causes"	47	25**	48	23**
"I know and understand the background of this event"	32	16*	47	29*
"I would like to know more about this subject"	51	32**	53	28***
"this is a topic I might discuss with my friends"	38	29n.s.	34	32 n.s.

Note: The statistical significance of the differences between the groups' proportions is tested under the null hypothesis of no difference. $*p<05$ (two tailed). $**p<01$ (two tailed). $***p<001$ (two tailed). n.s. not significant.

Table 6.3 Changes in Evaluative Attitudes toward Two
Terrorist Groups after Exposure to Television Coverage

	South Moluccan case			Croatian case		
	Averages before	Averages after	Matched t-test	Averages before	Averages after	Matched t-test
Good - Bad						
Experimental	2.11	2.98	ns	2.21	2.45	ns
Control	2.07	2.17		2.24	2.43	
Just - Unjust						
Experimental	2.09	3.12	3.56*	2.54	3.46	2.98*
Control	2.12	2.27		2.43	2.65	
Kind - Cruel						
Experimental	1.79	1.92	ns	1.75	2.87	2.27*
Control	1.96	1.87		1.97	1.80	
Fair - Unfair						
Experimental	1.87	2.01	ns	1.96	2.78	2.26
Control	1.89	1.72		1.91	2.00	
Honest - Dishonest						
Experimental	1.62	2.11	2.09*	1.70	2.43	2.21
Control	1.65	1.68		1.98	2.09	
Valuable - Worthless						
Experimental	1.64	1.87	ns	1.72	1.78	ns
Control	1.65	1.70		1.72	1.59	
Brave - Cowardly						
Experimental	2.18	4.19	3.32**	2.23	3.99	3.65**
Control	2.18	2.32		2.27	2.20	

Note: The statistical significance of the differences between the groups' proportions is tested under the null hypothesis of no difference. *p<05 (two tailed), **p<01 (two tailed), ***p<001 (two tailed), n.s. not significant.

Television coverage of the Croatian incident produced more change on more scales than did coverage of the South Moluccan event. The terrorists in the Croatian incident were less apt to be seen as cruel or unfair after exposure than was the case for the South Moluccans. There is good reason to believe that this difference is explained by the nature of the specific television reports on the two events. TV coverage of the South Moluccan event focused on the hijacked train and included dramatic footage of murdered hostages, masked gunmen, tense negotiations, and the terrorists' eventual arrest.

Given the macabre character of some of the footage, it is perhaps not surprising that the experimental group should not change its views of the terrorists' cruelty and unfairness. By contrast, coverage of the Croatian hijackers was essentially nonviolent in theme. The TWA aircraft was portrayed, the leaflet drop was described, and the eventual landing and surrender were photographed. The Croatian hijackers were guilty of murder, but the broadcast mentioned only very briefly the New York police officer whom they had killed. In sum, attitudes toward the Croatians became less unfavorable because the dominant image on television was one of the freed smiling hostages in Paris while images of the South Moluccan terrorists did not change because of the centrality of violence in the broadcast.

Table 6.4 The Impact of Television Coverage on the Public's Perceptions (percent agreeing with selected statements)

	South Moluccan		Croatian	
	expt	control	expt	control
"the problem which caused the event is important"	52	17***	49	22***
"the problem should have been reported by the media"	57	24***	56	27***
"the problem should be solved by international institutions"	51	23***	48	27**
"people should know about this event and its causes"	44	21**	50	24**
"I know and understand the background of this event"	27	18*	31	24n.s.#
"I would like to know more about this subject"	46	30**	42	24***
"this is a topic I might discuss with my friends"	42	26**	38	27*

Note: The statistical significance of the differences between the groups' proportions is tested under the null hypothesis of no difference. *$p<05$ (two tailed), **$p<01$ (two tailed), ***$p<001$ (two tailed), # n.s. not significant.

While differences in the content of the broadcasts on the two terrorist events produced somewhat different patterns in attitudinal change, the broadcasts did not produce substantially differing perceptions of the importance of the events.

Table 6.4 presents the results of the experimental and control groups' evaluation of the importance of the issues and the value of media coverage. As in the case of press coverage, discussed above, television coverage conferred status on the problem and the participants, encouraging viewers to believe that the problem should be solved and that the public had a genuine interest in its resolution. The control groups generally rated the problems in question as relatively unimportant and expressed little or no interest in each case and its causes. In sharp relief, the experimental groups were convinced that the problem is indeed important (49-52 percent), that it should be reported by the media (56-57 percent), and that it should be solved by international institutions (48-50 percent). TV reports heightened subject interest in the event and its causes (42-46 percent), increased the likelihood of personal discussion of the issue (38-42 percent), and strengthened the subjects' assessment of the need to inform the public about the case (44-50 percent). All of these effects are statistically significant when compared to the matched control groups.

Table 6.5 presents the results of a comparison of the experimental and control groups with respect to their evaluative attitudes. While press and television reports engendered some important attitudinal changes, this was much less so in the instance of radio coverage. Exposure to radio coverage was associated with changes in only three of the seven semantic differential scales (just-unjust, honest-dishonest, brave-cowardly). Nonetheless, as in the case of the other two media, radio exposure did produce less unfavorable images.

The relatively weaker impact of radio can be explained by the form and content of the radio reports. Coverage by the older of the two electronic media consisted primarily of short and strictly informative reports that outlined the course of events and contained only modest background information. The average length of a radio report was a mere 40 seconds, an obvious limitation on the amount of information, interpretation, and imagery that could be transmitted to the audience.

Table 6.6 portrays the impact of radio with respect to status conferral. Given that radio exposure did not yield as profound an attitudinal change as was true for the other two media, it is perhaps unsurprising that radio exposure likewise exercised a more modest influence on status conferral. Experimental subjects were slightly more apt to attribute greater importance to the case, to believe that it should have been reported by the media, and to hold that the problem demands an international solution. But unlike subjects exposed to television and press reports, those who were exposed to radio coverage did not undergo a significant increase in interest and reported level of information. Thus experimental subjects did not differ from the control subjects with respect to their interests or reported knowledge. At this point we turn to a comparison of the effects of the different media.

Table 6.5 Changes in Evaluative Attitudes toward Two
Terrorist Groups after Exposure to Radio Coverage

| Averages | South Moluccan case | | | Croatian case | | |
	Averages before	Matched after	t-test	Averages before	Matched after	t-test
Good - Bad						
Experimental	2.12	2.46	ns	2.23	2.11	ns
Control	2.15	2.28		2.08	2.25	
Just - Unjust						
Experimental	2.06	3.12	2.12*	2.26	3.32	2.58*
Control	2.26	2.45		2.61	2.76	
Kind - Cruel						
Experimental	1.73	1.80	ns	1.84	1.72	ns
Control	1.76	1.97		1.76	1.56	
Fair - Unfair						
Experimental	1.96	1.87	ns	1.85	2.04	ns
Control	1.89	1.75		1.54	1.78	
Honest - Dishonest						
Experimental	1.69	2.23	2.18*	1.97	2.84	2.09*
Control	1.87	1.75		1.54	1.78	
Valuable - Worthless						
Experimental	1.67	1.79	ns	1.91	1.78	ns
Control	1.74	1.78		1.87	1.69	
Brave - Cowardly						
Experimental	1.87	3.21	3.32**	2.23	3.43	3.46**
Control	1.98	2.03		2.05	2.03	

Note: The statistical significance of the differences between the groups' proportions is tested under the null hypothesis of no difference. *$p<05$ (two tailed), **$p<01$ (two tailed), ***$p<001$ (two tailed), n.s. not significant.

Table 6.6 The Impact of Radio Coverage on the Public's Perceptions

Percent agreeing with selected statements

	South Moluccan		Croatian	
	expt	control	expt	control
"the problem which caused the event is important"	28	18*	32	23*
"the problem should have been reported by the media"	38	19*	40	32**
"the problem should be solved by international institutions"	33	27ns	37	26*
"people should know about this event and its causes"	34	26ns	31	23ns
"I know and understand the background of this event"	24	17ns	29	24ns
"I would like to know more about this subject"	34	30ns	37	27ns
"this is a topic I might discuss with my friends"	27	26ns	33	29ns

Note: The statistical significance of the differences between the groups' proportions is tested under the null hypothesis of no difference. *$p<05$ (two tailed), **$p<01$ (two tailed), ***$p<001$ (two tailed), n.s. not significant

Table 6.7 summarizes the comparative impacts of the media on the two different issues. All three media were found to play an important role in the process of forming images of the events and terrorists and in accessing the importance of the causes that were their apparent motivations. All three media contributed to less unfavorable attitudes toward the terrorists and to augmented salience for the problems that the terrorists claim to be at the root of their concern. The press and television were both appreciably more potent than radio, a phenomenon that we attributed to the greater brevity of radio coverage. In this particular instance, the print medium was the most powerful in terms of its ability to diminish perceptions of the nefarious character of the terrorists. However, we have no reason to believe that the press is necessarily more effective in this regard than the broadcast media.

Table 6.7 Comparison of Effects across Media:
Changes Recorded in Attitudes and Perceptions

	Press		Television		Radio	
Evaluative Attitudes	SM	C	SM	C	SM	C
good-bad	+	+				
just-unjust	+	+	+	+	+	+
kind-cruel				+		
fair-unfair	+	+	+	+		
honest-dishonest	+	+	+	+	+	+
valuable-worthless						
brave-cowardly	+	+	+	+	+	+
Perceptions						
"the problem which caused the event is important"	+	+	+	+	+	+
"the problem should have been reported by the media"	+	+	+	+	+	+
"the problem should be solved by international institutions"	+	+	+	+		+
"people should know about this event and its causes"	+	+	+	+		
"I know and understand the background of this event"	+	+	+			
"I would like to know more about this subject"	+	+	+	+		
"this is a topic I might discuss with my friends"			+	+		

Television was more effective at encouraging subjects to say that they might discuss the topic with their friends. Television indeed might be more inherently effective at encouraging interpersonal communication than the press for the simple reason that exposure to television is much more of a group experience. People often watch television together, interspersing news stories with personal comments shared among family and friends sitting before the set. By contrast the consumption of newspaper reports tends to be a lonely and isolated experience. The ensuing chapter examines some of the features of the media presentation of terrorism that may account for the media impacts.

Chapter 7

Media Presentations of Terrorism

Sociological Explanations of Terrorism— Their Appearance and Meaning in Media Reports

To this juncture in the book, we have suggested that international terrorists seeking media attention can take comfort from the evidence of coverage accorded their violent acts. Of course, the extent to which the terrorists' comfort is well founded depends on the degree to which media attention does become transformed into tangible benefits. For some terrorists, the desired benefit is stature vis-à-vis their terrorist competitors. For most terrorists, the minimal objective is increased public recognition that they are a political actor to contend with. The optimal objective is movement toward achieving their communal, revolutionary, or other political objective.

The preceding chapter outlined a number of the ways in which the media may impact upon public opinion and the policy process. These effects range from mere information transfer to agenda setting and thence to priming and attitude change. The chapter concluded by reporting the results of a controlled experiment showing the cognitive and affective impact on 300 adult subjects as a result of being exposed to media coverage of two terrorist events.

The previous chapter's report of experimental public opinion impacts was offered within the framework of the debate among scholars about the maximal and minimal effects of the media upon society. Although the debate is far from resolved, a growing consensus has emerged to unite both sides on certain aspects of the controversy. For example, it is now almost axiomatic that media impacts on public opinion are more apt to be exercised on issues that are experientially remote from the public than on issues of which the public has much prior knowledge or understanding.

In the same vein, it seems reasonable to assume that an increase in the *volume* of coverage is normally sufficient to influence public agendas but not sufficient to produce affective change. Affective change may arise in two ways: either by actual changes in public sympathies toward the parties in a conflict and/or by means of priming, when the public amends its criteria for evaluating a situation. A terrorist event that receives enormous media attention will likely prompt the public to ascribe importance to the terrorists as well as their situation. But, the contextual information provided in media reports is more important than the mere length of these reports in affecting whether the public places more emphasis on the terrorists' deadly deeds or on their allegorical aims (i.e., priming) and in affecting whether or not the terrorists are viewed with sympathy.

This distinction between ascribing importance to the terrorists' agenda and embracing their cause may be an "academic" question in the pejorative sense of the word. For practical policy purposes, the distinction may not matter. From the terrorists' perspectives, merely ascribing greater importance to the issues that they allege to be at the root of their concerns may be an adequate form of recognition.

Public sympathies are nonetheless a potentially important matter. These public sympathies may be influenced by the particular details of a news event. For example, in the research project reported in Chapter 6, experimental subjects tended to perceive Croatian terrorists more benignly than South Moluccans after exposure to television coverage of the respective hijackings and killings. The public's more benign portrait of the Croatians was attributed to the fact that the coverage of their hijacking placed less emphasis on death and victimization. The TWA aircraft was portrayed, the leaflet drop was described, and the eventual landing and surrender were photographed. Although the Croatian hijackers were actually guilty of murder, this fact was glossed over in television reports. By contrast, coverage of the South Moluccan event included emotive footage of murdered hostages, masked gunmen, and tense negotiations.

The findings from our experimental research are corroborated by observational evidence. In his five-country analysis of terrorist behavior and public reaction, Hewitt shows that terrorists' lethal conduct can undermine their public support. Meanwhile, terrorists can enhance their public base when their conduct is perceived as less lethal or more charitable than expected.[1]

Public sympathies for a terrorist group may be influenced not only by the specific details of an event that is reported but also by the broader meaning that the media attach to the event. Of signal importance is the kind of

---

[1]   Christopher Hewitt, "Terrorism and Public Opinion: A Five Country Comparison," *Terrorism and Political Violence* (1989), 144-70, passim.

explanation provided by the media. On the one hand, the media could place emphasis on the social setting that may nourish terrorism and on the idealistic motives proclaimed by the terrorists. On the other hand, the media could place emphasis on the deadly conduct of the terrorists and on the evil motives that are imputable to them as a result, downplaying the terrorists' objectives along with their social and historical context.[2] Whether the media portray the practitioners of violence as *terrorists* or *freedom fighters* may make a difference to public feelings or affects.

The apparently simple polarity between terrorists and freedom fighters actually confounds three distinctions—denotative, legal/moral, and evaluative/connotative. A politically neutral denotative distinction is often made between fighting for freedom and practicing terror, but these are not necessarily mutually exclusive. Under conventions governing the conduct of war, standing armies and guerrilla forces may legitimately utilize fear, particularly through surprise attacks, in order to destabilize and demoralize an enemy provided that noncombatants are not targeted. Freedom fighters sometimes resort to terror as a tactic.

In practice, the term *terrorist* is rarely utilized to describe conventional forces practicing psychological warfare. The term is more typically used to ascribe an illegal and/or immoral character to groups that disregard conventions governing the rights of noncombatants in wartime. Portraying an assault on civilians as terrorist but one on the police or army as guerrilla action would conform with this legal-moral distinction.[3]

The polarity between freedom fighter and terrorist also embodies a connotative or evaluative distinction because the two terms contain "surplus" meaning, as philosophers might say. "Freedom fighters" are often considered with sympathy and "terrorists," with alarm. Of course the adjectives used to label groups might carry slightly different connotations

2   Steuter makes a strong case that *Time*'s reporting of terrorism sensationalizes violence while trivializing terrorists' objectives as well as the social and historical settings from which terrorism emerges. More studies along these lines need to be undertaken. However, in the end it may emerge that the publication selected by Steuter for scrutiny fits his portrait of conservative, patriotic media better than many. See Erin Steuter, "Understanding the Media/Terrorism Relationship: An Analysis of Ideology and the News in *Time* Magazine," *Political Communication and Persuasion* 7 (1990), 257-78.

3   For instructive discourse on moral-ethical aspects of the use of violence, see David C. Rapoport and Yonah Alexander, eds., *The Morality of Terrorism: Religious and Secular Justifications* (New York: Pergamon, 1982), passim and especially A. James Gregor, "Fascism's Philosophy of Violence and the Concept of Terror," ibid., 152-68.

for different audiences as well as different connotations for the same audience at different points in time. Winn conducted an exploratory study in 1988 among adults in Ottawa, Canada to assess the valence of certain key labels. In this small random sample survey, the term *freedom fighter* was found to generate unexpected negative rather than positive affects. The negative response to this particular label may reflect the fact that Canadians were most exposed to the term as it was used by spokesmen of the Reagan White House to characterize Nicaraguan contras and other groups about whom many Canadians had misgivings.

Some labels possess an essentially unchanging affective valence. All societies make efforts to control the use and display of violence so that the term *gunman* is not normally favorable. Democratic societies value compromise and moderation so that the term *extremist* tends to be opprobrious.

Many labels used by journalists in describing terrorist actions carry affective ramifications because they imply causal explanations that are not morally neutral. Thus, to describe a terrorist group as a "national liberation movement" is to imply that its violence is motivated by the normally laudable motive of liberating its nation from the yoke of a conquering power.

A social science-type explanation is often invoked in media reports to show the link between terrorism and national liberation. As the source of terrorism, this social science-type explanation typically points to an appalling social setting rather than to the terrorists' own unscrupulous intent. Terrorism is attributed to poverty, repression, and other antecedent social conditions rather than to the individual terrorists' evil or ambition. Individual terrorists are not seen as exercising free will or volition and are not held morally responsible for their actions. Media backgrounders may repeat the terrorists' own prepackaged justifications of violence as a situation of "no choice."

Reporters are not necessarily won over personally by the terrorists whose actions they cover. But the journalists' attempt at a social scientific explanation may lend an air of legitimacy to the national, religious, or political grievances that terrorists portray as their raison d'être.

In principle, the "root cause" social science-type explanations of terrorist behavior provided by the media need not accept uncritically the motives proclaimed by the terrorists themselves. In principle, the media could reject some terrorists' apparent grievances as unreasonable and treat the grievers as bent on the perpetration of new evils rather than the atonement of old ones. However, North American journalists share with the North American-based social sciences an underlying paradigm of liberal internationalism with its charitable view of foreign cultures, especially those that once fell under colonial rule. In the wake of the demoralizing Vietnam quagmire of the 1960s and by way of reaction against chauvinist tendencies at home, liberal internationalism in the United States has become especially disposed to granting a non- or anti-American view the benefit of the doubt.

Contemporary social scientists are a far cry from early anthropologists, who saw as their task to chronicle and account for the diminution of culture as one moved farther away from the world's ostensible cultural core in Europe. Social scientists today believe firmly in the moral equality of peoples, nations, and races. Social scientists are cautious about asserting that any particular foreign or non-Western culture may be disposed to intolerance, expansionism, or violence for fear that such invidious distinctions could be used to justify Western imperial traditions that they, as liberal social scientists, are anxious to bury. Because all peoples are equal, therefore all values and value systems must be treated as equal and all grievances must be treated as if they are equally deserving of rectification. No less liberal than social scientists, journalists may be moved by the same kind of largely unspoken and essentially benign reasoning.[4]

Intriguingly, the media's willingness to entertain sociological explanations for the violence of international terrorism contrasts with the media's lack of interest in pursuing social science explanations for domestic criminal acts. Journalists normally focus on the simple facts of an indigenous criminal act, rarely venturing into a consideration of the criminal's personal history or of the experiences that may have prompted his antisocial behavior. And yet, sociological explanations are objectively as well suited to indigenous criminal acts as to international terrorism.

It might be difficult to offer a social science explanation of crime if the incidence of crime were evenly distributed among all groups in society, but crime is not evenly distributed. In the case of the United States, blacks are four times more likely to reside in federal or state prisons than whites. While constituting only 12 percent of the nation's total population, blacks represent 47 percent of those who reside in prison.[5] In the western Canadian

---

4   On the liberal beliefs of journalists, see Stanley Rothman and R. Lichter, "Personality, Ideology and Worldview—A Comparison of Media and Business Elites," *British Journal of Political Science* (Jan. 1984), 29-49, and their "Media and Business Elites—Two Classes in Conflict," *Public Interest* (1982), 117-25.

5   Sources: *Statistical Abstract of the United States* (1988), 175, and *U.S. Bureau of the Census* (1986).

provinces of Saskatchewan and Manitoba, native Indians constitute less than 7% of the general population but more than half of prison admissions. In Saskatchewan, teenaged and young male aboriginal adults have a 70% chance of being incarcerated.[6]

Few domestic crimes are too idiosyncratic for social science explanations to be entirely inappropriate. A major portion of nonwhite collar crime is rooted in the demoralization found among low income groups and among those ethnic and racial groups where psychological well-being has been undermined by a history of slavery or subordination. This history of domination can be related to the poor self-images held by individual criminals as well as by the other members of the ethno-racial groups to which they belong.

Canadian Indians and African Americans are by no means the only descendants of conquered peoples to be represented disproportionately in the ranks of criminals. One of the most powerful underworld organizations, the Mafia, is a residue of centuries of subjugation of Sicily by the Italian mainland, dating to ancient Rome's plundering and deforestation of the island.

The incidence of crime is higher not only in politically troubled locations but also on politically troubled occasions. Crime rates apparently rose in the Soviet Union during *glasnost.* Palestinian crime rates have risen in times of political tumult and fallen in times of quiescence.

Social science explanations can account for many facets of criminal behavior. For example, recidivism can be related to the role of prisons as criminal learning centers, to the role of prisons as catalysts of anger, and to the insufficient supply of work force entry programs for prisoners upon release. Sexual crime can be related to childhood case histories and, in some instances, to the consumption of pornography. There is no dearth of social science-type theory. Indeed, there is probably a surfeit of potential hypotheses to account for every individual crime in terms of social conditions beyond the criminal's own control.

Ordinary crime is not only just as well suited to sociological explanation as terrorism, but ordinary criminals are less likely than terrorists to muddy the analysis by interjecting their own self-serving justifications. Domestic criminals are less prone than international terrorists to conjure up

---

6   Source: Official position of the Canadian Bar Association as made public on "As It Happens," CBC radio (August 26, 1988).

rationalizations of their conduct for the benefit of mass audiences. There are few real life counterparts to the expressive underworld characters in Bertolt Brecht's *Threepenny Opera* who excoriate capitalism as the source of their own criminality.

Domestic criminals rarely grandstand and typically face their sentencing courts in a dejected state of mind. The low incomes, low life expectancies, and high incarceration rates of conquered peoples such as Canadian Indians ought to stimulate the emergence of sociological explanations of their violent conduct, either from the mouths of aboriginals themselves or in journalistic reports. Yet criminals, aboriginal or European, tend to remain silent. The despondence of ordinary criminals suggests that their human condition may indeed contain a genuine element of subjugation and subordination.

When criminals do occasionally articulate social science-type explanations for their brutality, they tend to direct these self-serving thoughts to a tiny audience of court-appointed counselors. A much publicized criminal case in Canada illustrates the extent to which the self-justifying or rationalizing conduct of criminals and terrorists can reasonably be compared.

An extensive coroner's inquiry was conducted after Melville Stanton committed his fifth known rape and second murder while at a supervised halfway house in Toronto on leave from prison. The inquiry uncovered two decades of documentary evidence of the man's desire for revenge against a society that, he believed, had badly mistreated him, had permitted his own rape, and had threatened him with lobotomy. The coroner's official counsel concluded that psychologists had consistently underestimated Stanton's penchant for violence because they had been misled by his rationalizations and were never fully aware of the precise details of his criminal record.[7] In the wake of his second murder, the most recent court-appointed psychologist testified that she was torn between her conclusion that the multiple rapist-murderer was probably unsuited to normal life and her view that his "beliefs" about society were nonetheless somewhat "valid."

From the record of the coroner's inquiry into his crimes, it appears that Melville Stanton was as capable of articulating rationalizations as many terrorists. But he directed his rationalizations to a limited audience of

7   "Rapist Sought Revenge on Society, Psychologist Testifies," *Globe and Mail* (Nov. 2, 1988), A3.

court-appointed custodians and psychological assessors rather than to the mass media and general public. As in the case of terrorists, Stanton's quasi-social science rationalizations of his brutality were not entirely devoid of truth. Stanton did not have a happy childhood. He was himself raped. And he did have reason to fear lobotomy, mooted when he first showed signs of unconscionable brutality as a young adolescent.

Unlike the rationalizations of international terrorists, the rationalizations of Melville Stanton did not reach a wide audience for the simple reason that he sought to avoid rather than cultivate publicity. Without the criminal's own commitment to media exposure, the coroner's inquest into his case was only able to achieve recognition on the back pages of a small number of newspapers. The explanations of criminals such as Melville Stanton do not reach a wide audience at least in part because reaching a wide audience is not a criminal's objective. The explanations of terrorists are widely disseminated to the extent that such is the terrorists' goal.

The contrasting publicity wishes of international terrorists and domestic criminals are important factors, but not the only factors accounting for the media's lesser enthusiasm for liberal sociological explanations of domestic crime. Another factor may be an implicit ideological consensus among journalists that the peace and cohesion of the domestic society deserves special consideration. A generation ago in some communities in North America, the journalists' consensus went so far as to prohibit reports of bank robberies and other dramatic crimes in order not to arouse undue alarm or encourage too much imitation.[8] Following this line of reasoning, the ideological consensus among journalists today takes the form of withholding social science explanations of crime that could be interpreted from within a society as either moral justification or incitement.

Proffering any kind of sociological explanation of domestic crime risks sowing deep discord. The dominant groups in society may be enraged by explanations that highlight the historical subjugation or inferior socioeconomic position of groups that display a higher than average incidence of crime. Meanwhile sociological explanations that are sympathetic to subordinate groups may embolden them to strengthen their redistributive claims on government and society.

8 On the *demonstration effect* of domestic crime reports, see George Comstock, ed., *Public Communication and Behavior*, vol. 1 (Boston: Academic Press, 1986), passim.

Conceivably, sociological explanations need not necessarily be sympathetic to subordinated groups. Sociological explanations could focus on the maladaptiveness of subordinated groups with supranormal crime rates given that not all groups respond to subordination and exploitation by adopting antisocial behaviors. But this ideologically conservative type of explanation risks enraging the subordinate groups and those members of the dominant groups who are anxious not to arouse tension. In the final analysis, journalists are loyal nationals of their own country, honoring their society's taboos against disseminating ideas that could be seen as excessively destructive.

The international system lacks the sense of community of a developed national system. The international system has not produced the degree of integration and concern for collective survival that prompt the emergence of both formal law and informal taboo within national systems. If the international system were to become as closely integrated as it was in past centuries thanks to the supranational ties of aristocracy, both national governments and the media would begin to apply intranational standards of conduct to the international system.

For the short run, the pressure on the media to deprive terrorists of air to breath, to paraphrase Marshall McLuhan, is apt to be rooted less in a consensual desire for peace and stability and more in the rage of governments and peoples over the apparent legitimation of terrorist groups brought about by media explorations of terrorism's "root causes." In autumn 1988, Margaret Thatcher, one of the longest-ruling heads of government in the world's oldest continuous democracy, issued a decree prohibiting British television from diffusing interviews with IRA leaders. These interviews provided recognition not only for the individual terrorists themselves but also for the explanations of the Irish situation that they put forward.

Thatcher's effort to control news coverage of the IRA but not of other international terrorist groups illustrates our point about the normally greater taboos about the reporting of domestic as opposed to international violence. Indeed, it was the weakening of such taboos that prompted Thatcher's actions. From her perspective, the IRA propaganda threat struck at the core of the United Kingdom's domestic tranquillity.

To this point in the chapter, we have explored in an informal and hypothetical way the role of sociological explanation in media reports of international terrorism. Some hypotheses about the incidence of sociological explanations in media reports are difficult to test empirically. For example, it would be difficult to design a project to test the hypothesis that cohesion within a national or international system plays a role in the willingness of journalists to disseminate social science-type explanations that could lend an air of legitimacy to the perpetration of violence. And yet, abundant circumstantial evidence points to the influence of social cohesion on reporting. For example, in his widely respected book *The First Casualty*, Philip Knightley traces the historical impact of patriotism as a major factor in the misleading reports sent home by war reporters. Truth, as the title implies, is war's first casualty.

Not all hypotheses about when and why journalists resort to sociological explanations of violence are difficult to assess quantitatively. Indeed, our own dataset on media content and terrorist behavior allows for some empirical exploration. The passages that follow examine quantitatively a number of the factors that may help explain when, why, and to what degree the media discuss the proclaimed background motives or factors that are said to drive the behavior of international terrorists. We discuss the incidence with which the media transmit terrorists' motives as well the incidence of positive and negative labeling of various terrorist groups. Specifically, the pages that follow examine

- terrorists' motives in media reports
- violence as a means of securing media attention for terrorists' motives
- inequalities in the recognition given to the proclaimed motives of different terrorist groups
- the significance of affective labeling
- who does the labeling
- who and what are labeled.

The chapter concludes with a discussion of terrorist influence over media portrayals of their motives as an indirect consequence of the "Stockholm syndrome."

Terrorists' Motives in Media Reports

At the core of the explanation of terrorist behavior are the terrorists' own motives. From biblical times to the present, observers of the human condition have never taken motives entirely at face value. In the post-Freudian age, motives have become a phenomenon of particular complexity, involving both the conscious strategic deception of others and the unconscious deception of oneself. Daily journalism, however, tends to treat motives at face value.

Both the philosophical raison d'être of journalism in a free society and its methods of operation render difficult the complex portrayal of motive. To report unquestioningly the proclaimed purpose of a group is more consistent with the paradigm of journalism as verifiable reporting than to aver that the group's true purpose is other than what is proclaimed. Journalists, furthermore, operate under time constraints that limit their ability to assimilate background information and to transmit complex information to their audience. Even if journalists possessed the leisure to assimilate historical and other contextual knowledge, the time constraints of television news would limit the transmission of such information.

The time available for a story, say, on a Shia hijacking of Americans might be sufficient for describing the bare facts of the event. But few television producers or news editors would feel able to make room for a description of the various historical backgrounds—Christian-Moslem history in the Middle East, Sunni-Shia relations in the Moslem world, relations among the Arab states, Arab-Persian relations, Jewish-Moslem relations, Arab-Israeli relations, third world-U.S. relations, and so forth. For all these reasons, the discussion of motive in news reports of terrorism normally amounts to a discussion of the motives directly or indirectly proffered by the terrorists themselves.

Figure 7.1 portrays the frequency with which the media in our sample include a discussion of motive in their reports on terrorist events. As many as half of all stories explore motives. Because the space constraints of daily newspapers are less serious than the time constraints of nightly news broadcasts, the printed press tends to mention motives somewhat more frequently. For example, motives appear in 60% of *New York Times* stories as compared to fewer than half of the stories broadcast on the American networks.

The single biggest exception among the sample of 12 media is the *Pakistan Times*, which reports motives far less frequently than the others. The south Asian paper's disinterest in motives may be explained by a pattern of relatively parochial international interests and by the abbreviated length of its wire service-dependent stories. The *Pakistan Times*'s disinterest in motives may also be explained by its diffidence as a government-owned paper in an authoritarian state that experienced frequent changes between military and civilian rule as well as frequent changes of policy. For example, the anti-secular military regime of 1969-1971 was preceded by a secular military regime and succeeded by a secular civilian regime, which was overthrown in 1977 by a theocratic military regime. The instability of regime, not to mention the vagaries of policy within any given regime, make it difficult for the editors of the paper to know what line to follow. For

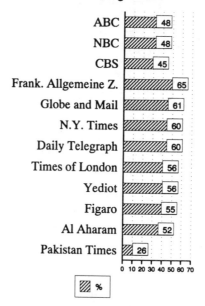

Figure 7.1 Motives — Proportion of
Stories Mentioning Motives

example, in 1971 the paper was embarrassed because it initially welcomed as "heroes" the Kashmiri hijackers of an Air India aircraft, only to discover that Pakistan's military government would soon imprison the hijackers as Indian agents.

Among the sample of media as a whole, terrorists achieve an approximately 50% success rate in securing media recognition for their purported motives and also achieve a certain locational prominence on the pages of the newspapers and in the sequence of stories selected for news broadcasts. The motives of terrorists have a good chance of being mentioned on the first page of a daily newspaper or among the first three stories in a nightly television newscast. Among terrorist stories broadcast by the U.S. networks, approximately two-thirds discuss the terrorists' motives and do so among the first three stories in the program (see Figures 7.2 and 7.3).

CBS, NBC, and ABC are remarkably similar to each other in their attention to terrorists' motives, as they are indeed with respect to other aspects of reporting. The daily newspapers, by contrast, reveal some heterogeneity. The *Daily Telegraph* leads the sample, reserving a discussion

Figure 7.2 Locational Prominence of TV
Terrorism Reports (% in first 3 items)

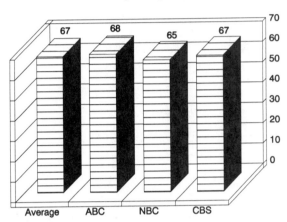

of motives for the first page in more than three-quarters of cases whereas the corresponding figure for the *Pakistan Times* is fractionally under 40%. The locational prominence given by the *Daily Telegraph* to terrorists' motives can be understood in terms of that newspaper's general preoccupation with the phenomenon of terrorism.

Over the period of our study, the media tended to heighten the locational prominence given to both terrorist events and their purported underlying motives. For example, the dailies tended to assign discussions of terrorist motives more frequently to page one in the later years than in the earlier while the newscasts tended to upgrade such discussions to positions one, two, or three. Indeed, the rates of locational prominence doubled over the course of the study in both newspapers and television.

The preceding chapter examined at some length the issue of agenda setting and the role of the press in influencing public and policy elite agendas as a result of the prominence given to a particular issue. The increasing locational prominence given to terrorists' motives in the media during the 1970s has some important ramifications for agenda setting. To the extent that publics and governments can be said to have grown more concerned about the issues that purportedly catalyze terrorism, the media can be assumed to have been a major factor accounting for the change. The research question to which we now turn is what prompts the media to pay attention to motives.

Figure 7.3 Locational Prominence of Press Reports on Terrorism

Figure 7.3 Locational Prominence of Press Reports on Terrorism

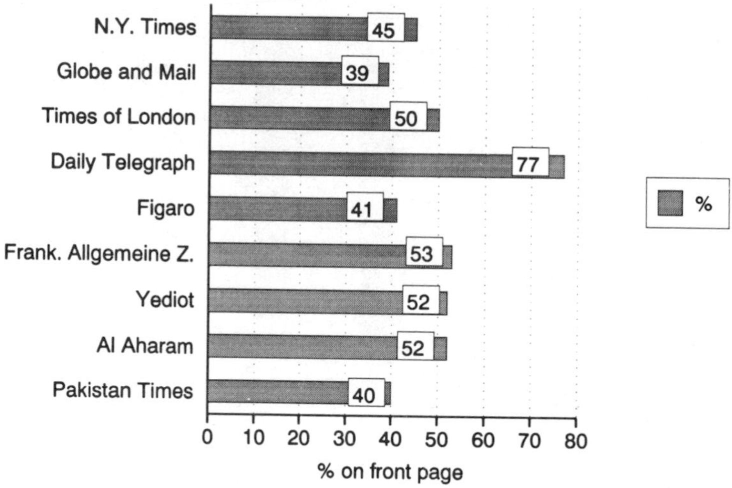

Over Dead Bodies—
Gaining Media Attention for Terrorists' Motives

Paradoxically, the more terrorists victimize innocent people, the more the media grant attention to the motives of terrorists *qua* victims. Figures 7.4 and 7.5 displays the frequency with which the 12 media in the sample report the motives of terrorists according to the number of fatalities in a specific encounter. For each media outlet, the probability of reporting the terrorists' apparent or purported motives increases as the number of fatalities increases.

The rate of victimization of innocents has a particularly strong impact on the reporting of motive in the case of television. The stronger link between victimization and the transmission of motive in the case of television may stem from the fact that the visual medium is better suited to the portrayal of the macabre. For all three networks, fewer than half of terrorist events entailing one to five fatalities are attributed a motive. By contrast, motives are attributed to almost three-quarters of events in which six or more people are killed.

Figure 7.4 Terrorist Motives Reported
by Fatality Rate: Television

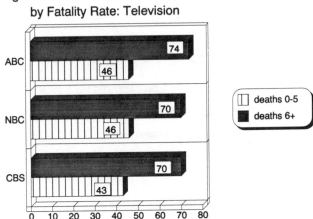

% stories reporting terrorists' motives

The relatively staid *New York Times* is the most immune to the influence of fatalities. Thus, the frequency with which this pivotal newspaper mentions motives rises only modestly from 59.7% in the case of events involving fewer than six fatalities to 68.6% in the case of events involving six or more fatalities.

Fatalities exercise a certain fascination among the Egyptian and Pakistani papers as well as upon *Yediot* and the *Daily Telegraph*. These Middle Eastern, British, and south Asian papers are more apt to discuss motives as the number of terrorist victims rises.

The link between the terrorists' willingness to victimize and their capacity to secure a platform for a reporting of their proclaimed raison d'être entails complex ethical and empirical ramifications. The media's behavior is understandable from the perspective of organizations whose economic survival and growth depends upon audience response. To the extent that news is a commodity rather than a social good, media treatment of international terrorism may not be astonishing. Audiences are fascinated by the macabre. A protracted discussion of a terrorist event that includes an examination of terrorists' motives may help fulfill an audience's profound psychological needs to manage anxiety and ascribe meaning to ethically meaningless acts. Violence is frightening, but terrorist violence is especially so because its victims are innocent. A frightened audience seeks information to help give meaning and structure to a world that seems

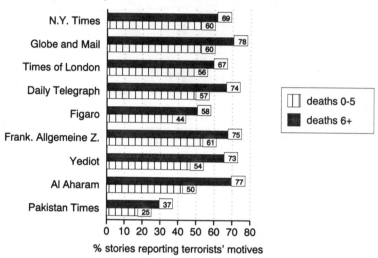

Figure 7.5 Terrorist Motives Reported
by Fatality Rate: The Press

% stories reporting terrorists' motives

anomic and to help control its own fear. At least if there is an apparent reason for unreasonable behavior, audiences can get some solace. Media that provide a platform for terrorists' motives meet audiences' informational and psychological needs, thus helping to solidify audience loyalty and strengthen the media's own economic situation.

Some Terrorists' Motives Are More Important than Others'

We reported earlier in this book that some terrorist groups are more likely to be covered than others. Middle Eastern and Palestinian terrorists are especially successful in having their motives acknowledged in press reports. Figure 7.6 shows that almost three-fifths of stories on Palestinian terrorists encompass a report of motives. The proportion of stories involving the motives of non-Palestinian Middle Eastern terrorists is 53%. By contrast, barely one-third of events involving Spanish or Armenian terrorists encompass a discussion of motive. The relative advantage of Palestinian and other Middle Eastern terrorist groups over non-Middle Eastern terrorists is particularly striking if one takes into consideration both the

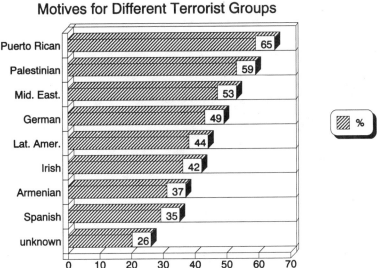

Figure 7.6 Frequency of Reporting
Motives for Different Terrorist Groups

likelihood of any coverage *plus* the likelihood of attention to motive for any given coverage.

The networks are relatively alike in their pattern of attention to motive (see Table 7.1). All three accord much attention to the motives of Palestinian, German, Middle Eastern, and Puerto Rican groups undertaking international terrorist actions but relatively little or no attention to the raison d'être of Irish, Spanish, and Armenian terrorism.

All 12 media display a certain element of parochialism in their pattern of attention to the motives of terrorists. The pattern of attention to motives tends to coincide with the home country's traditional foreign policy interests. Thus, the motives of terrorists are most apt to be reported if the terrorists pose a threat either to the media outlet's own country, to an ally, or to an international opponent. For example, because Puerto Rican terrorists pose a threat to the United States, their motives are most apt to be highlighted in the media of the English-speaking countries as well as in the German newspaper included in the sample. Puerto Rican terrorist motives have a greater than 75% probability of being mentioned in the *New York Times*, *Globe and Mail*, *Daily Telegraph*, and *Frankfurter Allgemeine Zeitung*.

Table 7.1 Frequency of Reporting Motive (in percent)

	CBS	NBC	ABC	NYT	GM	TL
Puerto	78	93	89	81	88	47
Palest.	54	59	53	54	74	57
Mid.E.	40	36	40	65	67	56
German	43	34	42	43	66	43
L/Amer	25	38	32	59	56	60
Irish	25	29	30	58	64	47
Armen	0	0	0	43	47	51
Span	0	0	0	37	64	83
Unkn	17	24	30	32	24	26

	DT	FI	FR	YD	AA	PK
Puerto	75	8	89	50	51	13
Palest.	64	52	72	54	70	41
Mid.E.	61	48	67	67	56	33
German	55	78	62	42	67	10
L/Amer	53	40	60	61	37	12
Irish	62	33	45	47	48	13
Armen	60	44	81	40	36	40
Span	31	71	41	60	22	10
Unkn	26	26	32	33	33	12

Palestinian and other Middle Eastern terrorists are likely to gain coverage for their motives in the North American media in part because the targets of these terrorists are so often American nationals. An additional incentive for New York and Toronto-based media to provide coverage for these particular terrorist groups is that these two cities possess large Jewish populations, whom journalists could expect to be interested in the conduct of Arab terrorists. Palestinian and other Middle Eastern terrorists are the focus of attention of the Israeli and Egyptian papers for obvious reasons of international politics.

Palestinian motives share equal billing with Armenian motives in the case of the *Pakistan Times*, followed closely by the category of other Middle Eastern terrorists. More than two-fifths of the *Pakistan Times*'s reports on Palestinian and Armenian terrorist attacks identify their purposes. Palestinian and Armenian terrorists are three to four times more successful in gaining exposure for their motives than are German, Irish, Puerto Rican, Spanish, and Latin American terrorists. The south Asian paper may be the most parochial among the 12 different media, caring only about the actions and purposes of terrorists with a direct bearing on Pakistani national interests.

Pakistan's Palestinian interest has two historical elements. On the one hand, as a leader of the Moslem world, Pakistan is interested in the fact that a Moslem population confronts a nonMoslem enemy. On the other hand, Pakistan's actual involvement in the region has included providing King Hussein with troops who participated with the monarch's forces in the lethal suppression of the PLO in 1970, out of which emerged the "Black September" terrorist group.

The parochialism of *Le Figaro* is simpler to account for. Terrorists based in France's most important neighboring countries, Germany and Spain, are the most likely to gain attention for their motives on the pages of the Parisian daily. Almost four-fifths of stories about German terrorists mention motives as compared to only 50% involving Palestinians and 8% in the case of Puerto Ricans. Germany and Spain are of course France's most important neighbors.

The pattern of attention given to terrorist motives is not always fully or effectively explained by traditions of national interest in foreign policy. The Frankfurt paper's interest in Armenian motives may be related to Germany's traditional interest in Turkey but it may also be related to the existence of Germany's sizeable Turkish immigrant groups. The German paper's interest in Puerto Ricans may be explained by West Germany's special relationship with the United States, rooted in the postwar period of occupation. *Yediot*'s willingness to transmit the motives of Latin American terrorists has no obvious single explanation. Perhaps it is because the region became a refuge for Nazis fleeing the ruins of the Third Reich and/or because the region hosts large Jewish and Arab populations.

The two London papers, the *Times* and the *Daily Telegraph*, manifest a diverse conception of national interest in their coverage. More traditionally toryish, the *Times* places enormous emphasis on Spanish terrorists, presumably because of a vision of Britain's overseas interests linked to her presence at Gibraltar. Perhaps because of its more upscale readership, the *Times* may also have been more interested in meeting the informational needs of middle class Englishmen who increasingly vacationed in and retired to the Iberian peninsula. By contrast, the *Daily Telegraph* is North American in its focus, placing less emphasis on the motives of Spanish terrorists than on those of Puerto Rican, Palestinian, and Middle East terrorists.

From Sociological Motives to Affective Labeling

The motives attributed by journalists to terrorists are not the public's only source of information about the terrorists' ultimate purposes. Media audiences can also draw inferences from the terms associated with a terrorist group, including both the group's formal name and the various synonyms that the media might use interchangeably with its formal name. To use some obvious examples, a group might be labeled murderers, gunmen, or saboteurs or alternately a national liberation movement, nationalists, or patriots.

The affective or propaganda significance of the terrorists' formal names or informal labels derives from how these terms are perceived. Weimann undertook public opinion research to measure the affective valence of a wide range of labels using seven-point semantic differential scales. His analysis of public perception data yielded a relatively simple threefold division into negative, neutral, and positive categories, as illustrated in Table 7.2.[9]

The political significance of language is so enormous that political leaders overlook it at their peril. Tyrants normally place the best light on their deeds from a calculated realization that domination is more economical if misunderstood by those who might resist. Orwellian examples of *newspeak* abound—France's imperialism as a civilizing mission, South Africa's racial exploitation as separation of the races, Nazi genocide as a final solution, Stalinist tyranny as democratic centralism, and countless examples of conquest as liberation.

On occasion, terms that originally embody positive affective meaning are utilized so blatantly for ulterior purposes that they lose their positive affect. For example, the Soviet Union's cultivation of foreign "peace" front groups as an instrument of its foreign and defence policies during the 1950s and 1960s was so widespread that peace almost became a dirty word. Meanwhile in North America, the McCarthyite temper of the times permitted unsavory fascists and Nazis to be paraded as anticommunists with the result that the term *anticommunist* lost some of its original patina.

---

9   G. Weimann, "Terrorists or Freedom Fighters?" *Political Communication and Persuasion* 2 (4)(1985), 433-45.

Table 7.2 The Affective Valence of Terrorist Labels

negative	neutral	positive
murderers	guerrilla	freedom fighter
gunmen	army	liberation organization
saboteurs	underground	liberation movement
terrorists	separatists	nationalists
criminals	organization	independence movement
kidnappers	movement	independence organization
hijackers	commandos	patriots
assassins	group	
	front	

Terrorists are aware of the ramifications of language. They do not always communicate effectively. Revolutionary groups sometimes get entangled in ideological rhetoric beyond the comprehension of a broad audience. But terrorists are usually sensitive enough to language to select favorable labels. Their titles appeal to the resounding political principles that emerged out of the European Enlightenment. A simple word count shows the terms most frequently used in the titles of the world's hundreds of international terrorist groups:

- liberation
- national
- people
- popular
- unity
- salvation
- democracy
- and resistance.

Other frequently used terms are *justice, order, oppressed, peasants, workers, homeland, fatherland, patriots, freedom, victims,* and *sovereignty.*

The positive valence of the terms used by terrorists to designate themselves has a potential propaganda value among the audiences of all the mass media. The propaganda value may be especially strong among those outlets such as the *Pakistan Times* that prefer using the terrorists' own name rather than synonyms.

The positive valence of terrorists' own appellations may also have an indirect propaganda benefit insofar as they affect how journalists think.

Indeed, in their own choice of substitute terms for terrorist groups, journalists do not often resort to negative labels. For example, negative terms are employed only about one-third of the time in the British and American press and less than half the time in the French, West German, and Israeli press.

As discussed more fully below in Chapter 9, neo-Marxist and other leftwing critics condemn the U.S. media for selective biased labeling and for excessively negative labeling of "terrorist" groups. Meanwhile, conservative or rightwing critics express dismay about what they perceive to be a degree of proterrorist labeling in news reports in the same media. Our findings lend some support to both sides.

Leftwing critics are probably on their strongest ground when they point to selective labeling. Simmons and Lowry conducted an extensive content analysis of terrorism reporting in *Time, Newsweek,* and *U.S. News and World Report,* and found evidence of greater negative labeling where the offending group opposed U.S. policy or selected American nationals as victims.[10] Our analysis below reveals cross-national evidence of selective labeling. *Le Figaro,* the *Frankfurter Allgemeine Zeitung,* and other papers make more frequent use of negative labels in portrayals of terrorist groups that they see as antagonistic to their own traditional national interests.

Leftwing critics are probably on weaker ground when they decry excessive negative labeling. Steuter[11] as well as Simmons and Lowry[12] have demonstrated that negative labeling is widespread in the terrorism coverage of major U.S. newsmagazines. Our own data also point to widespread negative labeling. For all nine newspapers in our study, the frequency of negative labeling far outweighs the frequency of positive labeling (see Figures 7.7 and 7.8). However, a full perspective on media labeling needs to compare not just negative vs. positive labeling but also negative vs. all other forms of labeling. Except for the single case of Canada's *Globe and Mail,* negative labels are less frequent than nonnegative labels, i.e., less frequent than the sum of neutral and positive labels plus the groups' own normally favorable names.

10   Brian K. Simmons and David N. Lowry, "Terrorists in the News, as Reflected in Three News Magazines, 1980-1988," *Journalism Quarterly* 67 (Winter 1990), 692-96.
11   E. Steuter, "Understanding the Media/Terrorism Relationship: An Analysis of Ideology and the News in *Time* Magazine," *Political Communication and Persuasion* 7 (1990), 274.
12   Simmons and Lowry, "Terrorists in the News," 692-96.

Any given level of negative labeling in the media can benefit some organizations while harming others. A strong political party in an authentic electoral contest might be dismayed if its media portrayals entailed negative labels far more often than positive ones. A small political party experiencing a similar pattern might be far less dismayed, perhaps even emboldened. A terrorist group hijacking the media agenda by means of violent action might take comfort from the evidence that the negative labeling of terrorists typically appears in only a plurality of media reports.

Turning from the issue of whether terrorists gain or lose from plurality negative labeling, one needs to consider whether U.S. media labeling is unusually negative from a cross-national perspective. Steuter's content analysis of *Time*'s treatment of terrorism led him to see the magazine as "reproduc[ing] and legitimiz[ing] conservative values..." and reflect[ing] a "conservative North American political culture."[13] Our own data do not yield a similar portrait of the *New York Times*. The New York paper resorts to negative labeling of terrorists less frequently than every other paper in our sample except the Egyptian and Pakistani. Steuter's and our own analysis may both be valid. As a traditionally middle-of-the-road Republican weekly, *Time* may be less receptive to terrorists' claims of injustice than the liberal *New York Times*.

Who Does the Labeling

There is a certain consensus or *zeitgeist* among the newspapers studied. With the single exception of Toronto's *Globe and Mail*, each of the newspapers in the sample is less apt to use negative labeling than positive and neutral labeling combined. The rank order correlations for usage of labels are all positive, albeit more so among the English-speaking and Israeli newspapers than between any of them and the Pakistani or Egyptian papers. The correlations among the *New York Times*, *London Times*, and *Yediot* are all above + .40, suggesting that these three form a kind of media subculture in terrorism reporting.

In spite of the general consensus about labeling shared by all the papers in the sample, certain labeling differences nonetheless persist (see Figures 7.7 and 7.8). Predictably perhaps, the Pakistani and Egyptian papers are

13   Steuter, "Understanding the Media/Terrorism Relationship," p. 274.

Figure 7.7 Affect of Terrorist Labels, English-speaking Press, 1968-1980

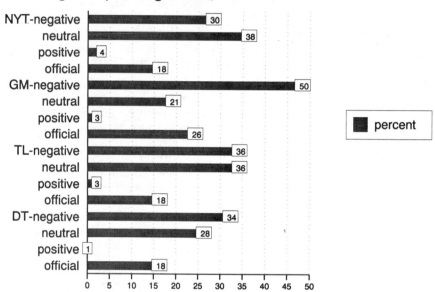

much less likely to resort to negative labels, much more likely to rely on the terrorists' own moniker, and somewhat more likely to use positive labels. In both third world papers, positive (i.e., proterrorist) labels plus terrorists' own appellations outnumber negative labels by more than 2 to 1. Thus, from their labelling behavior, one could reasonably conclude that the two third world papers manifest a certain sympathy towards international terrorism.

The labeling behavior of the Western papers is slightly more resistant to interpretation. The frequency of negative labelling is more frequent than the combined category of positive labels and official names; yet negative labeling is nonetheless less frequent than positive and neutral labeling combined. Because negative labels always outnumber the joint category of positive labels plus terrorists' own appellations, one could conclude that western papers are somewhat antiterrorist. Yet, with the exception of the Toronto paper, labeling is negative only on a minority of occasions. Thus,

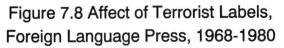

Figure 7.8 Affect of Terrorist Labels, Foreign Language Press, 1968-1980

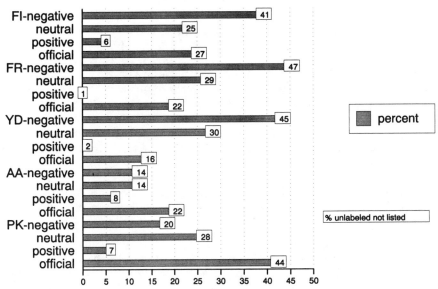

one could also make a case that Western press reports reveal a vague tolerance or even sympathy for terrorism.

The Western press reveals some patterns of internal difference. Among the papers on the eastern side of the Atlantic, the German paper is the most antiterrorist in its labeling behavior, almost one-and-a-half times more so than the New York paper and fractionally more so even than the Israeli paper. The Frankfurt paper's antiterrorist labeling practices may reflect some residual authoritarian tendencies in German political culture, impeding the ability of this important paper to adhere to the liberal democratic ethic of neutral reporting. Chapter 10, below, discusses evidence of authoritarian tendencies in the German media. Apart from possible authoritarianism, the paper's antiterrorist labeling tendencies may reflect an intense anxiety that German electoral democracy be made to work after the darkness of the Third Reich.

Perhaps the most intriguing difference among the Western papers is that which distinguishes Toronto's *Globe and Mail* from the *New York Times*.

One would have little reason to expect a major difference between the two papers given the physical, cultural, and communications proximity between them. Canada is by far the world's biggest consumer of American cultural products, accounting, for example, for about half of all U.S. book exports. As a result of the advanced state of cable rediffusion in Canada, Canadians actually have had greater opportunities to watch American television programming than have Americans. Most Canadians have had access to the three commercial and one public U.S. networks both off-air and through regular, nonpremium-priced cable service. Canadians have also had enormous opportunities to view American programming on Canadian public and private networks.[14] The cultural integration of the two countries is such that Toronto has become a major regional production center for the American film and movie industry. The Canadian television industry has been a supplier of newscasters, writers, and other creative personnel for its sister industry in the United States; for example, ABC and PBS suppertime newscasts are hosted by Canadians. There is no structural reason to expect the *Globe* to differ sharply from the American press, with which it is contractually linked and from which it draws much wire service material.

The Toronto paper nonetheless diverges sharply from its New York counterpart. The *New York Times*'s 30% rate of negative labeling is appreciably lower than at all other papers except *Al Aharam* and the *Pakistan Times*. By contrast, the rate of negative labeling at the *Globe* is 50%, two-thirds higher than at the American paper and by far the highest level among the sample of papers.

When discussing, above, the pattern of motive portrayal among the newspapers, we suggested that a significant factor was the host country's conception of national or foreign policy interest. This collective national view of the world could be said to help account for the English-speaking press's interest in Puerto Rican motives, the German and Pakistani papers' interest in Armenian motives, and the French paper's interest in the motives of Spanish and German terrorists. National or foreign policy interests may also help account for some patterns of positive and negative labelling, for example the Egyptian paper's limited use of negative labels in reports of terrorism by Palestinians,

---

14   *Report of the Task Force on Broadcasting Policy* (Ottawa: Supply and Services, 1986), 93.

A host country's foreign policy orientation is by itself only one of several possible factors in newspaper reports. For example, if foreign policy were a prime consideration, one might expect the highest rate of negative labeling to appear in the influential American newspaper because American citizens are the most frequent targets of terrorism and because the United States heads the western alliance. By the same token, one might expect a low rate of negative labeling in Canada's leading newspaper because Canada is a mainstay in the United Nations system of institutions and has displayed some neutralist, even anti-American, tendencies in foreign affairs. These anti-U.S. tendencies, expressed for example in staunch opposition to the Free Trade Accord between the two countries, have been much stronger in Toronto than in the western provinces and especially strong among Toronto-based journalists.

Foreign policy alone cannot explain the *Globe*'s high rate of negative labeling and the *New York Times*'s low rate. The *Globe*'s propensity for negative labeling is better understood when considered alongside the paper's high coverage of terrorists' motives. The Toronto paper's attention to motive reflects the country's tendencies to liberal internationalism in foreign policy while its pejorative labeling reflects the country's traditional commitment to lawfulness, as reflected for example in Ottawa's obligation under the Canadian constitution to provide "peace, order, and good government." In sum, the *Globe*'s treatment of terrorism can be characterized as highly ambivalent, reflecting elements of ambivalence in Canadian political culture as well as in the Progressive Conservative party, which the paper tends to embrace editorially.

The *New York Times*'s comparative avoidance of negative labeling is better understood in terms of American domestic politics than in terms of U.S. foreign policy. The newspaper and the local audience it serves are among the most ideologically liberal in the United States. Eastern seaboard liberals often see themselves as embattled defenders of liberal internationalism in a sea of xenophobic countrymen. In their moderate use of negative labeling, *New York Times* staff may have been motivated by a concern that jingoistic and chauvinist strains in American society can whet the nation's appetite for adventurism in foreign policy. Thus, for the journalists of the *New York Times*, the anti-American animus of the Communist and third worlds may have been a negative reference, but a negative reference point of less pressing importance than the anti-Communist, anti-third world animus of a nativist America.

While the *New York Times* may have seen its mission as tempering a strain of anti-Soviet or anti-third world chauvinism among fellow countrymen, the *Globe* was more apt to see its mission as tempering a strain of anti-Americanism among Canadians. Indeed, during the fierce 1988 federal election debate about the merits of the Free Trade Accord with the United States, the *Globe* became the leading media protagonist of the American economic link, perhaps the only such protagonist in English Canada.

To this point, we have suggested that the *New York Times* is characterized by a somewhat greater ethno-cultural and/or political liberalism, as reflected in its lesser overall proclivity for negative labelling of terrorists. The section that follows provides evidence of the New York paper's liberalism in the pattern of its positive and negative labeling.

Who and What is Labeled

Any chauvinistic paper might be expected to praise terrorists who share its worldview and condemn those who do not. As documented in Table 7.3, the West German, French, and Egyptian papers fit this mold well. For each paper, Table 7.3 identifies the terrorist group, location, type of action, and target most apt to elicit negative, neutral, and positive labels. As shown in the table, *Le Figaro* uses negative labels to describe French terrorists 58% of the time, more often than in the case of any other group. In the same paper, Spanish terrorists elicit neutral labels more often than other groups (58% of the time) while anti-Castro Cuban terrorists earn positive labels (52% of the time) more frequently than others. The *Frankfurter Allgemeine Zeitung* likewise condemns German terrorists and praises Cubans. *Al Aharam* uses positive labels in reporting the terrorist actions of Palestinians, some of whose goals are shared by Egypt. Meanwhile the Egyptian paper uses negative labels to describe other Middle Eastern terrorists, who pose a threat to the stability of the region of which Egypt is leader and also potentially to the Egyptian regime itself (see Table 7.3).

The two British papers reveal a pattern of labeling somewhat consistent with the analysis provided earlier of their general orientation. More quasi-American, the *Daily Telegraph* emphasizes the negative aspects of Palestinians and the positive aspects of anti-Castro Cubans. Meanwhile, the *Times* of London retains its toryish imperial strain, targeting Spanish terrorists for negative labeling and Armenians for positive labeling.

Canada's *Globe and Mail* persists in its middle-of-the-road North American portrait of terrorism while the *New York Times* displays its proclivity for liberal internationalism. The *Globe* is most apt to label negatively Middle Eastern terrorists while the New York paper singles out Spanish terrorists. The *Globe*'s most favored terrorists are Cubans while that privileged position is occupied by Armenians in the case of the *New York Times*.

Table 7.3 Predictors of Negative, Neutral, and Positive Labels: Probabilities for Terrorist Groups, Forms of Action, Targets, and Continents

Negative	NYT	GM	TL	DT	FI
Group	Sp (.43)	ME (.60)	Sp (.67)	Pal (.50)	Fr (.58)
Action	Kid (.43)	Kid (.60)	Kid (.49)	Assn (60)	Kid (.51)
Target	Air (.35)	Air (.59)	Air (.44)	Govt (.59)	Air (.52)
Locus	Afr (.80)	Afr (.83)	Afr (.70)	Asia (.58)	Asia (.56)
Neutral					
Group	LA (.54)	LA (.40)	LA (.47)	Cubn(.50)	Sp (.56)
Action	Thrt (.75)	Thrt (.80)	Thrt (.75)	Hijk (.44)	Thrt (.50)
Target	Unkn (.6)	Busi (.41)	Reli (.75)	Air (.47)	Unkn (.50)
Locus	LA (.53)	LA (.34)	LA (.41)	NA (.50)	Afr (.36)
Positive					
Group	Arm (.60)	Cubn (.53)	Arm (.62)	Cubn (.40	Cubn (.52)
Action	Thrt (.25)	Bomb (.35)	Thrt (.22)	Bomb (.36)	Thrt (.50)
Target	Govt (.33)	Unkn (.80)	Unkn (.50)	Mil (.60)	Mil (.44)
Locus	Eur (.26)	NA (.40)	NA (.30)	Afr (.28)	NA (.49)

Negative	FR	YD	AA	PK
Group	Ger (.63)	Sp (.60)	ME (.40)	Unkn (.29)
Action	Hija (.53)	Kid (.47)	Hija (.32)	Assn (.42)
Target	Air (.58)	govt (.54)	Citz (.50)	Dipl (.29)
Locus	Afr (.80)	ME (.53)	ME (.30)	LA (.25)
Neutral				
Group	Arm (.71)	LA (.56)	LA (.50)	LA (.48)
Action	Bomb (.32)	Thrt (.30)	Kid (.40)	Kid (.40)
Target	Unkn (.50)	Unkn (.50)	Govt (.50)	Govt (.50)
Locus	LA (.42)	LA (.60)	LA (.44)	Afr (.75)
Positive				
Group	Cubn (.54)	Arm (.42)	Pal (.71)	Arm (.67)
Action	Thrt (.75)	Thrt (.28)	Thrt (.80)	Bomb (.69)
Target	Mil (.36)	Unkn (.50)	Busi (.67)	Mil (.57)
Locus	NA (.41)	Afr (.44)	Afr (.77)	NA (.73)

Key: Arm=Armenian; Fr=French; Sp=Spanish; LA=Latin American; NA=North American; ME=Middle Eastern; Pal=Palestinian; Thrt=threat; Hija=hijacking; Kid=kidnapping; Assn=assassination; Unkn=unknown; Reli=religious; Busi=business; Mil=military; Citz=private citizen; Dipl=diplomat.

Tel Aviv's *Yediot* is most apt to assign negative labels to Spanish terrorists and positive labels to Armenians. The source of the Israeli paper's especially negative portrayal of Spanish terrorists is unclear to us. The choice of Armenians as virtuous is too easy to explain. On the one hand, for the sample of media as a whole, Armenians share primacy of favor with the Cubans. Thus, there is no particular reason to explain the Israeli paper's proclivity for the Armenians. On the other hand, post-Holocaust Israelis and Jews are frequently well disposed to the Armenian cause in part because they are aware of the parallel Hitler saw between the world's acquiescence to the Turkish massacres of Armenians and his own anticipated freedom of action.

The actual conduct of Armenian terrorists cannot be said to be a direct cause of the favorable press treatment provided by a number of newspapers because the actions of the Armenian terrorists were especially gruesome. Yet, Armenian terrorists' brutality may be an indirect cause or catalyst for the media's favorable labeling. By their brutality, the Armenians incited the press to focus on their proclaimed concerns. The Armenians' leitmotif, the Turkish genocide, aroused sympathy because of its moral clarity. The Armenians' leitmotif entailed neither class struggle nor institutional devolution of authority nor boundary dispute and rectification: it was a matter of life.

For the sample of newspapers as a whole, there is a considerable consensus about *neutral* acts of terrorism. Threats against unknown targets by Latin American terrorists and/or on Latin American soil are the most apt to be treated with equanimity in the press. This portrait of equanimity in labeling is consistent with the empirical findings, reported in earlier chapters, of a general disposition of the press to downplay terrorist events on the predominantly Spanish-speaking continent.

For the sample of newspapers as a whole, there is a moderate agreement about *positively labeled* acts of terrorism. Threats against military or unknown targets by Armenians or Cubans are the attributes of events that are most apt to be portrayed in a kindly light. Thus, actions are apt to be labeled positively when noncombatants are not targeted and when the perpetrators are thought to have some moral authority, in one case by virtue of a past genocide and in the other by virtue of opposition to dictatorship.

The world press in our sample are least agreed with respect to negative labeling. Spanish, Middle Eastern, Palestinian, French, German, Spanish, and "unknown" terrorists each lead in the negative labeling category in at least one newspaper. If the press agrees on any negative aspect of terrorism, it is the form of the violence. For seven of nine newspapers, kidnapping and the closely related phenomenon of hijacking are the most negatively perceived acts. Once again, the press implicitly abides by a moral order in which the canons of combat prohibit assaults on noncombatants.

The Special Role of the "Stockholm Syndrome"

To this point in the chapter, we have highlighted the willingness of the press to accommodate terrorists' causes either by providing quasi-apologetic sociological explanations or by providing news coverage with only a limited amount of negative labeling. The Stockholm syndrome is another, albeit extreme, method for terrorists to acquire influence over the way in which the media portray their activities.

The Stockholm syndrome is a concept used to describe the views and pronouncements of kidnap victims who have been brainwashed under the duress of terrorist captivity. The term *brainwashing* has its roots in a Mandarin Chinese concept of the possibility of changing a person's basic convictions and attitudes through a course of intensive indoctrination. The term entered the popular lexicon in the wake of the experience of American soldiers captured during the Korean War.

The concept of a "Stockholm syndrome" entered the popular lexicon in the wake of a protracted bank robbery in Sweden's capital in August 1973. The event gained lasting notoriety because of intensive media attention and because of the psychological transformation of the hostages held captive by the robbers over a five- day period. The transformation of the hostages took place in captivity and persisted even upon rescue. During captivity, one of the hostages asserted in a telephone call to the prime minister that "the robbers are protecting us from the police." For some time after their release, a number of the kidnap victims harbored especially warm feelings toward their erstwhile captors. One puzzled victim wondered, "Is there something wrong with me? Why don't I hate them [the robbers]?"[15]

Perhaps the best-known case of the Stockholm syndrome involved a domestic American example of terrorism. California newspaper heiress

15   D. Lang, "A Reporter at Large," *The New Yorker* (Nov. 24, 1974), 118.

Patricia Hearst learned to identify with her Symbionese Army kidnappers, embracing the group's "revolutionary goals," and actively participating in the group's schedule of armed and violent robberies.[16] However, the Stockholm syndrome has been manifested in international terrorism as well.

In the case of the Croatian hijacking of a TWA flight from New York in September 1976, many of the innocent passengers grew deeply sympathetic to the kidnappers and their cause. At episode's end, some of the victims proclaimed that they would take leave from their jobs to attend the terrorists' trial while others undertook fundraising for the terrorists' defense. One of the hijack victims portrayed the emotional complexity of the situation in the following words:

> After it was over and we were safe I recognized that they had put me through hell, and had caused my parents and fiance a great deal of trauma. Yet, I was alive. I was alive because they let me live. You know a few people, if any, who hold your life in their hands and give it back to you. After it was over, and we were safe and they were in handcuffs, I walked over to them and kissed each one of them and said "Thank you for giving my life back." I know how foolish it sounds, but that is how I felt.[17]

A Stockholm syndrome-like change took place among some Jewish passengers on the Air France flight hijacked by German and Palestinian terrorists to Entebbe airport in Uganda in July 1976. After liberation by Israeli commandoes, one passenger told the press that he had conversed at length with a German terrorist, who had been deeply moved on learning the significance of the death camp number tattooed on the passenger's arm. The kidnapper, declared the victim, became more solicitous and, during the rescue operation, fired on the commandoes rather than the hostages.[18]

Scholars have proposed a variety of theories to account for the profound transformations involved. Anna Freud wrote about the victim's identifica-

---

16 For discussions of many of the broad issues relating to terrorists' victimization, see F. Ochberg and D. Soskis, eds., *Victims of Terrorism* (Boulder, Colo.: Westview Press, 1982), *passim*.

17 See T. Strentz, "The Stockholm Syndrome: Law Enforcement Policy and Hostage Behavior," in ibid.

18 W. Stevenson, *90 Minutes at Entebbe* (New York: Bantam Books, 1976), 116. The Hanafi Muslim siege in Washington, D.C. engendered predictably positive feelings among the hostages. A number of them opined that they had been treated fairly.

tion with the aggressor as a psychological defense mechanism triggered in a state of intense anxiety.[19] Other scholars have written about a process of introjection, whereby victims embrace the values of the persecutor as a means of avoiding punishment.[20]

Terrorist kidnappings often entail the killing of some hostages or the use of some other palpable punishment, but the threat of punishment is sometimes subtle rather than heavy-handed. Fear itself may not be the only stimulus for victims to identify with their aggressors. The intensely personal and psychologically intimate relationship between aggressor and victim is another factor. Victims may learn to identify with their captors even if and/or because they do not themselves experience beatings, rape, or torture. Hostage-takers emphasize that they "have nothing against the hostages personally."[21] Close contact begets a realization that the terrorist is a simple human being. "Stockholm syndrome victims," observes a specialist in the subject, "...sense and identify with the human quality of their captors."[22]

The contrived character of the captors' "human quality" may not be readily apparent to either the victims or the news media who subsequently report their story. In their own theatrical script, the terrorists often formulate "good cop" and "bad cop" roles for their participants. Their intention is for the victims to develop an emotional bond with the conciliatory kidnappers by way of reaction against their more brutal captors.

T. Strentz, an expert on the subject, has written at some length about the ambivalent feelings of Stockholm victims. In discussing the Hanafi incident, he noted that "those hostages who gave glowing accounts of the gentlemanly conduct of some subjects did not generalize to all subjects. They evidenced dislike, even hatred, toward one hostage-taker whom they called an *animal.*"[23]

---

19 *The Ego and the Mechanisms of Defence* (New York: International University Press, 1974).
20 Strentz, "The Stockholm Syndrome," 159.
21 L. Eitinger, "The Effects of Captivity," in Ochberg and Soskis, *Victims of Terrorism.*
22 ibid., 157.
23 Strentz, "The Stockholm Syndrome," 12.

The phenomenon of the Stockholm syndrome would have little bearing on the relationship of terror and the media if it were not for the vulnerability of the media to the terrorist orchestration of events in kidnap settings. Journalists can succumb to the Stockholm syndrome when they are in captivity. They can also succumb indirectly to the Stockholm syndrome by becoming unreflective channels for the views of terrorists that emerge from the mouths of those traumatized victims who are not themselves journalists.

Many newspapermen have experienced kidnappings, death threats, and actual assassination at the hands of terrorists. The impact of intimidation on journalism is a broad and important subject, but beyond the boundaries of this book.[24] The first and less important point which we would make is that journalists themselves are not immune to Stockholm syndrome personality transformations. The second and more important point, to which we shall return below, is that journalists have often done an inadequate job of reporting the Stockholm-like experiences of others.

Gerard Vaders was a Dutch newspaper editor aboard a train bound for Amsterdam in December 1975, when it was commandeered by masked gunmen calling themselves the Free South Moluccan Youth Movement. Their list of demands included their homeland's independence from Indonesia, the release of ostensible political prisoners from Indonesian and Dutch jails, and safe passage for themselves. Vaders wrote extensively about the experience. After one hostage was taken away for execution, he recalled:

> When they came back I saw at least two of the three had tears in their eyes. One of them, whom I later got to know as Paul, had a sensitive and intelligent face. He asked, "Can you understand us, sir?...We don't hate you, but we have no choices. The Bible says there is a time to kill. The time has come."...Another young man who was called Djerrit said, "How can I hate you? My wife is Dutch." We found out later that this was a lie. They must have wanted us to like them.[25]

In his extensive reporting on the 12-day episode, the Dutch newspaperman wrote about the growing compassion that he felt for the Moluccan terrorists. Vaders and his fellow captives realized that the terrorists were

---

24 For a recent overview, see Robert G. Picard, "Journalists as Targets and Victims of Terrorism," in Yonah Alexander and Robert G. Picard, eds., *In the Camera's Eye* (New York: Brassey's, 1991). On the implications of threats for reporting, see David Bar-Illan, "Israel, the Hostages and the Networks," *Commentary* (Sept. 1985), 33-37, esp. 37.

25 Frank Ochberg, "A Case Study: Gerard Vaders," in *Victims of Terrorism*, 13.

killers but "you try to suppress it in your consciousness. And I knew I was suppressing that. I also knew that they were victims, too. In the long run they would be as much victims as we."

After liberation, Vaders became a vigorous critic of his government's handling of the episode, but his criticism was looked at askance by some of his fellow countrymen. Vaders, some felt, had fallen victim to the Stockholm syndrome. One particular threat to the integrity of his personality arose, it was said, from his 11th-hour success in persuading his captors not to execute him. After an emotional debate over whether to spare him, his kidnappers sent him away with the declaration "We have others to kill."[26]

The main value of tracing the outlines of Dutch editor Gerard Vaders's experience lies in illustrating the vulnerability to the Stockholm syndrome of even newsmen. But journalists are not the only victims of terrorist kidnappings. The dangers for the media in a democratic society arise less from the brainwashing of newsmen held in captivity than when the free media gullibly accept the verisimilitude of the pronouncements of terrorists and their victims in Stockholm-like situations.

Media treatment of the TWA hijacking to Beirut in the summer of 1985 illustrates many of the difficulties of the media when confronting Stockholm-like situations. As in the case of other highly threatening kidnappings and hijackings, the hostages developed enormous empathy with as well as considerable sympathy for their captors.

Upon his release, TWA pilot Testrake described his feelings this way:

> We were involved on a daily intimate basis with these people. We got to observe them on a human basis as differently from a political basis. It was a sort of a split personality thing. On the one hand they had us prisoner....But they were continually exhibiting small kindnesses to us which, of course, is, I grant you, an exact opposite of their cruelty, their murderous intentions and so on. But yet they were thoughtful toward us, they did bring us little special things. Any time there was a picture of one of us in the paper, boy, we got it quicker than you folks did almost. So this exhibits their interest in us, their concern for us. And this was on a human basis so when they would bring us things like this, we appreciated it. We could see then that these people have just the same

26   Ibid., 17.

hopes and aspirations that we all do. They hurt for their country, they see that their country is prostrate and bleeding, that they're really in almost a hopeless situation. And yet they're people just like we are....We empathized with that aspect of it, it's a purely human thing.[27]

The emotional bonds developed between captive and captor would provide the terrorists with a harvest of propaganda benefits. The Shia captors' initial pronouncement called for the release of their fellow Shia terrorists imprisoned in Kuwait, Greece, Spain, and Israel as well as sundry political changes including the reversal of United States policy in the Middle East. The initial panoply of demands was pared to a single simple theme once the Shia leadership grasped the communications advantages of doing so. The single simple theme was a quid pro quo exchange of the TWA captives for 700 Lebanese detainees in Israeli prisons.

The Shia drew an exact parallel between the two groups, calling both hostages. The TWA hostages obligingly repeated the theme, particularly through the person of Allyn Conwell. Conwell, an oil company salesman based in Oman, became the hostages' spokesperson because he was the terrorists' choice, one of a number of finer points largely omitted in media reports.[28] Conwell declared, "If my wife and children were abducted and taken illegally across the border, I guess, I, too, would have resorted to anything at all to free them."[29]

Both Conwell's rhetoric and the media's uncritical acceptance of it likely exceeded the terrorists' expectations. Other hostages and the Western media repeated the terrorists' portrayal of moral symmetry between Arab hijackers and the Israeli military. In fact, all of the detainees in Israel were Shia fighters captured in attacks on Israeli targets; none were women or children. Their capture and imprisonment were lawful. Unlike the fate of the TWA passengers and crew, none of the detainees in Israel had reason to fear impromptu execution.

---

27 Citations from the TWA episode are drawn from D. Bar-Illan, "Israel, the Hostages and the Networks," *Commentary* (1985), 33-37; "Excerpts from News Conference of TWA Crew," *New York Times* (July 4, 1985), 7; and "Transcript of News Conference Held by Freed Hostages in Syrian Capital," *New York Times* (July 1, 1985), 7.
28 For a discussion of other points missed in U.S. coverage, see the articles in the September 21, 1985 issue of *T.V. Guide*.
29 See note 27.

The victims' assimilation of the terrorists' view of the world persisted for some time following their liberation. For example, freed copilot Maresca observed to a press conference afterward that the detainees in Israel "were hostages in every sense of the word, just as we were, and since we were hostages we knew what the life was like and we have empathy for those people and we wanted them released just as quickly as we."[30] Freed hostage Robert Trautmann, Jr., emphasized that the hostages had all been treated "well" and that the terrorists "like the [American] people...it's the government they object to." Freed spokesperson Conwell warned against "any retaliation or revenge...I think we all need to find a deeper understanding of the circumstances that led up to people taking a desperate act."[31]

As in other terrorist kidnappings, the Shia prepared a script that called for the pretense of a conflict between moderates and hardliners, with hardliners guilty of brutality and moderates responsible for negotiation and conciliation. The hostages succumbed to the deception that the killers who commandeered the aircraft were unconnected to the gunmen who assumed authority on the ground, that Shia leader Nabih Berri was an honest broker seeking to moderate the gunmen, and that Syrian President Assad was a potential and then an actual savior.

As Bar-Illan notes, the media succumbed to these deceptions as well:

> During the entire crisis, the networks faithfully adhered to another bit of Shia fiction: that the only "bad guys" were the first two hijackers who killed Navy diver Robert Stethem, that the dozen reinforcements who took over on the second Beirut stop were much more moderate and civilized, and that the Amal militiamen who removed the hostages from the plane and guarded them until their release were kind, gentle, and considerate saviors. It was one thing to hear such naive nonsense from the hostages, who, after witnessing a murder and expecting to be murdered themselves, would naturally consider anyone who did not kill them a savior; it was another thing to hear it from presumably impartial and free agents.[32]

In fact, observes the author, the Shia reinforcements belonged to the same unit as the gunmen who had commandeered the flight and worked closely with them throughout the ordeal.

The Western media portrayed Shia leader Nabih Berri as a humane peace-seeking broker who abhorred violence but comprehended the frustrations that drove the terrorists to do what they did. Berri relished the

---

30   See note 27.
31   See the September 21, 1985 issue of *T.V. Guide*.
32   Bar-Illan, "Israel, the Hostages, and the Networks," *Commentary* (Sept. 1985), 35.

role, which called for him to pull the hostages from the clutches of "extremists" just in the nick of time. Adhering to the Shia script, the media portrayed Syrian President Assad as a good guy working independently of Berri's Amal to see what he could do to win the freedom of the hostages.

"What the networks did not deem worthy of telling their viewers," notes Bar-Ilan, "was that Berri had been responsible for *eight* hijackings before the TWA incident; that he had called for suicide attacks on the withdrawing Israeli army; that he personally commanded the Amal militia, which had mercilessly slaughtered Palestinian women and children in Sabra and Shatila; that during the hostage crisis his militiamen killed two Palestinian nurses who had stumbled on the hostages' hiding place; and that neither Amal nor any other armed group could make a major move in Lebanon without Syrian approval."[33]

At the press conference immediately after the TWA passengers and crew were released, Allyn Conwell, who had been chosen by the Shia as the hostages' spokesperson, addressed words of praise to the Syrians:

> We do indeed wish to take this opportunity to thank President Assad and all of the people in Syria for the part they played in gaining our freedom. We are sure, without their assistance, without their help, without their concern over our welfare, we would undoubtedly still be in Beirut with an uncertain future. So for them I give a hand.[34]

One of the minority of passengers who had resisted the Stockholm syndrome effect was Peter Hill. Hill quickly insisted that all the various groups had collaborated in a charade. For this, spokesman Allyn Conwell called him emotionally unstable and a racist. Two years later the press began to reveal a number of the elements of President Assad's complicity in the events.

33   Ibid., 36.
34   See note 27.

Chapter 8

The Contagion Effect

Media Violence and Contagion

From the origins of history, keen analysts of the human condition have noted the impact of unusual behavior upon those who are proximate enough to observe and susceptible enough to imitate it. Plato, who was alert to the impact of emulation, advocated isolating children from potentially harmful role models, including their own parents, as a precondition for imbuing a new generation of citizens with exceptional reasoning and moral capabilities.

Against Plato's sensitivity to the importance of nurture there has always been a contending school of thought that placed its emphasis on nature or genetics as the principal explanation for human behavior. In some fields of scholarship, notably the inchoate field of criminology, the *nature* school tended to hold sway, at least until the nineteenth century.

A hundred years ago, scholars began to experience a shift in how they understood the roots of criminal behavior. A major factor in the changed perspective was the increasingly visible influence of the new penny press and other innovations in telecommunications. Thanks to the penny press and the telegraph upon which its existence depended, extraordinary criminal and other behaviors could become known to an exceptionally wide audience capable of replication. Sociologists gradually became less comfortable with the idea of genetic inheritance as an explanation for crime, proffering instead the concept of imitative behavior.

Leading the assault on genetic explanation, French sociologist Gabriel Tarde postulated the concept of "suggestive-imitative" assaults to account for the link between a single sensational incident and a series of similar crimes patterned on it. For Tarde, the "Jack the Ripper" murders became an archetype of the great act of villainy that arouses intense public interest and spawns imitators as a result. In the "Jack the Ripper" case, eight identical homicides were committed within London itself and many others outside Britain's capital and across the channel. "Epidemics of crime," noted the French sociologist and criminologist, "follow the line of the telegraph."[1]

The emergence of quantitative empirical sociology in the second half of the twentieth century has produced a great deal of evidence in support of Tarde's thesis that highly mediated crime becomes an archetype that inspires derivatives. It has been shown that rates of violent crime increase after the reporting of spectacular murders such as the assassination of President John F. Kennedy.[2] In an analogous fashion, well-publicized suicides of famous people engender higher rates of suicide among the general population. Well-publicized suicides are also followed by an increase in the rate of quasi-suicides, i.e., traffic accidents involving a single vehicle. Fictional, soap opera suicides produce a similar result. Meanwhile, homicide rates increase in the wake of widely covered championship fights.[3]

The evidence of media-inspired cloning is not limited to crimes that are personal or nonpolitical in nature. Thus evidence of contagion has emerged in studies of racial disturbances, threats against nuclear power systems, generalized political violence, and international terrorism.[4] The burden of evidence about telecommunications-induced crime is unequivocal. "Real and fictional depictions by the media of violence—killings, shootings, or suicide," observes a reviewer of the scholarly literature, "can prompt audience members to act aggressively towards others or themselves."[5]

---

1   G. Tarde, *Penal Philosophy* (Montclair, N.J.: Patterson Smith, 1912).

2   L. Berkovitz and J. Macaulay, "The Contagion of Criminal Violence," *Sociometry* 34 (1971), 238-60.

3   D. Phillips, "The Influence of Suggestion on Suicide," *American Sociological Review* 30 (1974) 39, 340-54, "Suicide Motor Vehicle Fatalities, and the Mass Media: Evidence Toward a Theory of Suggestion," *American Journal of Sociology* 84 (1979), 1150-74, "The Impact of Fictional Television Stories on U.S. Adult Fatalities: New Evidence on the Impact of Mass Media on Violence," *American Journal of Sociology* 87 (1982), 1340-59, and "The Impact of Mass Media Violence on U.S. Homicides," *American Sociological Review* 48 (1983), 407-11.

4   A. Mazur, "Bomb Threats and the Mass Media: Evidence for a Theory of Suggestion," *American Sociological Review* 47 (1982), 407-11; S. Spilerman, "The Causes of Racial Disturbance: A Comparison of Alternative Explanations," *American Sociological Review* 35 (1970), 627-49; and R. J. Hamblin et al, *A Mathematical Theory of Social Change* (New York: Wiley-Interscience, 1973).

5   L. Berkovitz, "Some Effects of Thoughts on Anti- and Prosocial Influences of Media Events," *Psychological Bulletin* 95 (3)(1984), 410-27.

The contagion effect of mediated violence can be explained from a psychodynamic or attitudinal perspective as well as from a cognitive perspective. With respect to attitude, two complementary concepts are available—an *arousal* hypothesis and a *disinhibition* hypothesis. According to the logic of arousal, violence begets violence by exciting the spectator. The complementary disinhibition perspective holds that the spectator's conscience or inhibition is weakened by exposure to violence, especially if violence is cast by the media in a favorable light.

Indeed, it is arguable that most mediated violence possesses a favorable aspect. Coverage in and of itself may entail a positive evaluation of violence simply because it provides recognition and status conferral. The style of media coverage may in turn downplay the baneful aspect of violence.

Acts of violence normally consist of two actional elements—the aggression itself and the consequent suffering. The aggression itself normally receives far more attention on television and in the press than the consequent anguish. Indeed, coverage given the grief of victims is often dwarfed by coverage accorded the ostensible idealism of the victimizers. Schmid and de Graaf take the view that the media's downplaying of sorrow reflects a combination of technological and cultural considerations peculiar to the mass media:

> In violence portrayals in the media, emphasis is put on...[aggression] while...[grief] is largely neglected. This is done for two reasons. One is that the aftermath of violence is long and the act of violence, short. Given the time constraints which govern media programming it is logical that the long sufferings of the victim, the weeks in hospital, cannot be covered adequately while a shooting or stabbing takes only seconds to depict. The second reason for this imbalance between aggression and suffering is that showing the agony of the victim is unaesthetic and upsetting to the audience.[6]

To the extent that the media's containment of grief truly results from aesthetic considerations, it is a situation of life imitating art. Producers of TV news and editors of newspapers who feel uncomfortable transmitting anguish may be influenced by the virtual absence of sorrow scripted into the hundreds of thousands of murders portrayed on prime time serial television.

Of course, the containment of anguish in media reports of terrorist violence may not be the fruit of aesthetic considerations alone. As patriotic

6   A. Schmid and J. de Graaf, *Violence as Communication* (Beverly Hills, Calif.: Sage, 1982), 119.

citizens, television and print journalists are often receptive to the conceptions of national interest adumbrated by foreign policy officials and elected
politicians. Makers of foreign policy are mindful of the dangers to their
country's national security and to their government's domestic political
position as a result of lachrymose coverage. Mournful media reports may
arouse a populace to demand instant retaliation. Governments may feel
obliged to choose between hasty military action on the one hand and
electoral disenchantment with their governance on the other. Prudent
foreign policy-makers may caution the media against highlighting bereave-
ment. By so doing, policymakers may contribute inadvertently to the
success of the media-motivated terrorism that they would like to suppress.

Whatever the reasons for the relative absence of mediated grief, its
absence may affect the perspectives of audiences. The American television
system and those many national television systems that depend on U.S.
program producers for their content are awash in violent entertainment
and news programming. The relative inattention of television to victim as
compared to aggressor does not make it easier for viewers to comprehend
anguish. Insulated from the moral and emotional facets of human sorrow,
viewers may come to feel that violence is an inevitable element of daily life.[7]
Habituation and desensitization to violence may facilitate the process of
contagion.

Habituation is nonetheless not the only contributor to contagion. Cogni-
tion plays a role too. *Social learning theory* is said to help account for
contagion because potential perpetrators of violence may model themselves
upon aggressors portrayed in the media, replicate their specific acts of
aggression, and embrace their proclaimed justifications. Phillips is a major
proponent of "social learning theory" as a means of understanding mediated
contagion. He argues persuasively that mediated violence inspires duplica-
tion. From his extensive survey of the scholarly literature, he concludes
that "the effect of imitation, suggestion, and modelling has also been
extensively documented...there have been more than 2,300 studies on this
topic."[8]

---

7   For a classic overview of the evidence on television violence, see the U.S. Surgeon
     General's Advisory Committee on Television and Violence, *Television and Growing
     Up: The Impact of Televised Violence* (Washington: Government Printing Office, 1972).
8   D. Phillips, "Suicide, Motor Vehicle Fatalities...toward a Theory of Suggestion," 1151.

In their study of violence and communication, Schmid and de Graaf present many examples of aggression learned from the media. One memorable example involves an extortionist hijacker who called himself "D. B. Cooper." Cooper parachuted from his commandeered aircraft with $200,000 in cash and three extra parachutes, never to be seen again. The subject of a feature film, Cooper became virtually a folk hero as a result of his antics. Indeed, he inspired more than two dozen would-be imitators, each of whom hijacked an aircraft, demanded cash, and requisitioned extra parachutes.[9]

D. B. Cooper's emulators were not habitual criminals and few, if any, had a previous record of hijacking. But media reports of Cooper's exploits furnished psychologically maladjusted and/or financially desperate would-be mimics with a recipe for resolving their personal angst.

The Contagion of Terrorism

The process of emulation that accounts for the emergence of would-be Cooper mimics also applies to terrorist hijackings and other violent acts that have an apparently political foundation. As in D. B. Cooper's case, media reporting of terrorist malfeasance tantalizes would-be emulators with the promise of recognition, reward, and release. The processes of terrorist and criminal emulation are nonetheless different from each other in scope and magnitude.

The wider coverage afforded terrorism makes it possible for the details of terrorist exploits to touch audiences of tens and hundreds of millions of people. The quasi-global reach of media-motivated terrorism necessarily encompasses large numbers of maladjusted individuals, receptive to ideas about how they might act out their malaise on a stage far grander than that of their family or neighborhood. One expert in the field of terrorism has described the nexus between media coverage of terrorism and psychopathology in the following terms:

> Typical reporting of a terrorist event here in the United States might reach an audience of, say, conservatively, forty million people. What's the chance that may come to the attention of some borderline psychopath who may be stimulated to take part in some future episode? If we were to consider that just

9   *Violence as Communication,* 122-37.

one-tenth of one percent of the audience were borderline psychopaths, that would be forty thousand potential maniacs. If we took one-thousandth of one percent we've still got four hundred. If we took one-hundred-thousandth of one percent, we would still have the four that are necessary to carry out a typical terrorist episode.[10]

The concept of psychopathology as an important factor in politics lacks the cachet among social scientists that it possessed in the post-World War II period. During the late 1940s and early 1950s, a consensus united North American scholars with respect to the macabre character of the Third Reich under Hitler and Soviet totalitarianism under Stalin. Social scientists' certainty about the merits of Western democracy and the evil nature of the main contending regimes helped fashion a climate of academic opinion in which individual and/or global acts of violence could be accounted for in terms of psychopathology. Psychological tools were used to understand individual tyrants such as Hitler and Stalin as well as authoritarian cultures such as that of Imperial Japan.

During the 1960s, psychological explanations of politics waned. Scholars became diffident about accounting for the violent repudiation of Western democratic institutions in terms of psychopathology or psychological dynamics. The decline of psychological explanations of politics coincided with the diminished confidence of Western scholars in the effectiveness of Western institutions and scholars' heightened desire to cast nonjudgmental eyes on non-Western institutions. The academic world's growing preference for economic or sociological explanations of alienation from the West over psychological explanations reflected a desire to treat non-Western and anti-Western perspectives more respectfully.

The desire of scholars to treat non-Western perspectives less pejoratively is meritorious on both scholarly and ideological grounds. And yet, psychopathology remains a serious phenomenon that needs to be addressed. Millions of people do harbor irrational, unfounded, and potentially destructive ideas about their own place in the universe. The World Health Organization estimates that 10 percent of the planet's population is mentally ill. Terrorist exploits that are broadcast to a quasi-global audience of, say, 500 million people necessarily reach a large reservoir of suggestible, maladjusted people. As Schmid and de Graaf observe,

---

10   Michael T. McEwan, cited in Y. Alexander, "The Media and Terrorism" in D. Carlton and C. Scaerf, eds., *Contemporary Terror* (London: Macmillan, 1981), 55.

> A lunatic fringe of 10 percent is in such a context an awful lot of people. Many of them might already have lost the inhibition against acting violently, others might also have a personal motive to do so, some have both and all that is needed is a model which they can copy. The media can provide it.[11]

The suggestiveness of mediated terrorism operates on the minds not merely of the maladjusted but also on the minds of the relatively normal. Sane people may see the terrorist model as a plausible outlet for their sense of rational grievance. For suggestive normal people, mediated terrorism disseminates the precedence of violence and reinforces the sense of righteous anger. After the Hanafi incident in Washington D.C., Yale professor of psychiatry R. J. Lifton observed that when the press makes "the person of the terrorist something close to the total news of the week, the imagery of terrorism becomes much more active psychologically for the average person. Therefore it must contribute to stimulating similar acts among people who feel frustrated and other avenues are closed."[12]

In the absence of extensive and elaborate survey research, Professor Lifton's proposition about the impact of terrorist reporting on otherwise normal people must be treated as a very plausible hypothesis awaiting empirical confirmation. The impact of mediated terrorism on the terrorists themselves requires little verification; it has been amply documented in the case histories of terrorists. Horst Mahler, one of the founders of the German Red Army Faction, recalled years later how television newscasts had triggered the "shock...[which led to] self-liberation...[and]the basis for the RAF ideology."[13] Several biographical studies of terrorists showed that many were motivated by a desire to emulate the publicity achievements of

---

11 *Violence as Communication*, 125.
12 *New York Times* (March 19, 1977).
13 Interview in *De Groene Amsterdammer* (September 5, 1979), quoted in Schmid and de Graaf, *Violence*, 138.

their precursors. Hijackers, notes the author of a book devoted to the phenomenon, often interpret media reports of hijackings as "instructions from God to go and do likewise."[14]

The accumulating empirical evidence pointing to terror as a contagion and the role of the media as the agent of dispersal is not limited to or based primarily on biographical anecdotes. Strong evidence emerges from quantitative studies of waves of terrorism.[15] Skyjacking received its first main impetus from the seizure of an El Al aircraft by Palestinians in the summer of 1968. A wave of hijackings followed shortly thereafter.[16] Many academic and journalistic observers wrote about a *skyjack virus* transmitted through the media and underscored the role of mass communications as a catalyst of contagion.[17] A statistical analysis was undertaken of skyjacking within the United States over the period 1968-1972. Holden distinguished between those undertaken strictly for transportation (N=111) and those planned with extortion in mind (N=26). The author of the study found that each successful transportation-motivated hijacking generated an average of .758 emulative attempts with a median delay of 60.6 days. Meanwhile each extortion-motivated hijacking was followed by an average of as many as 2.014 attempts with a median delay of only 44.8 days. Altogether, the contagion effect accounted for 53% of transportation-motivated hijackings and as many as 85% of hijackings with extortion as the leitmotif. "The results tend to support the common belief," concluded Holden, "that hijacking spreads as a result of publicity."[18]

The passages that follow seek to build upon Holden's intriguing analysis. Our data analysis has the advantage of involving

14   D. G. Hubbard, cited in Schmid and de Graaf, *Violence and Communication*, 140. See also Hubbard, *The Skyjacker: His Flights of Fantasy* (New York: Macmillan, 1971) and F. J. Hacker, "Contagion and Attraction of Terror and Terrorism," in Y. Alexander and J. M. Gleason, eds., *Behavioral and Quantitative Perspectives on Terrorism* (New York: Pergamon Press, 1981), 73-85.

15   See G. Weimann and H. B. Brosius, "The Predictability of International Terrorism: A Time-Series Analysis, *Terrorism* 11 (1989), 491-502.

16   Consider, for example, Bandura's study of hijackings in the 1947-1970 period as reported in L. Berkovitz, *A Survey of Social Psychology* (Hinsdale, Ill.: Dryden Press, 1975), 44.

17   C. Whelton, *Skyjack* (New York: Belmont/Tower, 1972). Also, E. Rich, *Flying Scared* (New York: Stein & Day, 1972), and *U.S. News and World Report* (February 17, 1968), 68.

18   R. T. Holden, "The Contagiousness of Aircraft Hijacking," *American Journal of Sociology* 91 (1986), 902.

- a longer time frame
- a conglomeration of different terrorist acts
- terrorist acts taking place anywhere
- press coverage in more than one country.

The wealth of our dataset permits a comparison of the effects of terrorist actions that are ignored by the media with the effects of those events that are covered. We are sympathetic to Holden's view that the contagion he observed did result from media coverage. But his dataset does not actually allow such an inference. The vast majority of hijackings in Holden's dataset were reported on American television, thereby making it difficult to contrast the rates of reproduction for mediated and nonmediated events.

Measuring Contagion by Means of Time Lags

The measurement of the media's role in contagion requires that the incidence of behaviors subject to contagion should be compared according to whether the initial suggestive assault did or did not receive media coverage. The actual contagious symptoms to be measured could vary. Thus, one could either compare the rates of *identical* terrorist behaviors or compare *all* terrorist behaviors. One could likewise compare the length of the time lag between the initial suggestive assault and its first emulation.

Figures 8.1, 8.2, 8.3, and 8.4 present the average time lag in days for terrorist events reported and not reported on each of the three commercial American networks. Time lags are present for all actions as well as for each of six main categories—kidnappings, attacks on installations, hijackings, bombings, barricades, and assassinations. Time lags are substantially shorter for terrorist events that are covered in the case of *all events* overall as well as in the case of five of the six specific categories. The sole exception is barricades, in which instance the time lag to first emulation is not shorter in a statistically significant sense.

The data portrayed in Figure 8.1 demonstrate that any terrorist event that secures network attention is apt to be followed by some form of terrorist action after a significantly shorter delay than would be the case without coverage. Between the years 1972 and 1980, the period for which our dataset contains television data, a total of 1,752 incidents of international terrorism took place. The time interval between these events, regardless of their character or target, is strongly related to their being reported by the American networks.

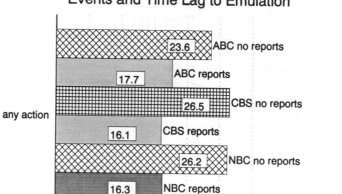

Figure 8.1 TV Coverage of Any Terrorist Events and Time Lag to Emulation

We know from data reported in earlier chapters that the American networks are highly intercorrelated in the types of terrorist acts that they report.[19] Hence, it may not be surprising to find that the time lags are similar across the three networks. For American network television as a whole, the average time lag after a reported event is 16.7 days as compared to 25.4 days in the case of an unreported event. Expressed somewhat differently, the lapse of time between an initial terrorist attack and its first emulation will be 52% longer if the U.S. networks choose not to mention it than if they do.

The impact of news coverage on time lags is stronger for specific types of action than for terrorism as a whole (Figures 8.2 to 8.4). The impact of news coverage on time lags is especially strong in the case of those types of action that are most apt to be reported, namely kidnappings, hijackings, and assassinations as opposed to bombings and attacks on installations. The average time lag for an unreported kidnapping is 50.3 days as compared

---

19 See Michael X. Delli Carpini and Bruce A. Williams, "Television and Terrorism: Patterns of Presentation and Occurrence, 1969 to 1980," *Western Political Quarterly* 40 (1987), 45-64.

Figure 8.2 TV Impact on Time Lags for Kidnapping and Attacks on Installation

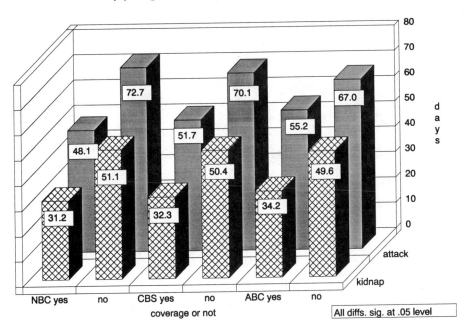

to 32.5 days for one that is reported. Corresponding time lags for hijackings are 72.3 and 34.6 days and for assassinations, 82.5 and 42.0 days, respectively. For hijackings and assassinations, it would appear that a decision to avoid coverage would virtually double the world's period of respite from a terrorist act's emulation. By the same token, a decision to cover would halve that period of respite.

The time lags for attacks on installations and bombings are shorter in the case of events reported on television, but not much shorter. In the case of barricades, television reporting is not associated statistically with shortened time lags.

The time lag analysis applied to television was replicated in the case of the press, albeit for a longer time period. In the case of press analysis, our dataset encompasses all 2,239 terrorist events recorded by the RAND Corporation for the 1968-1980 period. The data in Table 8.1 show that the

Figure 8.3 TV Impact on Time Lags for Hijackings and Bombings

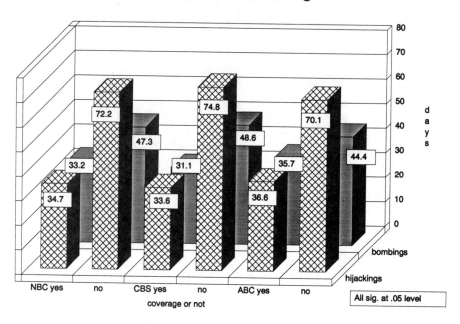

impact of *New York Times* coverage is similar in magnitude and structure to the impact of the networks. As in the case of television, the time lag between initial suggestive action and first emulation is significantly shorter for the category of *all acts* as well as for five of the six specific types. Thus, for all terrorist acts, the time lag falls from 27.2 days to 15.3 days if an event is covered. The time lag is especially affected in the case of assassinations and hijackings, somewhat less so in the case of kidnappings, and substantially less in the case of bombings and attacks on installations. In the specific instance of assassinations, a decision by the *New York Times* to provide coverage is associated with a reduction in the planet's respite from this form of terror from 80.4 days to 49.7.

The time lag data displayed in Table 8.1 suggests that the non-North Atlantic press plays a negligible role in contagion. For the category of *any* type of terrorist act, there is no statistically significant relation between

Figure 8.4 TV Impact on Time Lags for Barricades and Assassinations

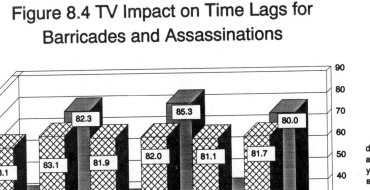

coverage and time lag to replication in the case of the Israeli, Egyptian, and Pakistani press. Thus, terrorist acts as a whole are no more likely to be emulated quickly if they are covered by *Yedlot, Al Aharam*, and the *Pakistani Times* than if they are not.

By contrast, coverage in the European and Canadian press is statistically linked to speed of replication. In the case of each of these non-U.S. North Atlantic papers, coverage is linked in a statistically significant sense to time lag to first emulation. The difference in time lag between coverage and noncoverage is less for the non-U.S. papers than for the *New York Times*. For example, the time lag to first emulation drops from 27.2 days to 15.3 days in the case of *New York Times* coverage. The differences in time lags are correspondingly smaller at the *Globe and Mail* (22.9 and 18.7 days), *Times* of London (23.5 and 18.4 days), and the *Daily Telegraph* (22.8 and 17.9 days). The pattern of time lags is closest to that of the New York paper among the French and West German dailies.

Table 8.1 Impact of Press Reporting on Time Lags

Action type	NYT yes	NYT no	GM yes	GM no	TL yes	TL no	DT yes	DT no	FI yes	FI no
any	15.3*	27.2	18.7*	22.9	18.4*	23.5	17.9*	22.8*	16.8*	26.3
kidnap	37.6*	56.9	43.1*	50.9	42.4*	52.4	40.0*	54.8	43.6*	52.8
attack	53.1*	68.9	58.3*	61.4	54.6*	67.2	55.0*	66.9	59.6	61.8
hijack	36.9*	71.1	39.6*	67.4	67.4*	70.2	37.3*	70.3	39.4*	68.0
bomb	38.1*	45.0	39.8*	41.2	37.8*	46.6	36.1*	47.3	40.4	40.8
barri.	77.9	84.3	81.4	81.9	80.0	82.2	79.0	83.8	79.3	80.9
assass.	49.7*	80.4	47.3*	76.7	46.6*	79.6	40.6*	82.1	47.1*	77.3

Action type	FR yes	FR no	YD yes	YD no	AA yes	AA no	PK yes	PK no
any	16.6*	26.8	19.8	21.2	20.1	20.3	19.7	21.4
kidnap	39.1*	55.0	44.4*	50.5	46.1	49.3	47.3	47.8
attack	58.1	61.4	57.9*	63.1	58.1*	62.9	59.8	59.7
hijack	37.1*	70.3	39.8*	67.8	40.1*	67.3	41.6*	66.5
bomb	39.9	41.0	39.7	42.1	40.6	41.2	41.8	41.7
barri.	78.0	83.7	82.1	82.0	81.8	82.7	82.8	81.3
assass.	45.3*	78.9	49.1*	74.9	47.3*	78.1	51.1*	73.4

*Differences are statistically significant at the .01 level

When terrorism is examined separately by type of action, the *New York Times* emerges once again as having the greatest impact on time lags. Indeed, the impact of the American paper is virtually as strong as that of its sister television networks. The far greater impact on time lag of the U.S. media helps give meaning to the hypothesis, explored in previous chapters, that the United States is the principal target of media-oriented international terrorism. Thus, international terrorist groups target American citizens in order to acquire recognition from the American media, and recognition by the American media in turn exercises the greatest impact on contagion.

It is true that terrorist coverage by non-American newspapers such as *Yediot* is associated with shortened time lags. But the effect of *Yediot* and other non-American papers is at most secondary and quite likely spurious. Coverage by the non-American papers appears to be related to time lags because their coverage is highly correlated with that of the *New York Times*, which exercises the predominant influence.

The net effect of each newspaper on terrorist emulation is unfortunately almost impossible to measure. Events are rarely reported by only one newspaper. And those events that are reported by only one paper are often unique to a given country or region.

Our dataset and analysis may lend themselves to an argument that each newspaper in the sample makes a separate contribution to contagion or emulation. The supporting evidence emerges from the fact that wall-to-wall cross-national coverage—the true media event—is associated with the shortest possible time lag between suggestive event and first emulation. A counter-argument can be made as a result of the fact that wall-to-wall cross-national coverage is correlated with *intensity* of coverage by the *New York Times* in its role as the world's leading newspaper. Following this line of reasoning, the intensity of coverage by the leading American paper is the crucial factor, affecting terrorism on the one hand and cross-national coverage on the other.

Our data analysis confirms that intensity of coverage by the New York paper is associated with the presence or absence of coverage in the entire sample of newspapers. But our data analysis does not allow a resolution of the debate between cross-national coverage as opposed to intensity of *New York Times* coverage as the main factor in contagion. Our data analysis cannot resolve the debate in part because of the nature of actual media coverage. Media coverage tends to be either highly correlated in matters of global terrorism or relatively uncorrelated in matters of local or unique concern. Thus, the pattern of media coverage is not sufficiently varied to test quantitatively the hypothesis that each medium makes a separate contribution to contagion or the alternative hypothesis that U.S. coverage is key and non-U.S. coverage incidental or derivative.

Measuring Contagion by Means of Frequency of Emulation

To this point in the chapter, we have measured the impact of media-induced contagion by comparing the time lag to first emulation of terrorist events that are reported with those events that are ignored. An alternative approach is to compare the frequency of events for set periods following an initial suggestive event.

Table 8.2 displays the frequency of terrorist events for each of 30-, 60-, or 90-day intervals following an event depending upon whether the event was or was not reported on the American television networks. For the case of *any action*, Table 8.2 shows that an average of 7.4 events took place within 30 days of an event not covered by NBC as compared to an average of 11.3 events in the same time period if NBC did report it. For the 90-day time interval, the average was 18.6 events if not covered by NBC as compared to 34.1 if left unreported by this network.

The pattern of contagion is essentially the same for the three networks. And, for each of the three networks, the major impact takes place in the second month. The average net difference in overall rates of terrorism between reported and unreported events jumps from 3.7 incidents in the first month to 13.7 incidents in the second month. The net rate difference levels off at 15.2 incidents after the third month.

For specific categories of terrorism, the data in Table 8.2 present a relatively uniform portrait of television coverage leading to emulation, particularly for an interval of 60 or more days. For example, for a period of 90 days after an assassination, the average number of subsequent assassinations is 5.9 if the initial assassination is reported on CBS but only 1.7 if left unreported. For a period of 90 days after a kidnapping, the average number of subsequent kidnappings is 4.4 if the initial kidnapping is reported on ABC but only 2.4 if overlooked.

Table 8.2 Television Coverage and Average Frequency of Emulation

Action type	lag in days	NBC		CBS		ABC	
		yes	no	yes	no	yes	no
any	30	11.3	7.4*	10.9	7.7*	11.0	6.9*
	60	25.6	12.1*	26.2	31.7*	25.3	12.4*
	90	34.1	18.6*	32.1	19.8*	35.2	17.6*
kidnap	30	0.9	0.7	1.2	0.5	1.1	0.4
	60	2.4	1.3*	2.6	1.1*	2.3	1.3*
	90	4.6	2.4*	4.7	2.2*	4.4	2.4*
attack instal.	30	1.5	0.9	1.7	0.8	1.3	1.1
	60	3.8	1.7*	3.5	1.8*	3.3	2.0*
	90	5.7	3.2*	5.6	3.0*	5.4	3.5*
hijack	30	1.4	0.7	1.3	0.8	1.3	0.8
	60	2.9	1.5*	3.1	1.4*	2.8	1.5*
	90	5.4	3.1*	5.5	3.0*	5.2	3.2*
bomb	30	5.9	5.2	5.8	5.2	5.8	5.2
	60	12.2	9.1*	11.8	9.5*	11.7	9.4*
	90	18.5	11.3*	18.0	11.7*	18.7	11.0*
barri- cade	30	0.9	0.4	0.7	0.4	0.6	0.4
	60	1.6	0.7	1.6	0.7	1.5	0.8
	90	2.5	1.1*	2.6	1.0*	2.4	1.4*
assass	30	1.2	0.4	1.0	0.5	1.1	0.4
	60	3.0	0.9*	2.8	1.2*	2.9	1.0*
	90	5.7	1.9*	5.9	1.7*	5.5	2.0*

Note: * denotes a statistically significant difference at the 0.5 level. The category of threats was not analyzed because of the small number of such events.

Overall, Table 8.2 contains relatively unambiguous evidence of a contagion effect. For all terrorist actions considered as a whole, there emerges statistically significant evidence of emulation for each time lag and for each of the three networks. For specific types of terrorist activity, the average rate of replicated acts is always higher when the event is reported than when it is not. It is true that some of the increases in rates of replication are not statistically significant, but the lack of statistical significance is related to the small numbers involved. Thus, for a period of 90 days following an incident, there are always more acts of the same type after the initial event is reported than when it is not. There are 63 different possible comparisons of terrorism according to whether the type of event was reported by a network or not. Among these 63 possible pairs, there is not a single instance where the rate of terrorism was *lower* if it was covered than if it was ignored.

Table 8.3, which contains data relating the presence or absence of press coverage to the frequency of terrorist emulation, conforms with the portrait of contagion sketched in the preceding pages. Coverage by the *New York Times* is the crucial element among the print media, but the *New York Times* is a less vital factor than are the American television networks.

Coverage by the non-American papers is sometimes related statistically to the frequency of emulation but the statistical relation between coverage and emulation is weaker in the case of the non-U.S. papers than in the case of the *New York Times*. The stronger relationship between coverage and emulation in the case of the American paper is reflected in several ways. Among the nine papers in the sample, the *New York Times* is the only paper displaying a statistically significant relationship between coverage of *any* terrorist act and frequency of emulation within a time lag of 30 days. The New York paper also displays the highest number of statistically significant relationships among the 21 possible relationships (i.e., 7 types of terrorism, each with 3 different time lags). Among the 21 possible relationships between coverage and emulation, 11 are statistically significant in the case of the *New York Times* as compared to 6 in the case of the *Times* of London, 2 in the case of *Le Figaro*, and an average of 5.0 for the sample of eight non-U.S. papers as a whole. The *New York Times* is thus in a tier of its own.

In a second tier are the West German, British, and Israeli papers. Within the category of *any* terrorist act, the Frankfurt paper, the two London papers, and the Tel Aviv paper each exhibit statistically significant relationships between coverage and frequency of emulation after two- and three-month lags. The Canadian and Egyptian papers exhibit statistically significant relationships after one time lag but not after all three while the Pakistani and French papers exhibit no statistically significant relationships in this comprehensive category of terrorist acts. Among the six specific categories of terrorist acts, the *New York Times* displays a more consistent relationship between coverage and frequency of emulation than is true of the other papers. For example, in the case of bombings, *New York Times* coverage is statistically related to rates of replication after time lags of both 60 and 90 days. A statistically significant relationship also holds true in the case of the Frankfurt paper and the *Daily Telegraph*. But, the relationship between coverage of bombing and replication holds true at most for a 90-day lag period in the case of some of the remaining papers.

Taken as a whole, the data presented to this point in the chapter provide corroborating evidence in support of the thesis of contagion with particular emphasis on the role of American television and a secondary emphasis on the role of the *New York Times* among the print media. The purely statistical information on coverage and emulation lends support to the thesis of the special role of the New York paper among print media, but the paramountcy of the *New York Times* is not fully reflected in the data.

Table 8.3 Press Coverage and Frequency of Emulation

Action type	lag in days	NYT yes	NYT no	GM yes	GM no	TL yes	TL no	DT yes	DT no	FI yes	FI no
any	30	10.2*	8.4	9.3	8.9	9.4	8.8	9.2	8.9	9.1	9.0
	60	23.4*	15.1*	21.6*	17.8	20.2*	16.7	19.9*	12.4	18.9	18.6
	90	32.2*	21.3	29.4	24.3	29.7*	23.8	28.4*	22.3	8.0	26.7
kidnap	30	0.9	0.7	0.8	0.7	0.8	0.7	0.9	0.7	0.9	0.6
	60	2.0	1.4	1.7	1.9	1.5	1.9	1.5	1.8	1.6	1.8
	90	4.3*	2.0	4.1*	2.3	4.0*	2.5	4.2*	2.2	3.9*	2.4
attack	30	1.4	1.0	1.2	1.1	1.3	1.0	1.3	1.1	1.2	1.2
	60	3.3*	2.1	2.9	2.6	3.0	2.5	3.1*	2.3	2.9	2.6
	90	5.5*	3.4	5.3*	3.4	5.3*	3.3	5.3*	3.3	5.0*	3.8
hijack	30	1.3	0.9	1.1	1.0	1.2	1.0	1.2	1.1	1.1	1.1
	60	2.8*	1.6	2.2	2.0	2.6	1.8	2.5	1.9	2.3	2.0
	90	5.3*	3.2	4.8*	3.8	5.0*	3.5	4.9*	3.7	4.6	4.0
bomb	30	5.8	5.3	5.5	5.4	5.6	5.4	5.7	5.3	5.5	5.5
	60	11.7*	10.1	10.9	10.4	11.0	10.5	11.4*	10.5	10.8	10.6
	90	18.0*	11.8	17.3*	12.4	17.3*	12.5	18.0*	11.8	16.3	13.5
barri.	30	0.6	0.4	0.5	0.5	0.6	0.4	0.6	0.5	0.5	0.5
	60	1.4	0.8	1.2	1.0	1.3	1.0	1.3	1.1	1.2	1.0
	90	2.4*	1.2	2.0	1.6	2.0	1.6	2.1	1.5	2.0	1.6
assass	30	1.1	0.5	0.9	0.6	1.0	0.5	1.0	0.6	0.8	0.7
	60	2.6*	1.4	2.3	1.6	2.3	1.6	2.4	1.7	2.4	1.6
	90	5.4*	2.1	4.5*	3.0	5.0*	2.4	5.2*	2.4	4.8*	2.7

Action type	lag in days	FR		YD		AA		PK	
		yes	no	yes	no	yes	no	yes	no
any	30	9.6	8.7	9.0	8.9	9.1	8.9	8.9	8.9
	60	21.8*	16.3	19.1*	17.9	19.1	18.0	18.8	18.7
	90	30.1*	24.0	27.3*	24.9	28.3*	22.4	27.1	25.7
kidnap	30	.8	0.7	0.8	0.8	0.9	0.5	0.8	0.7
	60	1.9	1.5	1.8	1.6	1.7	1.7	1.8	1.7
	90	4.2*	2.3	3.5	2.9	3.4	3.0	3.6	2.9
attack	30	1.3	1.0	1.2	1.1	1.3	1.1	1.1	1.2
	60	3.1*	2.3	2.8	2.6	2.7	2.6	2.8	2.7
	90	5.4*	3.3	5.0*	3.9	4.7	4.1	4.8	4.0
hijack	30	1.3	0.8	1.1	1.0	1.2	1.0	1.2	1.1
	60	2.7*	1.7	2.5	1.8	2.4	1.8	2.3	2.0
	90	5.1*	3.4	4.8*	3.7	4.6	4.1	4.8*	3.6
bomb	30	5.7	5.1	5.6	5.4	5.6	5.4	5.6	5.5
	60	11.3*	10.1	10.9	10.4	10.1	10.2	11.0	10.4
	90	17.9*	12.0	16.7*	13.1	16.0	13.8	16.9*	13.0
barri.	30	0.6	0.5	0.5	0.5	0.6	0.5	0.6	0.5
	60	1.3	1.1	1.2	1.0	1.1	1.1	1.2	1.0
	90	2.1	1.4	1.8	1.7	1.7	1.7	1.9	1.6
assass	30	1.0	0.5	0.8	0.6	0.8	0.8	0.9	0.6
	60	2.5*	1.5	2.2	1.0	2.4	1.7	2.3	1.6
	90	2.0	2.5	4.6*	3.0	4.1	3.6	4.2	3.3

Note: * denotes a statistically significant difference at the 0.5 level. The category of *threats* was not analyzed because of the small number of such events.

Ideally, a multivariate statistical procedure ought to be utilized in order to isolate the specific contribution of the American paper to the process of contagion. But too much of the media coverage emerges in the form of wall-to-wall reporting of media events with the result that the variance in coverage is too limited to permit the effective use of multivariate statistical analysis.

Our thesis that the American media are the prime target of modern terrorism rests partly, but only partly, on the statistical evidence linking *New York Times* coverage to shortened time lags before first terrorist emulation and to high frequencies of emulation after one-, two-, and three-month time lags. Our thesis also rests on the even stronger evidence of a link between television coverage and emulation. Furthermore, our thesis rests on the evidence presented in earlier chapters of the terrorists' proclivity for American victims and on the evidence in earlier chapters of the media perspicacity and preoccupation of terrorists themselves.

Coverage by the *New York Times* is related in a statistically significant sense to rates of replication of every type of terrorist event following at least one time lag. For the other newspapers in the sample, statistically significant links between coverage and rates of replication are more sporadic. For example, in the case of bombings, *New York Times* coverage is statistically related to rates of replication after time lags of both 60 and 90 days. In the case of the *Times of London* and *Yediot*, the relationship between coverage and replication holds true only for a 90-day lag period.

Taken as a whole, the data presented to this point in the chapter provide corroborating evidence in support of the thesis of contagion with particular emphasis on the role of American television and a secondary emphasis on the role of the *New York Times* in preference to other newspapers. The data presented in this chapter lead to the following predictions about coverage of terrorism and emulation:

- An event covered by American television is apt to be replicated in 16.7 days while an event not covered by television is apt to be replicated after 25.4 days,
- An event covered by the *New York Times* is apt to reoccur after 16.8 days while an event not covered is apt to reoccur after 25.3 days,
- Sixty days after an event, it is apt to be reproduced 25.7 times if reported on American network television but only 12.0 times if ignored, and
- Sixty days after an event, it is apt to be reproduced 10.2 times if reported on American network television but only 8.4 times if left unreported.[20]

To this point in the chapter, we have looked at quantitative evidence of the existence of contagion and the role of the media in the process. The ensuing section considers the question of whether contagion is recognized as such by the general public and by significant elements of the public in particular. But, before turning to the issue of whether contagion is recognized by the public for what we believe it to be, it is necessary to consider the possibility that we may have reached a false interpretation of true but misleading statistical data.

---

20 A complex time-series analysis of the same data likewise produced evidence of contagion. See H. B. Brosius and G. Weimann, "The Contagiousness of International Terrorism," *European Journal of Communication* (1991), 63-75.

Critics of our interpretation could accept as true that terrorist events replicate themselves more frequently after receiving coverage than when coverage is denied. But the true explanation, according to this argument, is not that terrorists are motivated by media coverage but rather that journalists are especially astute in identifying the kinds of terrorists and terrorist acts that are harbingers of intensified activity in the future. Thus, journalists do not catalyze terrorism, they foresee it.

There is more than an element of truth in the argument that journalists use their judgment to report movements, including terrorist movements, that are in ascendency rather than decline. But the prognosticating ability of the media cannot fully or even substantially explain the media-terrorist nexus. The thesis of journalists' prognosticating ability cannot account for the elaborate preoccupation with the media revealed in terrorist documents and pronouncements. The thesis of journalists' prognosticating ability cannot account for the carefully chosen targets selected by media-motivated terrorists nor their fastidious orchestration of media events. Finally, if the media-terrorism nexus is explained better by the journalists' ability to prognosticate than by the terrorists' quest for media coverage, it is essential to account for why journalists are so especially farsighted in the domain of terrorism, but not so clearly so in other domains.

Perceptions of Contagion

Strong evidence supports the contention that the general public perceives the mass media as a contributing factor in contagion. In 1977, a national poll conducted by the American Institute for Public Opinion asked respondents the question, *Do you think news media coverage of terrorism encourages others to commit these acts or not?* The results, portrayed in Figure 8.5, show that respondents hold the proposition to be true by a majority of more than two to one.

Strikingly, the likelihood of perceiving contagion rises with the education of respondents. Thus, among respondents with only grade school, the proportion of people who discern contagion is only 52% while those who deny its existence amount to as many as 33%. Meanwhile, among college graduates, the proportion identifying the process rises to 71% while the proportion with the opposing view falls to 21%.

The link between higher education and recognition of the media's role in terrorist emulation is important because it helps lay to rest a potential anticontagion argument that public perception of media-induced contagion is merely evidence of simpleminded, antidemocratic, working class

Figure 8.5 Public Perception of Media Coverage as Encouragement for Terrorism

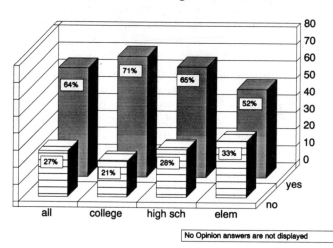

No Opinion answers are not displayed

authoritarianism. According to this anticontagion argument, when the public implicitly rebukes the media for abetting terrorism, it is a situation of "killing the bearer of bad news." However, the fact that recognition of contagion is strongest among the educated, who in the U.S. national culture are the least prone to be authoritarian, greatly undermines the counterargument based on authoritarianism.

The Gallup polling organization asked national samples of respondents in 1977 and 1986 if detailed coverage of terror encourages the replication of similar acts. Both sets of interviews yielded strong majorities favoring the contagion thesis. In 1986, 60% took the view that press coverage increases the chances of future terrorist acts while 7% felt that it reduced the chance of future terrorism and 21% took the view that media coverage has no effect.[21]

---

21 See C. De Boer, "The Polls: Terrorism and Hijacking," *Public Opinion Quarterly* 43 (1979), 410-18; The Gallup Opinion Index, Report No. 144 (July 1977), 13; and "The People and the Press," Part 2, *Newsweek* (Nov. 3, 1986).

Education is not the only factor that affects people's likelihood of discerning a process of contagion. People are also affected by their professional vantage point, both the intellectual perspective encouraged by their occupational experience and the material self-interest that arises from it as well. Elite interviews with national U.S. samples of police chiefs, television news directors, and newspaper editors corroborate the maxim that *where I sit is where I stand.* An overwhelming majority of police chiefs—93%—took the position that media coverage incites terrorism. A slight majority of newspaper editors shared this view (43% vs. 33%), while TV news producers were evenly divided (35% vs. 35%).[22]

---

22   J. P. Needham, *Neutralization of Prison Hostage Situations* (Huntsville, Tex.: Houston State University, 1977), 45, and M. Somer, "Nation's Police Chiefs, Media Differ on Terrorism Coverage," *Daily Variety* (August 17, 1978), 2.

Chapter 9

The Critical Perspective on Terrorism

Introduction

Our book has focused on one aspect of terrorism, transnational nonstate terrorism, and essentially one causal chain, the terrorism-media nexus and its impact on the public, decisionmakers, and the terrorists themselves. The approach of this book falls within the conventional mainstream perspective guiding much of traditional Western commentary and scholarship. Our outlook differs from mainstream writing less in broad outline than in an emphasis on the histrionic character and purposes of modern terror and in a quantitative orientation to organized violence, press coverage, and public opinion.

Though broadly shared by conservatives, liberals, and social democrats, the mainstream perspective is nonetheless not adhered to by everyone, especially among university communities. Vigorous dissension comes from radical, neo-Marxist and nondenominationally "critical" commentators. For many radicals, the mainstream perspective is a quasi-official sham designed to obscure the far more serious problem of state-sponsored terrorism conducted by capitalist states and their third world confederates. As Schlesinger, Murdock and Elliot observe,

> The official [i.e. Western mainstream] perspective is the set of views, arguments, explanations and policy suggestions advanced by those who speak for the [capitalist] state. The key users of these official definitions of terrorism are government ministers, conservative politicians and top security personnel. The official perspective is elaborated on by certain kinds of intellectuals—notably counter-insurgency theorists, academics and journalists—who are consciously engaged in waging the propaganda "war against terrorism."[1]

The radical perspective on terrorism can be decomposed into several arguments:

---

1 P. Schlesinger, G. Murdock, and P. Elliot, *Televising Terrorism* (London: Comedia Publishing, 1983).

- State-sponsored domestic violence by the United States and its third world client-states is widespread and serious;
- Excessive media emphasis is placed on anti-Western third world terror and insufficient coverage is allotted to the terror practised by the United States and its allies;
- The media stress on anti- rather than pro-Western terror reflects its commitment to serve Western capitalist interests;
- Scholars' and other experts' analyses of "terrorism" emerge from market demands for such intellectual labor from a "terrorism" industry organized and funded by Western governments and business;
- The portrayal of a central Soviet role in international terror prior to glasnost was overstated in order to serve capitalist interests.

These arguments are examined below in the context of two broad themes—the relative importance of terror conducted in the third world by the United States and its clients, and the link between media emphases on anti-Western terror on the one hand and capitalist interests on the other.

Third World Terror by the United States and its Client-states

The radical approach places a considerable accent on the terror practiced by third world states aligned with the United States. Many are military regimes employing violence to maintain control over populations that remain in impoverishment while ruling oligarchies partake of the material benefits of office.

Without specifically denying that violence was practiced on an enormous scale by the Soviet Union and its client states, radicals focus almost exclusively on Western and especially U.S. client relationships. In his *The Real Terror Network*, Edward Herman asserts that there is

> a huge tacit conspiracy between the U.S. government, its agencies, and its multinational corporations, on the one hand, and local business and military cliques in the Third World, on the other, to assume complete control of those

countries and "develop" them on a joint venture basis. The military leaders of the Third World were carefully nurtured by the U.S. security establishment to serve as the "enforcers" of this joint venture partnership....[2]

In his more recent book, The "Terrorism" Industry, Herman argues that Western governments and business have created an intellectual-ideological industry to serve the West's needs for tools of analysis and persuasion. Private sector think tanks join together with CIA and Pentagon offshoots in a "patriotic" effort to delegitimize "rebels and restive underclasses" resorting to violence out of desperation. Meanwhile, such experts seek to obfuscate the cruelties of "rightwing governments engaging in large-scale torture and killings or Western-organized and Western-funded insurgents attacking disfavored states."[3] From Herman's perspective, many analytic works, possibly including our own, reflect the broad economic interests and capabilities of Western governments and business. "Neither the African National Congress (ANC) nor the Mutual Support Group of Guatemala can fund data banks or theoretical analyses of the state terrorism that has killed scores of thousands in their countries and has posed an ongoing threat to the survivor populations."[4]

Herman and Noam Chomsky are the most prominent and prolific spokespersons for the "critical" school of thought.[5] Their far broader perspective than ours extends beyond transnational nonstate terrorism to encompass virtually all of United States policy. Chomsky's The Culture of Terrorism begins with a discussion of American domestic society including the nature of the power structure and the class system. Chomsky points to this class system as the impetus for what he perceives to be a global commitment to violence and terror in service of American national, i.e. corporate, interests.

In their global perspectives, Chomsky and Herman examine such client states and spheres of interest as the Philippines, Indonesia, Indochina, the

---

2   E. S. Herman, The Real Terror Network (Boston: South End Press, 1982), 3.
3   E. S. Herman and G. O'Sullivan, The "Terrorism" Industry (New York: Pantheon, 1989), 8.
4   Ibid., 7-8.
5   N. Chomsky and E. S. Herman, The Washington Connection and Third World Fascism (Nottingham: Spokesman Books, 1979), and The Political Economy of the Mass Media (New York: Pantheon, 1988); E. S. Herman, The Real Terror Network (Boston: South End Press, 1982); and N. Chomsky, The Culture of Terrorism (Montreal: Black Rose, 1988), Toward a New Cold War (New York: Pantheon, 1982), and Turning the Tide (Boston: South End, 1985).

Pacific rim, the Central American states, Brazil, Chile, and much of Africa, the Middle East and Europe. Their heterogeneous agendas include high-lighting evidence of U.S. government acquiescence in the militarization of the Philippines under Marcos, U.S. government support for the largely Nazi World Anti-Communist League,[6] and other practices at variance with proclaimed liberal democratic values.

If one assumes for purposes of argument that their assessment of U.S.-sponsored terror is faultless, one nonetheless does not necessarily have to conclude that their analysis and our own are completely incompatible. In principle, it is possible to study both U.S.-sponsored terror and international nonstate terror just as it is in principle possible to study both Soviet- and American-sponsored terror.

In practice, some radicals would condemn our study of nonstate terrorism on account of its emphasis on the cunning brutal means by which terrorists place themselves on public agendas. They would likewise decry an insufficient emphasis placed on the social conditions that ostensibly engender terrorist discontent.

Still other critics might lament an absence of attention to the potential contribution of the Reagan administration to the media salience of international terrorism. There may be some truth to the idea that the U.S. political right's preoccupation with and attention to international terrorism has made its own contribution to the media salience assigned to international terrorist events.

Some radical critics might accept our analysis as valid in its own terms, but would nonetheless castigate our study for exploring nonstate terrorism at the expense of U.S.-sponsored terror, deemed a far more oppressive problem. For many critics, to explore nonstate terrorism involves not only wasting resources on a lesser problem but also entails distracting one's audience from the fact that it is the lesser problem. According to this line of reasoning, the analysis of nonstate terror may amount to a propaganda effort on behalf of the United States and U.S. corporations.

Nonetheless, our analysis of nonstate terrorism need not be entirely incompatible with a radical agenda. Our analysis involves highlighting the media-motivated artificiality of international nonstate terrorism. The value-laden implication of this empirical finding is for journalists to moderate and nuance their attention to this subject. Radicals could welcome such

6   On retired general John Singlaub's involvement, see Chomsky, *The Culture of Terrorism*, 40, 58.

journalistic moderation if room were therefore made available for coverage of U.S.-sponsored terror.

This book on the media and terrorism is not the ideal venue to articulate a comprehensive stand on radical and neo-Marxist writing. To do so would require an overview of American foreign policy around the world as well as an analysis of power in American society, a challenge we are not prepared to take up here. From our *non*-Marxist perspective, to do proper justice to American foreign policy and the use of violence by U.S. agencies would require a comparative analysis of Soviet practices and the practices of other despotic regimes past and present.

Our general position is that the radical analysis of the use of violence by U.S. agencies and Washington's third world allies can contribute to an understanding of both terror and the ethical limits of liberal democracy. The work by Chomsky and other critics has value as a result of its examination of U.S.-initiated terror.

That value is limited by an exaggerated portrait of the magnitude of such terror and an unnuanced economic explanation of its causes. Even the most uncharitable cataloguing of U.S. violence abroad, while impressive in light of the self-proclaimed civic standards of liberal democracy, has been no match for the Soviet equivalent. Furthermore, the willingness of individual U.S. agencies to undertake or condone campaigns of violence abroad is not satisfactorily explained by capitalist profit-seeking alone. The long-standing interests of fruit companies may help explain traditional U.S. conduct in some of the countries of central America, including instances of opposition to democratic forces. However, U.S. interventions in many third world countries cannot be adequately explained by corporate economic interest since U.S. investments in such countries are often paltry by the scale of U.S. investments in the industrialized world and small compared to the magnitude of U.S. foreign policy interventions in a number of these countries.

The contemporary radical and neo-Marxist emphasis on corporate motivations for U.S. activity in the third world is reminiscent of Lenin's theory of imperialism, which centered on rational economic goals as the raison d'être of traditional European overseas colonialism. Decades of subsequent historical scholarship provide at best checkered evidence in support of the thesis.

An adequate account of U.S. foreign policy violence or terror abroad should not dismiss economic explanations but it should explore other considerations as well, for example:

- rivalry among competing organizations
  reign policy establishment about the effec-
       different ways of encountering anti-
       ces in the third world
  genuine American sense of patriotic and civic mission
- an authentic fear of communist intrusion and carnage
- the efforts of third world elites to appeal to and make
  use of American goodwill.

In the final analysis, the choice between an economic account of U.S. foreign policy interventions and a more pluralistic explanation is not entirely a scientific or value-free decision; it is also a matter of ideology and preference. A decision to focus exclusively on American violence abroad, as do many radicals, or to place American violence in a broader and therefore more charitable perspective cannot be made with absolute impartiality. By the same token, a decision to deem legitimate or illegitimate an academic inquiry into transnational nonstate terrorism is not entirely a matter of value-free objectivity.

Media Emphasis on Anti-Western Terror and Capitalist Interests

Chomsky and Herman contend that mass media attention devoted to [nonstate] "terrorism" is greatly overblown and that this misrepresentation of reality reflects United States propaganda strategy for distracting the public from the "real terrorism," the organized purposeful violence practiced by the United States and its third world allies. In *The Real Terror Network,* Herman argues that

> we have been living not only in an age of escalating "terrorism" but in an age of Orwell, where words are managed and propaganda and scholarship are organized so that terror *means* the lesser terror—the greater terror is defined out of existence and given little attention.[7]

The U.S. government-inspired perspective on the nature of terrorism, says Herman, leads to a widespread assumption that only the USSR and Libya engaged in terrorism, not the United States—"a patriotic lie of enormous dimension."[8]

---

7   (Boston: South End Press, 1982), 13.
8   Ibid., 23.

To assess Herman's point about a "lie of enormous dimension" would ideally require a cataloguing of U.S.-, Soviet-, and various other state- and nonstate acts of terrorism. American organizations such as the RAND Corporation have been able to assemble information on nonstate terrorism because such information is not impossible to assemble. Nonstate terrorists do seek publicity; that is their objective.

However, it is far more difficult to measure state terror because states that resort to violence by security officials usually make some attempt to disguise such violence. The concept of "state terror" may be a misnomer to the extent that a state successfully hides its violence from public view. Of course, states practicing terror in the third world would ideally prefer the terror to be known to and to exercise an intimidating effect on target populations while remaining hidden from the gaze of publics in the Western democracies. States such as Iran and Libya tend to execute a visible form of terror whereas states such as Syria are more discreet.

The United Kingdom, France, the United States, West Germany, Israel, Italy, and other liberal democracies have practiced terror and violence in varying degrees, albeit on a much smaller scale than the Soviet bloc. In the wake of the McCarthyite scare and then the Vietnam debacle, it was not always fashionable for Western academics and journalists to highlight the role of violence in Soviet rule. But if there were any doubts about the magnitude of Soviet domestic and foreign terror, *glasnost* may have brought about an end to such doubts. Soviet commentators, officials, and even retired KGB officers now speak with such abhorrence of the use of fear and brutality from Stalin to Brezhnev that Westerners making such observations in the past might well have been typecast as demented anticommunists.

The anti-Marxist writer Claire Sterling wrote in some detail about the role of the Soviet bloc in orchestrating a global network of terrorist states and nonstate groups.[9] She underscored the role of Moscow in providing terrorist organizations with weaponry, munitions, technical training, funds, intelligence, and logistical support including the use of diplomatic channels. Radicals highlighted the contribution of her work to the possible revival of a "red scare" and therefore to redirecting attention away from Western-sponsored terror.[10]

Radical writers have not confronted the paradoxical evidence that ideologically liberal journalists may have contributed to an under-reporting

9   *The Terror Network* (London: Weidenfeld and Nicolson, 1981).
10   See Herman, *The Real Terror Network*, 47-82.

of Soviet terror. Perhaps the best-known example of such a bias was the reticence of the *New York Times* and other Western papers during the 1930s about recounting evidence of the Ukrainian famine because reports of such an occurrence were reminiscent of anticommunist disinformation campaigns.

Radicals have pointed to the structure of the American economy and media system to account for the emphasis on anti-Western terrorism and deemphasis on pro-Western terrorism. Chomsky and Herman decry the "free press" as in effect "a state agency." Herman portrays the media as that part of the national power structure in the United States whose function is to shape public opinion:

> This is not accomplished by any conspiratorial plotting or explicit censorship—it is built into the structure of the system, and flows naturally and easily from the assorted ownership, sponsor, governmental and other interest groups pressures that set limits within which media personnel can operate....These interest groups find the National Security [i.e. client] States good, and this preference underlies U.S. sponsorship and support of this terror network.[11]

The many economic attributes of private ownership of the media converge to account for the capitalist bias in news production, according to the "critical" approach. The media themselves are owned by conglomerates with vast corporate interests. News and public affairs production depends on commercial sponsorship, and commercial sponsors possess their own set of corporate interests as well. By observing patterns of promotion and career advancement in media organizations, junior reporters learn to embrace the procapitalist values represented in the media executive suites. These procapitalist values, observe the radicals, are manifested in the media's suppression of unpleasant realities about the Western capitalist source of terror.

This *ownership and control* type of explanation of pro-Western media bias is useful for highlighting the potential significance of patterns of ownership, but it is unnuanced and incomplete. It does not take into consideration the structural heterogeneity of American capitalism nor the diverse goals of corporations. It would be difficult to account for the heterogeneity of media opinion on such foreign policy controversies as Vietnam and Nicaragua if American capitalism were in fact united on insurgency in the third world and if media conglomerates were truly able to command the journalists they employ. For example, it would be very difficult to account for the sustained misgivings of the *Wall Street Journal* and of the networks during

11   Ibid., 139.

at least the latter part of the Vietnam war. The overwhelming evidence is that American disengagement from Indochina did not take place over the opposition of the media.

Ironically, Chomsky and others base most of their evidence of U.S. terror on secondary sources, either U.S. government publications or in most cases news and opinion pieces appearing in American periodicals. It is exceedingly rare for their portrayals to be founded on direct testimony from eyewitnesses, coconspirators, or victims in the third world itself. If Chomsky's "system of state-private power"[12] were as commanding a media censor as he and his colleagues portray, it would be difficult to account for their own success in unearthing evidence of U.S. terror from the publicly available documents of this same "system of state-private power."

The highlighting of the conglomerate nature of the media is an important point, but interlocking corporate structures can make the media vulnerable to Soviet and third world pressure as well as to pressure from the American power structure. The fearful response of British and American book sellers and distributors to Iranian threats over the publication of Rushdie's *Satanic Verses* illustrates the vulnerability of conglomerates with far-flung exposed corporate interests when confronted by a purposeful antagonist.

Perhaps the most striking weakness of the ownership and control approach is its underrating of the individuality of corporate objectives. Consumer-based industries do not have the same interest in military matters as the aerospace and defense industries. American exporters to industrialized markets do not have the same interest in an American presence in the third world as do firms dependent on resource extraction or low-cost labor pools in nonindustrial countries. The principal concern of commercial sponsors of television programming is not ideology but the size and consumer purchasing power of program audiences. The CBS program "60 Minutes" and other television series that uncover disreputable aspects of capitalism and the American political system prosper because of the size and quality of the audience they can provide sponsors.

12   *The Culture of Terrorism*, 39.

The ownership and control account of the media's accent on anti-Western terrorism and minimization of pro-Western terrorism may be a less adequate explanation than another neo-Marxist account, which focuses on the process of news production. The respected leftwing British scholar, Stuart Hall, has placed an emphasis on the "practical pressure of constantly working against the clock," as a result of which deference is shown toward the opinions and outlooks of those in "powerful and privileged institutional positions."[13] Following the neo-Marxist logic, powerful persons, linked to the corporate structure, would prefer a stress on anti-Western violence.

A study of terrorism coverage in the *New York Times* corroborates Hall's point insofar as the evidence points to a special emphasis on the views and interpretations of people in authority.[14] This phenomenon belongs to a larger pattern of media dependence on authoritative and powerful institutions for the raw material of news production. The networks, news services, and individual news organizations rely mainly on governmental and corporate sources. As we noted earlier in this book, much media content amounts to *subsidized* reporting in the sense that the newsmakers contribute financially and organizationally to the production of news involving or relating to themselves. Sigal's study of the information sources of the *New York Times* over a 20-year period found that almost half the sources were U.S. government and agency officials, with the business community as the second most important source of information.[15]

Stuart Hall's emphasis on the news process and the "practical pressure of constantly working against the clock" can help account for the media emphasis on anti-Western terror in light of the motives and modus operandi of terrorists themselves. Because of time pressures, journalists depend greatly on news sources for their raw material. Nonstate transnational terrorists, disproportionately based in the third world, are greatly represented in news coverage for the simple reason that their objective is news

---

13   Hall et al., *Policing the Crisis: Mugging, the State and Law and Order* (London: Macmillan, 1978), 58. See also H. Becker, "Whose Side Are We On? *Social Problems* 14 (1967) 3, 239-44; the Glasgow University Media Group's *Bad News* and *More Bad News* (London: Routledge and Kegan Paul, 1975 and 1980) as well as the empirical reanalysis of the Glasgow data and a rebuttal in Martin Harrison, *TV News: Whose Bias?* (Hermitage, U.K.: Policy Journals, 1985); and Todd Gitlin, *The Whole World Is Watching: Mass Media in the Making and Unmaking of the New Left* (Berkeley: University of California Press, 1980).

14   D. Paletz, P. A. Fazzard, and J. Z. Ayanian, "The I.R.A., the Red Brigade, and the F.A.L.N. in the *New York Times*," *Journal of Communication* (Spring 1982), 162-71.

15   L. V. Sigal, *Reporters and Officials: The Organization and Politics of Newsmaking* (London: Heath, 1973).

coverage. Whether in reality abundant or inconsequential, Soviet and Western state-sponsored terror is poorly covered in the mass media largely because the practitioners of such terror seek to conceal rather than highlight their conduct.

Paradigmatic Reconciliation— Limits and Possibilities

Competing paradigms or perspectives often overlap with regard to which problems merit academic study and how such study should be undertaken. The radical, sometimes populist and sometimes neo-Marxist paradigm and the conventional mainstream paradigm of which our book is a part overlap in respect of a common recognition that journalists' work practices and time pressures impact upon the nature of media coverage. From our perspective, the time pressures upon working journalists and their professional culture largely account for the preeminence accorded to international nonstate terrorists given that media coverage is the goal of such terrorists.

Radical observers go one step further, attributing the emphasis on anti-Western terror to a Western public opinion strategy designed to camouflage the ostensibly more serious terror practiced by the United States and its client states. For radicals, the mass media's emphasis on anti-Western nonstate terror reflects its role as a propaganda instrument of the "system of state-private power," to use Chomsky's term. Yet, for some mainstream observers, the media inadvertently "serve as propaganda agents of terrorism."[16] This is a point at which the radical and mainstream paradigms become essentially irreconcilable.

The irreconcilability of the two approaches is partly a matter of assessing the same facts differently as well as deeming different facts to be important. The irreconcilability is also a matter of values and ideological preference, matters not easily resolved by conventional scholarly and scientific methods.

And yet, some reconciliation between the two approaches is possible. The two approaches are in some respects profoundly complementary. One approach focuses on publicity-seeking nonstate terrorists; the other approach focuses on secrecy-seeking state actors. One approach highlights

---

16   F. Hacker, *Crusaders, Criminals, Crazies* (New York: W. W. Norton, 1976), 161.

media-oriented terror, the other media-avoiding terror. Together, the mainstream and critical paradigms portray the two faces of terrorism.

The notion of a "theater of terror" can be applied to state as well as to nonstate purveyors of violence. Metaphorically speaking, our own analysis directs its spotlight to front and center stage. The critical school looks behind the curtains at the contributions of democratic states, their military, and their security apparatus.

The critical school's emphasis on Western countries' highlighting of certain kinds of terrorism in order to divert attention away from other forms can be understood as broadly consistent with our focus on scripting and repertory direction in the theater of terror. Thus, the concept of a theater of terror allows for considerable reconciliation between the two seemingly irreconcilable schools of thought.

Chapter 10

Institutional Stress under the Theater of Terror

Introduction

This chapter focuses on the special responsibilities and perspectives of security forces, professional journalists, and political leaders. All three roles are greatly affected by the emergence of mediated violence. All three are subjected to intense momentary pressures when governments are all but paralyzed by terrorists' media events.

The chapter begins by exploring the general misgivings that security forces have about the press as well as some of the experiences that have given rise to these misgivings. How security officials and political executives have responded to the media-terror nexus is examined.

In concluding, the chapter returns to a consideration of journalism itself. Models of media restraint in the coverage of terrorism are portrayed and assessed.

Journalism, Security, and Political Leadership— Different Occupational Perspectives

Traditional terrorism, not as motivated by media access as an objective, presented police and security forces with traditional challenges. Security agencies responded with such established procedures as frontier controls, fortification of potential governmental and military targets, statistical tracking of eruptions, monitoring of the social conditions conducive to popular support for terrorism, proscription of certain political organizations, and sundry undercover intelligence efforts.

The *theater of terror* presented security forces with new situations—the dramatic live transmission of terrorist actions to millions of viewers, terrorists' negotiations with officials by means of "TV diplomacy," competition among journalists for access to terrorists and the events in which they are involved, competition among terrorists for access to the journalists, and competition among terrorists to manufacture those events that assure accessibility to the mass media.

According to the liberal democratic paradigm forming the basis of freedom of the press, an unfettered journalism enhances personal security because free media make the exercise of absolute power more difficult. Absolutist or dictatorial regimes may have a greater capacity to crush nonstate terrorism but they do so at the price of permitting state terrorism to be practiced against a regime's own populace. Unfettered by a critical press, absolutist regimes are apt to exacerbate the social conditions that may kindle nonstate terrorism.

Most commentators on terrorism agree in principle that nonstate terrorism can spring from genuine grievance over abusive conditions as well as from murderous impulses cloaked in high principle. Commentary on terrorism usually divides over whether the grievances of a particular group are genuine or feigned and, if genuine, whether they justify and/or are helped by the horror practiced by the particular group.

In those hypothetical situations where a consensus agrees that nonstate terrorism is nourished by objectively opprobrious conditions, the impact of a free media may be to place these discontents on the public agenda, thereby obliging authorities to embark on conciliatory solutions. Nonmilitary action by government to reduce group discontent may help tame the rancor that prompts publics to sustain terrorists in their midst. In Ulster, for example, new housing, industrial incentive, hiring and social policies plus the London-Dublin agreement for a joint condominium over the northern province could conceivably have provided Catholics with incentives to lessen support for the IRA or its political wing, Sinn Fein.

Because of the primordial essence of the conflict in Northern Ireland, many would argue that the conflict is intrinsically a *zero-sum game*, unsuited to compromise irrespective of the conciliatory efforts of the two governments involved. In such a climate, Irish terrorists, in common with many other terrorist groups, are incited by a mix of inordinate political ambition, irreconcilable group differences, and criminal intent, and are nourished by foreign governments waging war by proxy. Problems of such complexity may not be solvable by a free press and/or conventional liberal democratic institutions. Indeed, the parliament at Stormont was closed down a generation ago partly because the authorities in London saw the paralysis at Stormont as an incitement to more terrorism.

In situations of disorder, the ascendancy of the security apparatus typically places security on a collision course with the press. This mistrust has roots in different occupational roles and perspectives. As Miller notes,

> What the police see as intrusion the media see as the performance of their traditional role to gather information and disseminate it. What the police see as important tactical procedures—control and containment—the media see as unnecessary restrictions which violate the media's constitutionally guaranteed right to publish.[1]

Police misgivings about journalism can be seen in the context of a wider apprehension about the role of journalists in the theater of terror. Journalists have been termed "the terrorist's best friend" and "propaganda agents of terrorism."[2] An African journalist participating in a survey of editors' views on terrorist reporting termed members of his profession "blood brothers" of terrorists.[3] The United States Task Force on Disorders and Terrorism, under the aegis of the National Advisory Committee on Criminal Justice Standards and Goals, reached a conclusion that "in many ways, the modern terrorist is the very *creation* of the media."[4] An Australian security overview came to a similar conclusion. In a report to Canberra, Justice R. M. Hope expressed his view of the terrorism-media nexus by quoting from an article by U.S. scholar Chalmers Johnson:

> Equal to or greater in importance than new weaponry in the growth of terrorism is the global expansion of mass media of communications....Media contribute to publicity for a particular terrorist cause, the contagious triggering of other terrorists' decisions to act, the training of terrorists through a media-fed pool of experience and inspiration, and international linkages among terrorist organizations.[5]

Terrorists are rarely the creation of the media or of television, the medium that normally comes to mind first. Even media-motivated terrorism long predates the emergence of the electronic media. However, because of television's short reaction time, vast geographic reach, and intense emo-

---

1   A. H. Miller, "Terrorism and the Media: Observations from the American and British Experiences," in P. Montana and G. Toukis, eds., *Managing Terrorism* (Westport, Conn.: Quorum Books, 1983), 91.
2   W. Laqueur, "The Futility of Terrorism," *Harper's* (March 1976), 104, and Hacker, *Crusaders, Criminals, Crazies*, 161.
3   A. P. Schmid, "Editors' Perspectives," in Paletz and Schmid, eds., *Terrorism and the Media*, 117.
4   Report of the United States Task Force on Disorders and Terrorism, National Advisory Committee on Criminal Justice Standards and Goals, Washington, D.C. (December 1976), 9.
5   Chalmers Johnson, "Terror," *Society* (Nov-Dec. 1977), 119-20, in R. M. Hope, *Protective Security Review Report* (Canberra: Australian Government Publishing Service, 1979), cited in J. J. Hocking, "Government Perspectives," in D. L. Paletz and A. P. Schmid, eds., *Terrorism and the Media* (Newbury Park, Calif.: Sage, 1992), 92.

tional impact, the possibility of controlling television provides terrorists with a prize of exceptional value. It is the value of this prize that renders modern media-motivated terrorists more media-motivated than their antecedents.

The specter of journalists as witting or unwitting handmaidens of terrorists provokes intense feeling. The most severe critics of journalists have expressed a desire for limits on coverage: "What is at issue is not political censorship, which is inimical to our tradition and instincts, but crime control. Publicity is the sea in which terrorist fish, the handful of desperate isolated figures who commit these acts, swim in."[6]

Milder critics of the profession worry that cooperation between journalists and terrorists might produce a primeval public outcry, unleashing some form of censorship. Jaehnig has warned that

> the greater the collaboration between journalists and terrorists, the greater will grow community fears and calls for legal restraints that will intrude upon what journalists regard as their libertarian position. Only by forsaking this tradition, in developing a new ethical posture that will voluntarily control and intellectually regulate the instrumentality, can journalism preserve itself.[7]

The frustration and ire generated by media treatment of terrorism is acknowledged even by those who feel such reporting to be appropriate. Writing in the *Columbia Journalism Review*, J. Bowyer Bell has defended coverage as an essential requisite of liberal democracy:

> If open, democratic societies in the West cannot protect the liberty of us all from a handful of gunmen, accommodate legitimate dissent, and repress the politics of atrocity under the law—if we cannot tolerate the exaggerated horror flashed on the evening news, or the random bomb, without recourse to the tyrant's manual—then we do not deserve to be free.[8]

Critics of coverage have been incensed because of their abhorrence of violence, their fury that bloodshed is cloaked in high ideals, and their outrage that the media could be so readily mastered by antidemocratic forces. Occasionally, critics emphasize the journalism component of the media-terrorism nexus, focusing on what they deem to be a broader

6   S. S. Rosenfeld, "How Should the Media Handle Deeds of Terrorism?" *The Washington Post* (November 21, 1975).
7   W. B. Jaehnig, "Journalists and Terrorism: Captives of the Libertarian Tradition," *Indiana Law Journal* 53(4)(1978), 744.
8   "Terrorist Scripts and Live-action Spectaculars," *Columbia Journalism Review* 17 (1)(1978), 50.

professional deficiency. From this perspective, the media's susceptibility to terrorism constitutes part of a larger problem in the process of news production—time pressures on reporters; journalists' dependence on newsmakers for scripting, staging, and background information; and audience and commercial pressures for theatrical rather than analytic news content. In Miller's words, "terrorism does not bring forth a spectrum of new issues so much as it raises more distinct concerns which have potentially greater consequences for both the media and the larger political system."[9]

By this logic, the acquiescent or excessive reporting of terrorist violence and associated terrorist propaganda reflects the impact on the media of the kinds of audience and market forces said to cause the emergence of dramatic news presentations, stylized news formats, and other aspects of "infotainment."

Critics of media reporting tend to focus on the incentives provided by coverage for the replication of violence. Our own data lend weight to that concern. But media reporting also impacts on the security forces and political executives, albeit in more complex ways.

The impact on security forces is two-edged. On the one hand, intensive media scrutiny constrains the police and armed forces from overstepping their authority and transgressing due process. On the other hand, the mediated grief of victims' families puts security officials under relentless pressure to find a quick solution.

The content rather than the volume of media coverage may affect the extent to which security officials are propelled into or constrained from undertaking ill-advised actions. Just as economic theory posits that demanding consumers stimulate the emergence of successful companies, by the same token demanding journalists may give rise to competent, careful, and effective policemen. Paradoxically, demanding journalists can enhance the effectiveness of security forces by restraining officials under stress from impulsive acts that can alienate publics and by pressuring the judicial process to convict only the demonstrably guilty.

9   A. H. Miller, "Terrorism, the Media, and the Law: A Discussion of the Issues," in Miller, ed., *Terrorism: The Media and the Law* (New York: Transnational Publishers, 1982), 13.

The false conviction and incarceration of four men for IRA bombings and death in England illustrate the two-edged impact of the press. On the one hand, by their excess the tabloids may have been "guilty of bludgeoning the police to charge and the court to convict."[10] On the other hand, the "Guilford four" won their freedom by virtue of the unflagging and courageous scrutiny of a small group of individual journalists.[11]

With respect to the media-security nexus, a vital issue is how the freedom of the media to report terrorism impacts upon the performance of the security forces and other liberal democratic institutions.

Security Forces' Apprehensions

Security forces are rarely engaged in the broad questions about the role of the media in the political system, but they have had many practical concerns about the reporting of terrorism. They have been troubled that, merely by reporting news of terrorist events, the media nourish and provide support to the perpetrators. Short of this overarching concern, security forces have been fearful that the safety of innocent victims of kidnapping and other terrorist acts may be jeopardized by the professional ambitions of journalists vying for scoops, market share, and employer gratitude.

Security forces' apprehensions are frequently rooted in well-documented experiences of irresponsible media conduct, as illustrated in the following examples:

Revealing security forces' tactics and ruses

- In November 1974, terrorists hijacked a British Airways jet en route from Dubai to Libya, demanding the release of terrorists imprisoned in Egypt and the Netherlands in exchange for the passengers taken as hostages. When the exchange was scheduled to take place, journalists reported that the transaction was a ploy, prompting the terrorists to single out a West German banker among the hostages for execution as a reprisal.[12]

10   David L. Paletz and John Boiney, "Researchers' Perspectives," in Paletz and Schmid, eds., *Terrorism and the Media*, 6-28.
11   A. H. Miller, "Preserving Liberty in a Society under Siege: The Media and the Guilford Four," *Terrorism and Political Violence* (1990), 305-24.
12   A. Schmid and J. de Graaf, *Violence and Communication* (Beverly Hills, Calif.: Sage, 1982), 100-104.

- When an elite German antiterrorist team, GSG-9, was dispatched to rescue hostages aboard a Lufthansa aircraft in Mogadishu, Somalia in October 1977, an amateur radio operator intercepted messages from the antiterrorist flight to its home base, passing this information to Agence France Presse and Israeli television. The story was soon carried in the French, Israeli, and British press, placing in jeopardy the lives of 86 hostages in the five hours before the rescue operation actually took place. Only good fortune prevented the hijackers from learning of the operation since they had already executed the Lufthansa captain after hearing another broadcast on the hijacking.
- During the April 1980 seizure of the Iran embassy in London, security officials permitted cameras to carry live footage from the front of the embassy provided that no shots were taken of security forces' deployment or of eavesdropping equipment on the sides of the building. BBC personnel complied but an ITN cameraman, posing as a new arrival from London airport, smuggled a handheld camera in a suitcase through the police cordon at the rear of the edifice. He secured an excellent location in the window of a flat overlooking the embassy rear and switched on the moment SAS men appeared on the roof and started to lower themselves by rope. His electronic camera was capable of transmitting live. Had the footage been transmitted without delay, the lives of both the hostages and the rescue team members would have been at risk. But for no clear reason the network decided to wait four minutes rather than interrupt the program being broadcast.[13] In an analogous American incident, the on-location broadcast was not delayed and the SWAT team was less fortunate.[14]

Revealing victims' ruses

- In October 1977, a commandeered Lufthansa aircraft was forced to land in Mogadishu, Somalia. The captain somehow managed to radio information to the

13 Clutterbuck, *The Media and Political Violence*, 138ff.
14 M. McEwan, seminar on "Terrorism: Police and Press Problems", Oklahoma (April 14, 1977), mimeo, 35.

authorities on the nature of the terrorist threat aboard. The media report of his bravery was overheard by the terrorists, who responded by executing him.

- In March of the same year during the Hanafi hostage-taking in Washington, D.C., a basket of food was observed being hoisted to a floor that was not occupied by either the terrorists or their known victims. The press correctly concluded that the food was destined for people who had managed to evade a round-up and had barricaded themselves in a room. By broadcasting this information, the press put at considerable risk the lives of the group.

Provocative misinformation

- In March 1977, Hanafi Muslims took hostages at three separate buildings in Washington, D.C. including B'nai B'rith headquarters. A truck arrived at this latter building with boxes of food authorized by the kidnappers. A reporter broadcast the false story that the boxes surreptitiously contained weapons for an imminent police assault. Using this false report as a point of departure, another journalist in a live interview with the terrorists asked challengingly, "How can you believe the police?"[15]
- During the same episode, a prominent Washington newscaster called one of the terrorists a "Black" Muslim, prompting him to fly into a rage and threaten the hostages with death. The hostage-taker, whose family had died at the hands of Black Muslims, regained his composure after the police persuaded the broadcaster to issue an apology.[16]

Arousal

- During the 1977 Hanafi episode, a radio station interviewer provocatively asked a terrorist spokesperson if

---

15 See interview with Lt. F. Bolz, head of the New York Police Department's Hostage Negotiating Squad, reported by Robert Friedman in *More* (June 1977), 19. Only good fortune prevented vengeance against a hostage for the false alleged breach of faith by the police negotiator.

16 See "The Media and Terrorism," proceedings of a seminar (Spring 1977), 19.

the group had provided authorities with an ultimatum: "Have you set a deadline?"

- On March 30 1979, a small new terrorist group, the Irish National Liberation Army (INLA) murdered Shadow Secretary of State Airey Neave M.P. in the precincts of Parliament. In early July of that year, the most popular BBC television current affairs show, "Tonight," scheduled for its very last program a secret interview in Dublin with a representative of INLA. Disguised and with his back to the camera, the southern Irish representative of the INLA justified the killing by means of a Marxist critique of British society and by means of allegations that the victim himself had been an advocate of torture.[17] The BBC interview aroused widespread distress about the impact on the victim's widow, who was at home alone watching the program without the slightest inkling of what to expect. The BBC interview also sparked concern that so much publicity should be granted a small-scale organization merely because it had succeeded in committing murder. Former Northern Ireland and Home Secretary Merlyn Rees cautioned that the enormous media achievements of the fledgling INLA would galvanize the Provisional IRA to take whatever action necessary to reassert its lead in the contest for "who are the greatest guys in the terrorism business."[18] In late August, the Provisional IRA fulfilled Merlyn Rees's prediction, murdering Earl Mountbatten.

Agents of terrorist propaganda

- The general security of liberal democratic societies is undermined to the extent that terrorist organizations achieve success in winning hearts and minds. In their propaganda battles with security forces, terrorists have the advantage of surprise and secrecy. The Provisional IRA's momentary nighttime control of a part of the Ulster village of Carrickmore is often used to illustrate the propaganda advantage available to terrorists. While

17   Clutterbuck, *The Media and Political Violence*, 110ff.
18   BBC, "The Editors," July 15, 1979.

in Dublin to interview Provisional IRA leaders, a BBC crew was told that they would find something engrossing to cover if they rushed to Carrickmore, just 22 miles on the other side of the Republic-Ulster border. In Carrickmore, the television crew spotted 7 armed men in balaclavas stopping four or five cars to check for drivers' licenses. A total of 11 minutes of footage was shot before the journalists' departure. The Provisional IRA was able to embellish this kernel of truth into a phantasmal claim of 100+ heavily armed men policing the community over a period of several hours, a story that was carried without verification by newspapers around the globe.[19]

- One of the particular propaganda strengths of some terrorist forces has been to successfully misrepresent to the media their violent encounters with security forces. In the Ulster context, media misrepresentation has taken the form of portraying as unarmed civilians those armed terrorists who are shot in unsuccessful ambushes laid against security forces. In the Middle Eastern context, terrorists have succeeded in portraying one wing of a movement as neutral referee while another plays the role of violent revolutionary. In both geographic contexts, the terrorists' media advantage is nourished by a host of considerations: the credulity of peripatetic journalists without local roots; privileged access accorded sympathetic members of the press; journalists' professional and commercial rivalry for a story with dramatic content; ultimately the threat of reprisal against uncooperative reporters; the practical difficulty of authorities seeking to counter accusations directed against their own conduct; and the legal difficulty of authorities in rebutting allegations that are under investigation and are hence *sub judice*.[20]

---

19   Clutterbuck, *The Media and Political Violence*, 117ff.
20   See Clutterbuck, *The Media and Political Violence*, passim.

Security Responses to the Media-Terror Nexus

Media manipulation is essential to despotic regimes while it occupies an important, albeit much more subtle, form in liberal democracies as well. The concern of senior civil servants in democratic regimes with mass communication and public consent is reflected in the flowering of sizeable public sector markets for public relations expertise, media counsel, crisis preparedness, and public opinion polling. Developing effective media relations has been a preoccupation of senior officials in central agencies of government and line departments but, until recently, it has not been a concern of security forces. The success of terrorists in capturing the attention of the media and in affecting the media agenda has forced security forces to take note.

The most obvious institutional response of the security forces has been to create for the first time entire media or public relations units. These units are staffed by uniformed military personnel who, by virtue of lifetime careers in law enforcement, possess the occupational credibility to attract the interest of journalists. But these career officers are often paired with civilians trained in modern mass communications. These administrative marriages of uniformed military specialists and civilian media specialists are found in such organizational units as the Press Office of the Royal Ulster Constabulary, the United Kingdom's principal antiterrorist force in Northern Ireland.

The roles of such civilian media advisors include educating the security forces with respect to media rights and responsibilities in democratic societies as well as explaining the reality of career and peer pressures affecting how reporting is conducted. Another role of such civilian advisors is to demystify terrorists' media strategies in the eyes of on-site journalists. Still another role is to persuade journalists to abide by ground rules in the reporting of terrorism. For example, in 1988 Australia's Protective Services Co-ordination Centre (PSCC) presented new media guidelines to journalists attending a media briefing. Similar to guidelines in other Western democracies, Australia's ground rules included provisions for:

- no live coverage
- nonuse of slogans and inflammatory phrases
- reporting of terrorist demands to be free of rhetoric
- journalists to remain bystanders

- no telephone calls or other direct communication
- no action endangering the lives of hostages.[21]

The security forces' communications units are often staffed by former journalists. The units may be buttressed by research or strategy units staffed by graduates in the social sciences with training in how to interpret public opinion surveys and how to conduct quantitative content analyses of communication. Indeed, the growing supply of master's graduates in sociology and political science has been increasingly drawn to security service as traditional employers of their talents, domestic social policy departments of government, face constraints on hiring.

The major impact of the civilian social scientists and ex-journalists in the employ of security forces has been to enhance the ability of the uniformed personnel to contest the terrorists for control of the media. During crises, one of the daily functions of the security forces' press relations staff is to befriend visiting scribes and seek to delegitimize the terrorists in their eyes. Press relations staff try to persuade journalists to remove themselves from areas of turbulence on the grounds that the journalists' presence is itself a prime reason for such turbulence.

The press relations staff's role in delegitimizing terrorists may entail drawing the attention of journalists to the links between terrorism and organized crime. In the Ulster case, visiting journalists are often told of the role of the IRA in extortion, particularly in the taxicab industry. Quite a number of terrorist groups are involved in illegitimate economic activities, frequently narcotics trafficking. A number of terrorist leaders have succeeded in amassing a degree of wealth inconsistent with their proletarian pretensions.

It is conceivable that the press relations staffs of security forces have affected the character of terrorist reporting as a result of what they sometimes term their efforts at "demystification." But little research has been conducted on the apparent effects on reporting achieved by the security forces' press efforts. Furthermore, very little of the known evidence of links between crime and terrorism is actually reported.

Apart from their general efforts at demystification, press relations officers seek to affect the specific ways in which periodic crises are portrayed by the media. Prior to emergencies, they endeavor to persuade uniformed security personnel of the value of remaining accessible to journalists in the

---

21   J. J. Hocking, "Government Perspectives" in Paletz and Schmid, eds., *Terrorism and the Media*, 94.

event of a contingency. The absence of official statements and information might cede the media battle to the terrorists and arouse journalistic skepticism about the propriety of official conduct and the candor of official statements.

Both prior and subsequent to crises, press relations officers strive to explain to journalists the constraints on what governments can say, for example the legal limits on public statements relating to matters before court review. Press relations officers may also point out the human limits on the information that security forces can provide as a result of the fact that the only government witnesses at a violent incident may be unseasoned 18-year-old servicemen traumatized by their first experience of bloodshed. By contrast, terrorists, knowing the outlines of a planned event well in advance, have the luxury of carefully scripting their own "eye-witnesses."[22]

Security officials are not usually entirely candid in expressing their thoughts about the role of the media except at in camera conferences with their civilian superiors. But the perceptions held by security forces do sometimes enter the public domain through the comments of observers friendly to their point of view. One such observer in the United Kingdom, Richard Clutterbuck, wrote of terrorism as "a propaganda war supported by a shooting war."[23] A major general-turned-professor of international relations, Clutterbuck advocated the creation of a licensing body analogous to medical and legal authorities with the function of certifying and decertifying professional journalists. He also proposed empowering local police chiefs (chief constables) to declare local states of emergency and to prohibit media coverage for periods of up to six hours at a time.

The perceptions held by security forces have also become known thanks to survey research. Michael Somer compared the views of security officials and journalists in the 30 largest cities in the United States. Police chiefs, television news directors, radio news directors, and newspaper editors were each asked "to what extent...[they] consider live coverage of terrorist acts a threat to hostage safety..."—a minimal threat, a moderate threat, or a great threat. Not surprisingly, perhaps, 46% of police chiefs deemed it a "great threat" as compared to only 3%, 14%, and none of the TV news directors, radio news directors, and newspaper editors, respectively.

22 The preceding discussion is based on extensive off-the-record interviews with security officials, reporters, newspaper editors, and broadcasting officials in the United Kingdom in spring 1989.
23 See Clutterbuck, *The Media and Political Violence*, xlii, on the Provisional IRA.

Meanwhile, live coverage was considered a minimal threat by as many as 76% of newspaper editors, 47% of radio news directors, and 43% of television news directors but by only 7% of police chiefs.[24]

Quite apart from their misgivings about media coverage of terrorist events, police authorities are distressed about any kind of interaction between journalists and perpetrators during the course of an incident. Their concerns range from the possibility of inciting or inflaming gunmen to practical considerations such as preempting telephone lines when the authorities are themselves desperately anxious to make contact.

Political Leaders' Strategies

The cross-national consensus among political leaders in the liberal democracies is that media coverage of terrorism constitutes incitement and that coverage should ideally be curtailed, though not necessarily as a result of government action. For cabinets and legislators, the principal manipulative strategies are

- supervisory censorship
- prohibiting certain coverage and requiring approval for other
- exhorting the media to greater prudence
- news micromanagement or manipulation
- enunciation of official guidelines
- intimidation by means of coercive precedent.

The less coercive options, discussed in ensuing sections, are for political leaders to

- encourage police-media collaboration with candid information offered in exchange for prudent reporting
- hope that journalists will adopt and respect their own reporting guidelines, and
- wait for journalists' reporting styles to evolve from an emphasis on drama and emotion to one on cognitive substance.

Direct supervisory censorship has been common in Latin America and parts of Africa. But it has tended to be sporadic and surreptitious among the advanced democracies. During the October 1970 FLQ crisis in Quebec,

24   Michael Somer, "Nation's Police Chiefs, Media Differ on Terrorism Coverage," *Daily Variety* (Aug. 17, 1978), 2.

the prime minister's office sent an emissary to control the news at the English language television network of the government-owned Canadian Broadcasting Corporation. The government's half-hearted effort did not extend to the private networks or those operating in the French language.

In the United Kingdom during much of the cold war, supervisory censorship affected personnel decisions. An official from the MI5 intelligence service, a retired senior military officer, played a role in hiring and promotion at the British Broadcasting Corporation. MI5's man did not apparently intervene directly in reporting in general or in the reporting of terrorism in particular.[25]

The *Bastille Syndrome* is the term used in France to describe various presidents' intensive interference in broadcasting. Before Francois Mitterand inaugurated parallel public and private broadcasting systems along Canadian lines, each president traditionally decided who would staff broadcast news programs and precisely how he himself would appear and be covered on French public television. Governmental economic power was such that presidents could in some circumstances hire and fire staff at nominally independent privately owned papers.[26] The heritage of censorship permitted capitalist France to afford even the Communist party some perquisites. In the mid-1980s, the *Parti communiste* persuaded the broadcasting regulatory authority to ban a documentary portraying a role for the party in betraying its own fighters to the Nazis during the German occupation.[27]

Compared to supervisory censorship, a less costly and less provocative form of control is for government to specify the kinds of coverage which are prohibited or that require prior approval for dissemination. Under long-standing British law, the central government possesses dictatorial authority over the BBC in times of crisis, emergency and war. The privately

---

25   "How the BBC Escaped from its Minders," *Guardian* (August 22, 1985) and "BBC Likely to Review its Rules on Staff Vetting," *Financial Times* (August 19, 1985). Censorship was not new at the vaunted BBC. During the 1930s, the BBC had embraced the Foreign Office view that the threat of Hitler ought not to be exaggerated. Churchill was kept off radio as a person deemed "too controversial." For an overview of MI5's role in hiring and promotion and BBC's system of double personnel files, see Mark Hollingsworth and Richard Norton-Taylor, *Blacklist: the Inside Story of Political Vetting* (London: Hogarth Press, 1988), 97-121.

26   See "Under official pressure...," *International Herald Tribune* (May 3, 1985).

27   "M. Fillioud et le PS estiment que la Haute Authorité a outrepassé ses pouvoirs," *Le Monde* (June 1, 1985), and "L'annulation de la diffusion..." *Le Monde* (May 31, 1985).

owned Independent Television companies (ITV) have been themselves legally responsible to censor programs that "incite crime and disorder." For this reason, programs on IRA fund-raising, the strength of the Provisional IRA, and related matters were frequently disallowed by the Independent Broadcasting Authority or postponed.[28]

It is perhaps not difficult to understand how government officials might stretch the meaning of emergency or crime and disorder to potential emergencies arising from terrorist activities. In August 1985, the Thatcher government successfully exerted pressure on the government-funded BBC to cancel the showing of an interview with convicted IRA leader Martin McGuiness in a documentary to be entitled "Real Lives: At the Edge of the Union." Replying to a question from the press during an American tour, Mrs. Thatcher had declared her opposition in general to any showing of an interview with any IRA person on BBC. When the possible showing of the particular interview with McGuiness came to light, Northern Ireland Home Secretary Douglas Hurd declared that he was "alarmed" at the prospect— "giving space to terrorists has a very powerful effect and it is up to the broadcasting authorities to understand this." Conservative party chairman John Selwyn Gummer followed up with the view that "the BBC should look very carefully at what it's doing to do" and "think again." "If the BBC has interviewed the IRA's chief of staff," he added, "it ought to be ashamed of itself."[29] Meanwhile British Home Secretary Leon Brittan, the minister responsible for broadcasting, wrote a strong letter to the chairman of the network.

The Board of Governors of the British Broadcasting Corporation decided to prohibit showing of the program. An ensuing statement from the government read as follows:

> The Home Office naturally welcomes the governors' decision and will be writing to the chairman to express his [i.e. the Home Secretary's] gratitude and to confirm that he will be happy to meet and discuss the issues relating to terrorism and the way it is handled on television which were raised in his letter to the chairman.[30]

In 1988, the then Home Secretary Douglas Hurd introduced regulations banning all interviews with members and supporters of proscribed organizations, principally the IRA. In early spring 1989 the regulations were partially lifted for the local elections in Ulster as well as for the June

28   David Elstein, "Why Can't We Broadcast the Truth?" in *The British Media and Ireland* (London, 1978), 14-15.
29   Quoted in *The Sunday Times* (July 28, 1985), 1.
30   Ibid., (July 31, 1985), 1.

European Community elections in the United Kingdom as a whole. Under the partial lifting, journalists could quote the comments of proscribed groups only if these comments pertained directly to the proscribed group's candidatures. In this complex situation, the IRA's political wing, Sinn Fein, could field candidates for election but these candidates and their supporters could appear on the BBC only to the extent that their statements were directly connected to the election they were contesting.[31]

British journalists responded with rage both to the initial decision to withhold broadcasting of "Real Lives: At the Edge of the Union" and the subsequent regulations limiting interviews with proscribed organizations and their adherents. British journalists reacted to the "Real Lives" episode with a 24-hour strike and a wave of published criticism. The BBC governors' decision was branded "an act of editorial cowardice" by National Union of Journalists' organizer John Foster.[32]

During the *Front de libération du Québec* crisis of October 1970, the Canadian government used the climate of emergency to have Parliament pass Public Order Regulations along with the *War Measures Act*. Regulations specified that those who communicated on behalf of certain prohibited groups were liable to prosecution. As a result, several radio stations became fearful of retransmitting terrorist demands in their entirety.[33]

For constitutional-legal reasons and because of differences of political culture, it has been more difficult for political leaders in the United States than elsewhere to implement a regime of supervisory censorship or to specify coverage that is prohibited or that requires prior permission. Instead, American political leaders have resorted to a great deal of exhor-

---

31 See the discussion in the BBC's magazine, *Ariel* (May 2, 1989), 3.
32 *The Sunday Times* (July 31, 1985), 1.
33 Ronald D. Crelinsten, "Terrorism and the Media: Problems, Solutions, and Counterproblems," *Political Communication and Persuasion* (1989), 329. On the FLQ crisis, see Ronald D. Crelinsten, "Power and Meaning: Terrorism as a Struggle over Access to the Communication Structure," in Paul Wilkinson and A. M. Stewart, eds., *Contemporary Research on Terrorism* (Aberdeen: University of Aberdeen Press, 1987), 419-50, and his "The Internal Dynamics of the FLQ During the October Crisis of 1970," in David C. Rapoport, ed., *Inside Terrorist Organizations* (New York: Columbia University Press, 1988), 59-89.

tation. Former Secretary of State Henry Kissinger declared that "what the media ought to consider is not carrying anything, including the terrorists."[34] Representative Thomas A. Luken, a member of a House subcommittee examining the media and diplomacy in the Middle East in 1985, observed pointedly that coverage is "the ransom...now paid to terrorists who kill, particularly American hostages."[35] Congressman Lukens proceeded to decry the situation whereby "TV becom[es]...a coproducer of hostage drama, coproducer with the terrorists..." Sometime Undersecretary of State Lawrence Eagleburger called upon television to comprehend "the fact that...terrorists do what they do, at least in part, because of the publicity [television] gives them."[36] Representative Edward Feighan, cochairman of a House subcommittee on media and terrorism, denounced media coverage for excess, tastelessness, and irresponsibility.[37]

Presidents Carter and Reagan, Secretary of State George Shultz and countless less prominent politicians have bid the media to adopt more responsible norms of conduct. Several political leaders have argued that the roots of journalists' ostensible irresponsibility lie in cutthroat economic and professional pressures. Lawrence Eagleburger called upon the U.S. "networks...to think about...whether...they ought not eliminate the competitive factors between the networks and...work together." The media conglomerates vie with each other for priority access to terrorists and ignore lives and U.S. national interests because of "competitive instincts."[38] Were the networks to concert their efforts in terrorist situations, they would have more opportunity to reflect upon the implications for their society of the way in which they conduct themselves. Commenting in the wake of discussions of media coverage of the Beirut hijacking, Eagleburger expressed dismay that journalists continued to protest "their innocence, [and made] no real admissions that they [had done] anything wrong."

Not to be outdone, Prime Minister Margaret Thatcher also urged her views on her audiences:

> We must try to find ways to starve the terrorist and hijacker of the oxygen of publicity on which they depend. In our [democratic] societies we do not believe

34   Source: CBS News transcript, CBS News Special Report, "Continuing Coverage of the Hostages of Flight 847," June 20, 1985.

35   Statement to the Subcommittee on Europe and the Middle East of the Committee on Foreign Affairs of the House of Representatives, Hearing, July 30, 1985, Washington, D.C., 2.

36   "Viewpoint: TV Reporting under the Gun," ABC, July 30, 1985.

37   Ibid.

38   "Viewpoint: TV Reporting under the Gun," ABC, July 30, 1985.

in constraining the media, still less in censorship. But ought we not to ask the media to agree among themselves on a voluntary code of conduct, a code under which they would not say or show anything that could assist the terrorists' morale and their cause?[39]

Some backbench Members of the British House of Commons were less restrained in expressing their frustrations with the effect of the media coverage of outbreaks of domestic and international terrorist violence. Eldon Griffiths M.P., parliamentary advisor to the Police Federation, declared in the House in May 1980 that

we are in the presence of a concerted campaign in the fringes of politics, in the media and occasionally in this House, to denigrate the police service...as Cossacks...racialists...corrupter...and as fascists. No organ of opinion in this country has done more to disseminate and endorse these mendacities than the BBC.[40]

Intriguingly, polling data show that the British public views independent television as more leftwing and critical of Conservative government than the government-owned BBC.[41] The antagonism of the Conservative government toward the BBC may be ascribed in part to its misgivings about governmental institutions as a whole, but it is also attributable to a special rage about the ways in which BBC covered terrorism.

Apart from exhorting the media to "prudent" reporting, governments can themselves seek to micromanage or manipulate the news to their advantage. Public and media relations experts attached to cabinets, justice departments, or security offices can seek to dissuade individual reporters from covering particular events or to persuade them to cover them from a particular perspective.

Occasionally, Western governments have sought to transform to their advantage the apparent media successes of terrorist organizations and the states that provide them succor. The United States' bombing of Libya in April 1986 was an example of such an effort to turn media loss into media victory. The U.S. Air Force raid was portrayed by the White House as an attempt to punish the world's leading terrorist state. In spite of its substantial media profile, Libya was in fact rarely the main state sponsor of

---

39 Speech before the American Bar Association, July, 1985.
40 Clutterbuck, *The Media and Political Violence*, 67.
41 As many as 85% of respondents saw BBC1 and BBC2 networks as pro-Conservative compared to only 43% in the case of ITV and 17% in the case of the independent Channel 4. By the same token, more than 50% saw ITV and C4 as pro-Labour as compared to 15% or fewer in the case of the two BBC television services. See "Attitudes to Broadcasting," a study commissioned by the Independent Broadcasting Authority (Summer 1985).

international terrorism. Damascus's involvement in terrorism, including attacks on U.S. military personnel, was as ample, perhaps greater. But Colonel Qaddafi's achievements in media grandstanding provided his government with a far stronger image as a state sponsor of terrorism than was true of Syria's government under its more stolid president. Thus, it was easier for the White House to elicit the acquiescence of the American people and the cooperation of NATO allies in undertaking the raid than would have been the case had the target been other than Tripoli. New York University's Professor Neil Postman argues that "without television month after month showing Qaddafi's face and terrorism's carnage, Libya's presence would have been largely ignored."[42]

The Reagan White House was so excited about the opportunity for media countermanipulation that an elaborate campaign of *disinformation* was inaugurated in August 1986. Media reports were carefully seeded with false information about alleged turmoil within Libya, Qaddafi's ostensibly central role in a network of international terrorism, and an anticipated new confrontation between Libya and the United States. By so doing, National Security Advisor Admiral John Poindexter hoped that Qaddafi would be prone to ever more frantic behavior and his regime would become susceptible to more internal dissension and potentially a coup d'état.[43] Poindexter likewise sought to intensify Qaddafi's image among Americans as a terrorist and thus prepare the groundwork for public support for a military strike against Libya.

Governmental efforts in the United States and other liberal democracies to censor, micromanage, or countermanipulate the media on terrorist issues are less numerous than in the case of nonterrorist issues. Known governmental efforts to combat terrorism by means of censorship are less frequent than known efforts to manipulate media systems for partisan party or ideological advantage.

In both the United States and Canada, the funding of public broadcasting has been affected by the partisan fears or ambitions of particular governments in power. In each country, individual news programs are known to

---

42 Cited in "TV Brings Home Terror's Message," *U.S. News & World Report* (April 28, 1986), 29.
43 Poindexter's plan was enunciated in an August 14, 1986 memorandum to the President, as revealed in reports by Bob Woodward in the *Washington Post*.

have been cancelled at the behest of government. In Canada, the highest-rated public affairs show in television history, "This House Has Seven Days," was discontinued in the 1960s because its oppositional mentality rankled the Liberal government of the day. A generation later, the Reagan administration stopped the production of a PBS special on the Soviet Union by the expedient of withdrawing funding for it.[44] The fact that paymasters, governmental or private, have succeeded at times in influencing news coverage on nonterrorist issues could conceivably intimidate journalists in their reporting of terrorist events.

The last remaining quasi-coercive or manipulative strategy available to government is to enunciate guidelines for the coverage of terrorism. Such guidelines, often released through security officialdom, were discussed in the preceding section on security responses to the media-terror nexus.

Executive-media Concordance

A gentle alternative to governmental intervention is government-media collaboration. The most comprehensive attempt to strike an informal agreement between government and journalism took place in the United States under the aegis of the National Advisory Committee on Criminal Justice Standards and Goals. In December 1976, the Advisory Committee's Task Force on Disorders and Terrorism released a 661-page report, devoted in significant measure to proposing a working relationship between the state and the media for the coverage of terrorism. The Task Force acknowledged that "hard rules [could not] be prescribed" to govern media performance and that "whatever principles can be prescribed must be generated by the media themselves, out of a recognition of special public responsibility."

The Task Force's recommendations for news coverage were comprehensive. The detailed advice addressed such matters as

- the use of pool reporters
- limits on high-intensity lighting
- limits on soliciting interviews with participants
- primary use of official spokespersons for discussions of law enforcement operations

44 "Corporation for Public Broadcasting's Pfister Resigns as President," *Wall Street Journal* (May 21, 1985). For a discussion of a state government's politically motivated meddling in public television, see "This Network Is Brought to You by Trenton," *New York Times* (January 12, 1986).

- delayed reporting of information apt to inflame the situation, contribute to a contagion effect, or undermine tactical planning by law enforcement
- a reporting balance between terrorists' self-serving statements on the one hand and official statements and victim information on the other.

The recommendation for an accord between government and journalism fell completely on deaf ears, perhaps because of the vibrant tradition of mistrust of government upon which the country was founded. By contrast, (West) German authorities and media have developed a very close working relationship even in the absence of a blueprint as detailed as that of the U.S. Task Force.

The concurrence of the media and the Bonn authorities was reflected in their coordinated handling of the subsequently well publicized kidnapping and death of Hans Martin Schleyer in September 1977. Prior to the event, the chief of the federal press and information office had persuaded the heads of the significant broadcasting and press organizations to observe a news embargo or "rationing"; information received from terrorists and their confederates would first be vetted by government officials. The executives of the remaining media were subsequently asked to comply as well.

For the six-week duration of the kidnapping, the German press office monitored all German media including even magazines plus more than two dozen foreign agencies operating in the Federal Republic. When an occasional item deemed harmful appeared in a wire service transmission, the press office either succeeded in persuading the agency to block the item's appearance or promptly issued its own denial.

The embargo or "rationing" was largely successful. Less than one-tenth of the country's daily newspapers failed to fully observe the government's request for prudence. Most of the terrorists' 139 communications to 37 media were not reported. The frustrated terrorists' attempts to gain the attention of the media in neighboring countries were likewise blocked. Subsequent public opinion data showed that about three-quarters of the German public were supportive of the embargo.[45] In the midst of the crisis,

---

[45] On this point, see H. J. Horchem, *Terrorism in West Germany* (London: The Institute for the Study of Conflict, 1986). For a fulsome account of the six-week period, see Schmid and de Graaf, *Violence*, 148-55.

Klaus Bolling, the head of the press and information office, articulated the rationale for the "rationing" in a letter to media editors as follows: "We all know how much publicity matters to the terrorists and that they try to use press, radio and television as instruments for their purpose. Please help us in thwarting these intentions of the kidnappers."[46]

The experience of press-government collaboration in Great Britain falls somewhere in between that of Germany and that of the United States. In 1973, Sir Robert Mark, then Commissioner of the London Metropolitan police, introduced various rules as the basis of collaboration between the security forces and the press. Reporters were invited to agree to delay transmission of information that, in the judgment of the police, could place lives at risk. In turn, consenting reporters were granted special passes entitling them to frequent, detailed, and candid briefings.

Media Self-restraint

In a cross-national study of broadcasters' own rules for reporting on terrorism, Paletz and Tawney identified five levels of media prudence, ranging from a complete absence of recorded guidelines to detailed rules for covering terrorism in particular:

- level 1—no guidelines or even approaches
- level 2—only general philosophies or approaches to the coverage of terrorism
- level 3—rules for coverage of violence and disorder but not terrorism in particular
- level 4—standardized guidelines
- level 5—detailed codes.[47]

The general tendency is for the content of the guidelines at levels 4 and 5 to correspond to what the security forces and political executives of governments would desire. For example, at level 4, broadcasters specify that reporters should not contribute to the sensationalism of an event, should paraphrase terrorists' demands, and obey the police. At level 5, reporters are specifically enjoined to avoid any language that would portray

---

46   Letter dated September 15, 1977, 10 days after the abduction. Reprinted in J. K. Klein, "Der Deutsche Terrorismus in den Perspectiven der Konfliktforschung," *Beitrage zur Konfliktforschung*, 7(1977), 153.

47   David L. Paletz and Laura L. Tawney, "Broadcasting Organizations' Perspectives," in Paletz and Schmid, eds., *Terrorism and the Media*, 105-111.

terrorist groups as "legitimate," to cite the term used in the BBC codebook.[48]

According to the analysis of guidelines undertaken by Paletz and Tawney, British and other Commonwealth broadcasters (Canada excepted) tend to possess level 5 guidelines while North American broadcasters function at level 4. The apparently more sporadic commitment to self-regulation of American broadcasters appears consistent with other evidence of the lesser enthusiasm of the United States media for self-regulation. A press and radio survey undertaken in the late 1970s showed that 38% of U.S. newspapers and radio outlets possessed written rules on the reporting of terrorism while 52% did not.[49] Some prominent media organizations, notably the *New York Times* and NBC have repudiated guidelines on principle. The *Times*'s A. M. Rosenthal expressed deep concern lest the freedom and diversity of the press be undermined: "As soon as you start imposing guidelines, they become peer group pressure, then quasi-legal restrictions."[50] A spokesperson for NBC News expressed fear that guidelines would "limit our flexibility."[51]

In retrospect, the experience of CBS and the other media who adopted guidelines showed that any fear of constraint on media initiatives was groundless. Once in the midst of crisis, guidelines were overlooked. Our own comparison of CBS's guidelines and its actual coverage of the 1985 TWA hijacking showed that each of its guidelines was disregarded and that its coverage was indistinguishable from that of ABC, which lacked guidelines, and NBC, which expressed strong objection to them. R. A. Friedlander's study of guidelines and media coverage of the Iranian hostage crisis reached parallel conclusions:

> Throughout the Iranian captivity, these guidelines were ignored to a far greater extent than they were observed. All three television networks, taking advantage

48 ibid., 109.
49 Study conducted by Michael and Heidi Sommer and reported in the appendix in Miller, *Terrorism, the Media and the Law.*
50 Quoted in D. Shaw, "Editors Face Terrorist Demand Dilemma," *Los Angeles Times* (September 15, 1976).
51 Letter by Richard C. Wald to the United States Congress, Committee on Judiciary, Subcommittee on Civil and Constitutional Rights, *Federal Capabilities in Crisis Management and Terrorism*, 95th Congress, 2nd session, 1979, 115.

of the Iranian drama, developed a blind eye to professional ethical considerations in a fervent competitive quest for audiences.[52]

Though observed mainly in the breach, the guidelines formally adopted by CBS, UPI, the *Chicago Sun-Times*, and other media are intriguing for what they reflect about the culture of journalism. The content of the guidelines do reflect the existence of a professional ethic and a profound sense about how journalism should be conducted in a democratic society. As Miller has noted, these guidelines embody the main principles of good journalism transmitted in professional schools of journalism.[53]

Paradoxically and ironically, the guidelines also reflect the view of journalism in a democratic society articulated by journalism's most severe mainstream critics. Most of the guidelines are too lengthy to be explored here in great detail, but consider the following salient features:

- coverage should be "thoughtful, conscientious and show restraint," to use the particular language of UPI, and "not sensationalized," in the words of the *Chicago Sun-Times*
- terrorist demands ought ideally to be paraphrased and not presented live in order to avoid "fall[ing] into the trap of providing an unedited platform" (CBS)
- coverage should be low-key, "avoiding the use of inflammatory catchwords or phrases, the reporting of rumors, etc." (CBS)
- reporters should not "inject...themselves into the story as intermediaries or negotiators" (UPI) or take other action that would attract undue attention to the episode and "crowd out other important news" (CBS) or endanger or hamper police
- decisions about "information [to] be withheld or deferred" should be made by senior editors (*Chicago Sun-Times*).

Apart from these specific and detailed directions to their staffs, media guidelines for the coverage of terrorism are noteworthy because they frequently pay homage to the problem of "contagion." The guidelines of the

---

52   "Iran: The Hostage Seizure, the Media and International Law" in Miller, ed., *Terrorism, the Media and the Law*, 59.

53   A. Miller, "Terrorism and the Media: Observations from the American and British Experiences," in P. J. Montana and G. S. Roukis, eds., *Managing Terrorism* (Westport, Conn.: Quorum Books, 1983), 97.

Chicago Sun-Times and CBS begin by mentioning "the dangers of contagion," albeit in quotation marks in the case of the network document. Both documents pronounce the necessity of covering terrorism "despite the dangers of contagion." In the judgment of the *Chicago Sun-Times*, the "adverse effects of suppression are greater" than its benefits.

Paradoxically, the formal guidelines adopted by various media for their own regulation reflect a view of the world that is similar, perhaps even identical, to the views of many mainstream critics of the media. The guidelines are consistent with the perspectives often held by security forces and political executives functioning under stress. The American media's formal guidelines recognize the desirability of depriving terrorists of publicity without depriving citizens of information, the importance of avoiding theatricality, and the necessity of reporters' remaining nonparticipants. The guidelines even acknowledge the unfortunate potential contribution of the media to a contagion effect. And yet, the dramatic and sensationalist features that so many journalists feel should not receive excessive reinforcement are a good part of what journalists find seductive in terrorist actions.[54]

Journalists appear caught between competitive audience-seeking pressures for drama on the one hand and professional, ethical impulses for reasonableness on the other. In the words of Crelinsten, there may be "an inherent contradiction between the *ideology* of good reporting and the *practice* of good reporting."[55]

---

54   See A. P. Schmid, "Editors' Perspectives," in Paletz and Schmid, eds., *Terrorism and the Media,, 111-36.*

55   Ronald D. Crelinsten, "Terrorism and the Media," *Political Communication and Persuasion* (1989), 332.

Chapter 11

Must the Show Go On?

The book set out to examine one aspect of terrorism, the media, and one component of terrorism, international acts. It presented statistical and anecdotal information on the evolution of modern international terrorism, more media-oriented than in the past as a result of technological and social emergence of modern media. It examined how terrorists have sought to make use of the media and how and why the media made use of terrorism. The book assessed the impacts of this *ménage à deux* on public opinion, government decisionmakers, and the terrorists themselves.

The principal data examined quantitatively over the course of these pages consist of three parts: the RAND Corporation data on terrorist acts by international terrorist groups, the Vanderbilt Archive data on coverage of these events by the three principal American television networks, and our own content analysis of coverage of these same acts by nine newspapers around the world—in North America, Western Europe, the Middle East, and South Asia. In addition, we reported the results of an experimental examination of the impact of media coverage on public images of terrorists, and analyzed media guidelines governing the reporting of terrorist acts.

Chapter 1 began by exploring the histrionic aspects of the 1985 TWA hijacking in Beirut and ABC anchor Sam Donaldson's question, "The terrorists won, right?" The Beirut episode and Donaldson's question set the stage for our study. Our analysis was not concerned with the manifold psychological, sociological, economic, and other forces at the root of terrorism nor with organizational and technological aspects of violence. Our analysis has been concerned with the theatrical opportunities available to terrorists thanks to modern electronic communication and with the impact of these opportunities on terrorists as well as on their various audiences and opponents.

Chapter 2 began with a brief discussion of controversies in the definition of terrorism. The subsequent empirical analysis showed a continuing growth in the incidence of international terrorism and in the incidence of injuries and fatalities. As the symbols of state, diplomats were once the target of preference. But the data demonstrated the evolving primacy of businessmen and ordinary civilians as targets, presumably as a result of diplomats' enhanced security precautions.

International terrorist acts were most apt to involve American or perhaps Israeli victims and to take place in Europe rather than on other continents. We acknowledged that the targeting of Americans had roots in anti-U.S. objectives by terrorist groups. But the targeting of Americans was also rooted in the primacy of the American media and hence the special newsworthiness of American citizens as victims. The instrumental media value of American citizens as victims helped to explain, for example, the preponderant targeting of Americans rather than Israelis among Palestinians and other Middle Eastern terrorist groups.

A unifying theme in our analysis was that coverage by daily newspapers and television can be a major incentive for terrorist action. The technological evolution of television has enhanced the value of the incentive. This, we argued, helps to account for terrorists' more intensified concern for media attention.

Nonetheless, not all contemporary international terrorist groups have been equally media-motivated. The data showed, for example, that French, Irish and some other European groups fit relatively well the mold of traditional, multimotivated terrorists during the period under study. For example, Irish terrorists focused much more on military and governmental targets than on newsworthy diplomats or civilians while French terrorists emphasized business leaders and the police. Both categories targeted enemy nationals (i.e., British and French) rather than the more newsworthy Americans.

If Palestinian terrorists had been traditional and multi-motivated, they would have targeted their Israeli and Jordanian enemies during the period in question along with Americans. But the Palestinians tended to fit the mold of the modern, more single-mindedly media-motivated group. Thus, Palestinian terrorists were more than twice as likely to attack Americans as Israelis and more than 10 times as likely to attack Americans as Jordanians.

Chapter 3 on media-oriented terrorism began with an examination of the media within the terrorists' own paradigm. It explored media motivations among earlier terrorists and in the published writing of terrorist strategist Carlos Marighela and others. We explored in some depth the media practices of some European groups thanks to our interview with a retired European terrorist, code-named "D."

The systematic empirical component of this chapter reported on the coverage provided by 12 media around the world. Our factor analysis yielded a shared pattern of television coverage and a moderately shared pattern of press coverage. The *New York Times* emerged as the most typical or representative of the print media. Its coverage was relatively intercorrelated with other English language papers and with the Israeli paper in the study. The Egyptian and Pakistani papers tended to be the most independent of the others in their patterns of coverage.

Location and nationality of victims emerged as factors in coverage. The three American networks gave greater attention to incidents in North America and the Middle East. Patterns of coverage among the newspapers were more complex, reflecting national priorities, individual newspaper traditions, and other factors. For example, the Frankfurt paper provided very modest rates of coverage in the case of German victims, a phenomenon that may have reflected the pressure of security forces not to satisfy German terrorists' quest for media attention.

Events were especially apt to be covered if perpetrated by Palestinian or other Middle Eastern terrorists and especially if Israeli victims were involved. Unfortunately, too many different explanations were available for accounting for the significance of Israeli victims. Israeli victims may have been newsworthy because of the media skills of Palestinian and Middle Eastern terrorists, including their lethality, because of the region's strategically significant oil reserves, because of Israel's war against terrorism, or because Jews and Israelis are especially newsworthy for biblical, Holocaust and/or other interrelated reasons.

Chapter four looked at terrorism through the prism of the concept of the media event, an occurrence that secures its meaning and significance from its mediated nature. The chapter discussed various attributes of the media event such as preplanning, drama, and the priestly role of journalists.

The exploration of terrorist incidents as a subset of media events set the stage for an analysis of predictors of coverage in Chapter 5. After reviewing the anecdotal evidence of terrorist coercion against the press, the chapter provided a quantitative overview of predictors of coverage and patterns of terrorist conduct. The chapter showed that traditional conceptions of newsworthiness such as scarcity, drama, and intensity of human emotion did help account for patterns of coverage. For example, hijackings were more than twice as likely to be covered as attacks on installations.

In the case of television, terrorist events were apt to receive more attention if injuries and fatalities were involved, the perpetrators were Palestinian, and responsibility was known, whereas they were less likely to be covered if responsibility was unknown and the action was a bombing. The degree of press attention was explained by similar variables.

The data showed that an event was more apt to be covered at all if the perpetrators were Palestinian or perhaps Irish, if injuries and/or fatalities were involved, if a hijacking took place, and/or if Israelis were the victims. Thus, the data reported to this point in our analysis suggested that astute terrorists could enhance their likelihood of achieving news attention by purposeful injury and death.

Chapter 6 explored the question of the ultimate impact of terrorism on the public in the course of discussing the scholarly evidence about media effects, media power, status conferral, agenda setting, priming, and contagion. The chapter concluded with results from an experiment showing opinion change as a result of coverage of terrorist violence.

From our cross-national observational data, it is evident that international terrorists might enhance their likelihood of coverage by becoming more violent. From our experimental data, a conclusion is that coverage may enhance the position of terrorists' issues on the public agenda. And yet, Christopher Hewitt's findings suggest that terrorists are more apt to reap a public reward when their conduct is perceived as charitable, or at least less lethal than anticipated.[1] If, as Hewitt shows, public interpretations of terrorists' motives are important in public appraisals, media interpretations of terrorists' motives must be important as well. Chapter 7 focused on media presentations and interpretations of terrorism.

The chapter began with a discussion of the emergence of social science-type "root cause" explanations of violent and criminal conduct. We argued that these extenuating explanations could just as easily apply to domestic criminals as to international terrorists in light of the subjugating socioeconomic and racial conditions from which criminals often emerge. But criminals have been much less apt than terrorists to benefit from such interpretations because of the normally greater societal taboos governing the coverage of domestic as opposed to international violence.

Our empirical analysis showed that international terrorists achieved an approximately 50 percent success rate in securing media recognition for their purported motives. Our data showed that the proclaimed motives of terrorists had a good chance of being mentioned in the first page of a daily newspaper or among the first three stories in a nightly television newscast.

---

1   See Christopher Hewitt, "Terrorism and Public Opinion: A Five Country Comparison," *Terrorism and Political Violence* (1989), 144-70.

Self-serving motives were especially apt to be reported when the fatality rate was high. Thus, international terrorists had a double incentive to be lethal: the probability of coverage increased as did the likelihood of the terrorists' goals being reported.

Furthermore, while increasing the likelihood of event coverage and reporting of motive, lethality did not necessarily produce negative labeling. The *New York Times*, the most influential of the newspapers, resorted to negative labels in only 30% of cases. Furthermore, the most deadly of the groups, the Armenians, was tied with Cubans for the most positive labeling among the newspapers in our study. The moral clarity of the Armenian terrorists' proclaimed motives appeared to have more than made up for the deadly cruelty of their actions.

Chapter 8 turned to the measurement of a contagion effect. Our quantitative analysis yielded considerable evidence of a contagion effect wrought by coverage. The existence of television coverage was associated with a shortened time lag to emulation in the case of kidnapping, attacks on installations, hijackings, bombings, and assassinations. The one terrorist action not apparently affected by televised coverage was street barricades, perhaps the most spontaneous of deeds. Among the newspapers, the *New York Times* appears to have had the greatest impact on time lags to emulation. As in the case of television, *New York Times* reporting was associated with shortened time lags to replication in the case of every terrorist deed except barricades. In a somewhat similar vein, each of the 12 media appeared to exercise an impact on the frequency of emulation.

Chapter 9 examined briefly the "critical" perspective on the media-terrorism relationship. We acknowledged the radical and sometimes Marxist assertion that Western regimes and their third world allies have been responsible for some degree of state-sponsored terrorism but did not share the radicals' estimation of its magnitude relative to other sources of terrorism. In an analogous vein, we acknowledged the conservatives' assertions about state-sponsored terror by communist and radical regimes. But we did not accept that the existence of these two forms of state-sponsored terror warranted overlooking nonstate international terrorism, the focus of our analysis in this study. We suggested that the concept of a theater of terror may go part way toward reconciling the two approaches, permitting a joint understanding of media-seeking and media-avoiding terrorist behavior.

Chapter 10 discussed analytically and anecdotally the stresses experienced by security forces and political executives, the institutions held accountable by publics for combating terrorism. Their three main stresses were a perception that journalistic treatment of terrorism is an incentive for it, that journalistic interventions during terrorist acts can jeopardize life, and that journalists can place an undue limitation on the ability of government to combat terrorism.

From the particular stresses experienced by security forces and executives mandated to curtail terrorism have emerged desires, proposals, and actual actions to limit journalistic freedom in terrorist contexts. In light of our findings on the impact of terrorist lethality on coverage and especially on the impact of coverage on replication, we are deeply concerned about media practice. But the dangers of external controls on the media far exceed the harm done by immoderate, excessive, or ill-considered media treatment of terrorist outbreaks.

Thinking about how media in democratic societies should cover terrorism is not just an "academic" or hypothetical question. It would be a mistake to forecast the demise of international terrorism because of the collapse of the Soviet empire, which often provided succor to terrorist groups. If the demise of the Soviet system cut off support for some terrorist groups, it also offered new opportunities. Armenian terrorists, for example, have mounted several attacks for the first time within the boundaries of the former Soviet Union.

Thinking about how media should cover terrorism is an important issue because a fear of terrorism has contributed to the vulnerability of democracies to absolutist tendencies. Greece, for example, enacted a law banning the publication of terrorist proclamations. In 1991, the editors of seven newspapers were sentenced to jail terms of up to 10 months for having violated the legislation.[2]

Even in the strongest of the liberal democracies, political executives and security forces have shown an uneven ability to observe the niceties of liberal democratic theory whether or not terrorism is a factor. British intelligence's intrigues against Harold Wilson's Labour government, Canada's use of a *War Measures Act* against a phantom insurrection, and Watergate belong to a long list of perilous actions that are best counterbalanced by an unsubdued press.

An untamed press is indispensable not only for liberal democracy as a whole but also for effective counterterrorist efforts in particular. An everpresent self-confident press helps inhibit security forces under siege from

---

2   "Greek Court Sentences 7 Newspaper Editors for Publicizing Terrorists," *New York Times International* (September 10, 1991).

lashing out in ways that could debilitate the democratic regime they defend and enhance support for the terrorists they are combating.

Some polling has been conducted to measure public attitudes toward media coverage of terrorism, particularly in the United States. Public attitudes appear to be complex and multidimensional. On the one hand, respondents in U.S. polls believe that terrorism would persist with or without television (84%) and that television should cover terrorist incidents even if such coverage caused more such violence (60%).[3] On the other hand, majorities believe that television coverage incites other subsequent terrorist events (75%) and shows more sympathy for perpetrators than victims (55%), and that the press gives terrorists too much opportunity to promote their causes (56%).[4] An overwhelming majority (76%) believes that terrorist success rests on publicity from the media, who often do terrorists' bidding and exaggerate terrorist incidents.[5] Ninety percent take the view that television reporters should check with police before broadcasting information that might affect negotiations with perpetrators. A clear majority (62%) would simply prohibit television coverage in order to withhold the publicity that terrorists seek.[6]

The route to the temperate, considered reporting of terrorism lies partly with more reasoned consumer preferences by readers of newspapers and viewers of television. If audiences learned to prefer reasoned discourse on the news over "infotainment" and "terrorvision," media business managers would take notice, and so too would producers and editors of news.

The route to the temperate, considered reporting of terrorism also lies with the professional culture of journalists. Their professional culture has undergone many transformations in the past. The timidity and trepidation of television reporters toward national governments in the English-speaking democracies in the 1950s is nowhere to be seen today. It is only a matter of time before journalists will temper their enthusiasm at the theatrical prospects of terrorism coverage with an enhanced sensitivity to the impact of their reporting. Journalists' sensitivity to the impact of reporting is central to the notion of a responsible press, an issue that we addressed in Chapter 1.

---

3   ABC/WP poll, January 1986, cited in Ronald H. Hinkley, *People, Polls, and Policymakers* (New York: Lexington Books, 1992), 101.

4   ABC/WP poll, January 1986, and "The People & the Press," (Los Angeles: September 12 & 14, 1986), cited in Hinckley, *People, Polls, and Policymakers*, 101.

5   D/M/I poll, July 1-3, 1985, cited in Hinckley, *People, Polls, and Policymakers*, 101.

6   ABC/WP poll, January 1986, cited in Hinckley, *People, Polls, and Policymakers*, 101.

11 Must the Show Go On?

It is to be hoped that a more sensitive professional culture will emerge sooner rather than later. The world is witnessing an intensification of primordial loyalties, often a significant element in international terrorism, along with an increasing availability of inexpensive technologically advanced weaponry well suited to certain terrorist endeavors.

Appendix

Database Outline

Since its initial work on terrorism in 1972, the RAND Corporation developed specialized chronologies documenting actual cases of the use of political violence. These computerized events data are accessible via an enhanced data retrieval system developed by RAND.

The material for these databases is derived from a wide array of public domain sources. Over 100 newspapers, journals, and periodicals have been surveyed monthly in English and five other languages. Appropriate material is clipped and stored in a hardcopy file while information on events is abstracted and entered into the computer files. The oldest and most extensive of these files is of incidents of terrorism from 1968 to the present. The RAND Corporation adheres to the definition of terrorism as:

> The use of violence, or the threat of violence, calculated to create an atmosphere of fear and alarm. It is defined by the nature of the act, not by the identity of the perpetrators or the nature of their cause. All terrorist acts are crimes. Many would also be violations of the rules of war, if a state of war existed. All involve violence or the threat of violence, usually directed against civilian targets. The motives of most terrorists are political, and terrorist actions are generally carried out in a way that will achieve maximum publicity. The perpetrators are usually members of an organized group, and unlike other criminals, they often claim credit for their acts. Finally, a terrorist act is intended to produce effects beyond the immediate physical damage it causes.

This chronology includes only those incidents of an international nature in which terrorists went abroad to strike their target, selected victims or targets that had connections with a foreign state (e.g., diplomats, foreign businessmen, offices of foreign corporations), or created international incidents by attacking airline passengers, personnel, and equipment. Incidents in which groups such as the Irish Republican Army or the Red Brigades of Italy directed attacks against their own government or citizens in their own territory are excluded (the terrorist actions of some indigenous terrorist groups are recorded in separate chronologies). The Chronology of International Terrorism used in the present study contains over 5,000 incidents. Abstracts and data are accessed by the computer based database management system.

Appendix

Datebase Codes

All incidents in each RAND chronology are listed by date, and accompanying each event is a set of coded variables for ease of access. We used these codes to retrieve certain types of information rapidly, but only that information which readily lends itself to coding. Other relevant information is retained in the textual rendition and is amenable to full-text key word searches. The following symbols indicate the type of event and specific chronology:

Type of action (B)
B1 - Kidnapping

B2 - Attacks on installations, including grenade attacks, arson, sabotage other than by bombing

B3 - Hijackings

B4 - Bombings

B5 - Barricade and hostage

B6 - Assassinations, shootings

B7 - Threats, conspiracies, serious protests, others

Fatalities (F)

Exact number of fatalities

Injuries (I)

Exact number of injuries

Target (T)

T00 - Unknown

T01 - Diplomatic

T02 - Business

T03 - Military

T04 - Police

T05 - Airlines

T06 - Private citizens, communities

T07 - Utilities, energy (T07a for oil, T07b for electric), communications facilities

T08 - Government, including politicians in and out of office, government buildings, all of the host country

T09 - Exiles, immigrants

T10 - Religious

T11 - Other, and nonspecific multiple

T12 - Maritime

T13 - Nuclear facilities

T14 - Towns

T15 - Transportation (other than air, sea)

T16 - Terrorists as targets

Geographical location (G)
NA - North America

EU - Europe

LA - Latin America

AS - Asia

ME - Middle East/North Africa/Persian Gulf

SA - Sub-Saharan Africa

Responsibility (C)

C00 - Known, or otherwise evident

C01 - Claimed, meaning intention or act of taking public responsibility for an action, often in the name of the group

C02 - Attributed to, but no claim

C03 - Unclaimed and unknown

C04 - Disclaimed

C05 - Multiple, unsubstantiated claims

Appendix: Database Codes

Nationality of targets (N)
and country location of incident (S)
Nationality = NOOOO, State = SOOOO
'N' or 'S' preceding code

Country codes (numerical)
002 United States
020 Canada
030 Bermuda
031 Bahamas
040 Cuba
041 Haiti
042 Dominican Republic
043 Puerto Rico
044 Virgin Islands
046 Antigua
047 Grenada
050 West Indies Federation
051 Jamaica
052 Trinidad-Tobago
053 Barbados
054 Dominica
059 Montserrat
060 St. Kitts, Nevis. Anguila
065 Guadeloupe
066 Martinique
068 Netherlands Antilles
070 Mexico
080 British Honduras
090 Guatemala
091 Honduras
092 El Salvador
093 Nicaragua
094 Costa Rica
095 Panama
096 Panama Canal Zone
099 Latin nation, indeter.

100 Colombia
101 Venezuela
102 Curacao
103 Aruba
110 Guyana, British Guyana
115 Surinam, Dutch Guyana
120 French Guyana
130 Ecuador
135 Peru
140 Brazil
145 Bolivia
150 Paraguay
155 Chile
160 Argentina
165 Uruguay
196 Central Common Market
198 Alliance for Progress
199 Org. of American States
200 United Kingdom
201 Isle of Man
202 Guernsey
205 Ireland
206 Scotland
210 Netherlands
211 Belgium
212 Luxembourg
219 Corsica
220 France
221 Monaco
223 Liechtenstein
225 Switzerland
230 Spain
231 Gibraltar
232 Andorra
235 Portugal
255 Federal Republic of Germany

265 German Democratic Republic	400 Azores
266 East Berlin	402 Cape Verde
267 West Berlin Market	404 Guinea-Bissau
268 Latvia Trade Assn.	410 Equatorial Guinea
269 Estonia indeterminate	411 Spanish Guinea
270 Lithuania	420 Gambia
273 Northern Ireland	432 Mali
290 Poland	433 Senegal
291 Greenland	434 Benin, Dahomey
300 European, indeter.	435 Mauritania
305 Austria	436 Niger
310 Hungary	437 Ivory Coast
315 Czechoslovakia Republic	438 Guinea
325 Italy	439 Upper Volta
328 Vatican	450 Liberia
331 San Marino	451 Sierra Leone
338 Malta	452 Ghana
339 Albania	460 Togo
345 Yugoslavia	471 Cameroon
346 Croatia	475 Nigeria
350 Greece	476 Biafra
352 Cyprus	481 Gabon
355 Bulgaria	482 Central African Republic
360 Romania	483 Chad
365 USSR	484 Congo (Brazzaville)
375 Finland	490 Zaire (Belgian Congo)
380 Sweden	500 Uganda
385 Norway	501 Kenya
390 Denmark	510 Tanzania
393 Comecon	511 Zanzibar
394 Warsaw Pact	515 Ruanda-Urundi
395 Iceland	516 Burundi
396 NATO	517 Rwanda
397 European Common Market	520 Somalia
398 European Free Trade Assn.	522 Djibouti
399 United Nations or any UN org.	530 Ethiopia

531 Eritrea	664 West Bank
539 Cabinda	666 Israel
540 Angola	667 Palestine Inter Arab
541 Mozambique	670 Saudi Arabia
551 Zambia	671 Aden
552 Zimbabwe (Rhodesia)	678 Yemen
553 Malawi	680 South Yemen
560 South Africa	690 Kuwait
561 Ciskei	691 Persian Gulf
562 Transkei	692 Bahrain
565 Namibia	693 Arabs (Arab States)
570 Lesotho	694 Qatar
571 Botswana	695 Dubai
572 Swaziland	696 Trucial Oman States
580 Malagasy Republic	697 Abu Dhabi
581 Comoro Islands	698 Muscat and Oman
585 Reunion	699 United Arab Emirates
590 Mauritius	700 Afghanistan
591 Seychelles	710 China, People's Republic of
599 African nation, indeter.	711 Overseas Chinese
600 Morocco	712 Mongolia
601 Canary Islands	713 China, Republic of (Taiwan)
609 Spanish Sahara	720 Hong Kong
615 Algeria	721 Macao
616 Tunisia	731 Korea, North
620 Libya	732 Korea, South
625 Sudan	740 Japan
630 Iran	741 Ryukyu Islands
632 Qatar	750 India
640 Turkey	765 Bangladesh
641 Armenians	770 Pakistan
645 Iraq	775 Burma
651 Egypt	780 Sri Lanka (Ceylon)
652 Syria	782 Maldive
660 Lebanon	790 Nepal
663 Jordan	791 Kashmir

800 Thailand

811 Cambodia

812 Laos

815 Vietnam

816 Vietnam, North

817 Vietnam, South

820 Malaysia

830 Singapore

835 Brunei

840 Philippines

850 Indonesia

851 West Irian

852 South Molucca

860 Portuguese Timor

900 Australia

910 Papua-New Guinea

920 New Zealand

921 Nauru

955 Tonga

960 French Polynesia

990 Western Samoa

992 SEATO

993 OPEC

994 Transnational Corps.

995 Jewish, non-Israeli

996 International, multilateral

997 Unspecific foreign

998 Irrelevant

999 Worldwide, indeterminate

Perpetrators (P)

0000 - Unknown or claims that are not credible

0100 - Palestinian, general, indeterminate

0110 - Palestine Liberation Organization

0111 - Al Fatah

0112 - Popular Front for the Liberation of Palestine (PFLP)

0113 - Popular Front for the Liberation of Palestine, General Command (PFLP-GC)

0114 - Democratic Front for the Liberation of Palestine (DFLP)

0115 - As-Sai'qa

0116 - Arab Liberation Front (ALF)

0117 - Palestine Liberation Army

0118 - Popular Front for the Liberation of Palestine (Special Operations)

0119 - Black September

0120 - Black June, Al-Assifa (includes early PLO dissidents)

0121 - May 15 Organization for the Liberation of Palestine

0122 - Eagles of the Palestinian Revolution

0123 - Palestine Liberation Front (PLF)

0200 - Italian, general, indeterminate, or unknown

0210 - Red Brigades

0211 - Prima Linea (Front Line)

0300 - German, general, indeterminate, or unknown

0310 - Red Army Faction (RAF)

0311 - Baader-Meinhof Group

0312 - 2nd of June Movement

0313 - Revolutionary Cells

0315 - Neo-Nazis

0400 - French, general, indeterminate, or unknown

0410 - Action Directe

0420 - Charles Martel Group

0430 - Group Bakunin Gdansk Paris Guatemala Salvador (BGPGS)

0440 - Other French separatists, nationalists, general, indeterminate, unknown

0441 - Corsican National Liberation Front (FTNC)

0442 - Guadeloupe Liberation Army

0500 - Irish, general, indeterminate, or unknown

0501 - Provisional Irish Republican Army (PIRA)

0502 - Irish National Liberation Army (INLA)

0503 - Irish Republican Army (IRA official - no actions since 1972)

0600 - U.S., general, indeterminate, or unknown

0601 - Weather Underground, Weathermen

0602 - New World Liberation Front (NWLF)

0610 - Puerto Rican, general, indeterminate, unknown

0611 - Fuerzas Armadas de Liberacion Nacional (FALN) (Puerto Rico)

0612 - Macheteros (Puerto Rico)

0613 - Puerto Rican Armed Resistance

0700 - Spanish, general, indeterminate, or unknown

0709 - GRAPO

0710 - Basque (ETA) general, indeterminate, or unknown

0711 - ETA/PM

0712 - ETA/M

0713 - Spanish Basque Battalion (BBE) (rightist)

0800 - Asian, general, indeterminate, or unknown

0810 - Pakistani, Indian, Afghan, general, indeterminate, or unknown

0811 - Al Zulfikar

0820 - Thai, general, indeterminate, or unknown

0821 - Pattani United Liberation Organization (PULO)

0822 - Komando Jihad (Thai Muslims)

0830 - Philippine, general, indeterminate, or unknown

0831 - Moro National Liberation Front

0832 - New People's Army

0840 - Japanese, general, indeterminate, or unknown

0841 - Japanese Red Army

0850 - Chinese, Taiwanese, Korean, general, indeterminate

0900 - Latin American, general, indeterminate, or unknown

0910 - Peruvian

0911 - Sendero Luminoso

0912 - Bandera Roja

0920 - Brazilian, Colombian, Venezuelan, Guyanan, Surinami, general, indeterminate, or unknown

0921 - M-19 (Movement of April 19)

0922 - Revolutionary Armed Forces of Colombia (FARC)

0923 - National Liberation Army of Colombia (ELN)

0930 - Chilean, general, indeterminate, or unknown

0931 - Movement of the Revolutionary Left (MIR) (Chile)

0932 - Movimiento de Accion Popular Unida (MAPU) (Chile)

0933 - Partido Comunista Revolucionaria

0940 - Guatemalan, Mexican, general, indeterminate, or unknown

0941 - Guerrilla Army of the Poor (EGP)

0942 - Guatemalan Labor Party (PGT)

0943 - Rebel Armed Forces of Guatemala (FAR)

0944 - Organization of the People in Arms (ORPA)

0950 - El Salvadoran, Costa Rican, general, indeterminate, or unkown

0951 - Farabundo Marti National Liberation Front (FMLN)

0952 - Armed Forces of National Resistance (FARN)

0953 - People's Revolutionary Army (ERP)

0954 - People's Liberation Forces (FPL) (El Salvador)

0955 - People's Avant Garde Organization (often Echeverria Command) (Costa Rica)

0956 - February 28 Popular League (El Salvador)

0960 - Argentina, Uruguay, Bolivia, Ecuador, Paraguay, general, indeterminate, unknown

0961 - Tupamaros (Uruguay) Montoneros (Argentina)

0962 - Ejercito de Liberacion Nacional (Bolivia)

0963 - Ejercito Revolucionaria del Pueblo (ERP) (Argentina)

0970 - Caribbean, general, indeterminate, or unknown

0971 - El Poder Cubano (anti-Castro Cubans)

0973 - Omega-7 (anti-Castro Cubans)

0974 - Anti-Castro (general)

0980 - Honduran, Nicaraguan, general, indeterminate, unknown

0981 - Lorenzo Zelaya Revolutionary People's Command

0982 - Cinchonero Popular Liberation Front (Honduras)

0985 - Sandinistas (Nicaragua)

1000 - Religious fanatics, general, indeterminate, or unknown

1010 - Ananda Marga

1100 - Other groups, general, indeterminate, or unknown

1120 - Canadian, general, indeterminate, or unknown

1121 - Front de Liberation du Quebec (FLQ)

1200 - Armenian, general, indeterminate, or unknown

1210 - Armenian Secret Army for the Liberation of Armenia (ASALA)

1211 - Third of October Group

1212 - Ninth of June Organization

1213 - Orly Organization

1214 - New Armenian Resistance

1215 - September-France

1216 - Armenian Revolutionary Army

1220 - Justice Commandos for the Armenian Genocide

1221 - 28 May Armenian Organization

1300 - Libyan, general, indeterminate, or unknown

1400 - Middle East, North African, other than Palestinians, general, indeterminate, unknown

1410 - Turkish, general, indeterminate, or unknown

1411 - Dev Sol

1412 - Dev Yol

1413 - Marxist-Leninist Armed Propaganda Unit (MLAPU)

1420 - Lebanese, Jordanian, general, indeterminate, or unknown

1421 - Front for the Liberation of Lebanon from Foreigners 1422 - Lebanese Armed Revolutionary Faction (LARF)

1430 - Iranian, Iraqi, Syrian, general, indeterminate, unknown

1431 - Movement of Islamic Action of Iraq

1432 - Amal, Movement of Hope (Imam Musa Sadr) (Shia)

1433 - Kurdish separatists

1434 - Jihad (Struggle) Islamic Holy War

1440 - Israeli, Jewish extremists, general, indeterminate, unknown

1441 - Jewish Defense League (JDL)

1442 - Hatikva Leumi (Hope of the Nation)

1450 - Egyptian, Sudanese, Oman, general, indeterminate, unknown

1460 - Algerian, Moroccan, Tunisian

1500 - European, general, indeterminate, unknown

1510 - Yugoslav, Albanian, Croatian, general, indeterminate, unknown

1520 - Greek, Bulgarian, Romanian, general, indeterminate, unknown

1521 - Revolutionary People's Struggle (ELA)

1530 - Netherlands, Belgium, Denmark, Finland, Norway, Switzerland, Sweden, general, indeterminate, unknown

1531 - South Moluccan separatists

1540 - Soviet Union, Polish, East German, Czech, Hungarian, general, indeterminate, unknown

1545 - USSR Republics (Ukraine, etc.), general, indeterminate, unknown

1550 - Portuguese, general, indeterminate, unknown

1551 - Popular Forces of April 25

1600 - Sub-Saharan African, general, indeterminate, or unknown

1610 - South African, Namibian, Lesotho, general, indeterminate, unknown

1611 - African National Congress (South Africa)

1612 - Spear of the Nation (South Africa)

1613 - Pan Africanist Congress (South Africa)

1614 - South-West Africa People's Organization (SWAPO) (Namibia)

1620 - Angolan, Ethiopian, Sudan, general, indeterminate or unknown

1621 - National Union for the Total Independence of Angola (UNITA)

1623 - Eritrean Liberation Front (ELF)

1630 - Zimbabwean, Mozambiquan, Zambian, Botswanan, general, indeterminate, unknown

1631 - Zimbabwe African People's Union (ZAPU)

1632 - Zimbabwe African Nationalist Union (ZANU)

1633 - Mozambique National Resistance Movement (MNR)

1640 - Uganda, Zaire, general, indeterminate, or unknown

1650 - National Resistance Movement (NRM) (Uganda)

Media (M)

ABC - ABC Television Network

CBS - CBS Television Network

NBC - NBC Television Network

FR - *Frankfurter Allgemeine Zeitung*, Frankfurt, Germany

GM - *Globe and Mail*, Toronto, Canada

NYT - *New York Times*, New York, United States

DT - *Daily Telegraph*, London, England

TL - *Times* of London. London, England

YD - *Yediot*, Tel Aviv, Israel

FI - *Le Figaro*, Paris, France

AA - *Al Aharam*, Cairo, Egypt

PK - *Pakistan Times*, Lahore, Pakistan

Index

Index

TWA, 1-4, 66, 94-95, 97-98, 100-104, 106, 109, 114, 161, 167, 174, 204, 207-210, 270, 273

Task Force on Broadcasting Policy, 198

Task Force on Disorders and Terorrism, 267

Terrorism as a term, 4-7, 13-15, 21-24, 26-28, 31, 91, 93-94, 99-109 passim, 120, 124. 157, 160, 247-259, 273-274, 277

Theater of terror, 1, 15, 27, 51, 60, 65, 93, 97, 99, 111, 115, 126, 247-249, 277

Threats, 4, 8, 11, 21-22, 47, 56, 61, 64, 69, 98, 100, 109, 112, 114-115, 117, 120, 127, 179-181, 189, 200-202, 205-207, 254-256, 259-260

Time Magazine, 106

Times of London, 13, 68, 71, 74, 77, 112, 130, 140, 200

Tupamaros, 113, 157

Turkey, 19, 83-85, 155-157

TV diplomacy, 103, 247

TV Guide, 4, 97, 99, 106, 117

United Kingdom, 40, 54-55, 63, 67, 71, 77, 81-86 passim, 89, 257, 259, 261, 263

UPI, 271

USSR, 5, 83-84

Ustacha, 19

Vanderbilt Archives, 13, 67, 273

Victims, 3-6, 11-14, 19-49 passim, 93, 95, 98-104, 113, 115-116, 120-124, 127, 135-136, 174, 186-188, 193-194, 203-208, 251-255, 268, 274-276, 279

War Measures Act, 263, 278

Washington Post, 64, 116, 250

Washington Star, 64

West, 2-3, 9, 15, 18-19, 23, 43, 53, 86, 89, 100, 104, 109, 121-126 *passim*, 177, 196-197, 199, 208-209. 250, 257, 265

Yediot, 68-71, 77, 80, 85-87, 133, 162, 187, 191, 195, 202